The Yale Series of Younger Poets

Edited by Carl Phillips

Firsts

100 Years of Yale Younger Poets

Yale UNIVERSITY PRESS
NEW HAVEN AND LONDON

Every effort has been made to satisfy copyright requirements in the publication of this book. Should any errors or omissions become known, Yale University Press will gladly correct them in future editions.

Yale University Press books may be purchased in quantity for educational, business, or promotional use. For information, please e-mail sales.press@yale.edu (U.S. office) or sales@yaleup.co.uk (U.K. office).

Designed by Nancy Ovedovitz and set in Quadraat type by Newgen North America. Printed in the United States of America.

ISBN 978-0-300-24317-8 (hardcover : alk. paper)
ISBN 978-0-300-24316-1 (paperback : alk. paper)

Library of Congress Control Number: 2019937272
A catalogue record for this book is available from the British Library.

This paper meets the requirements of ANSI/NISO Z39.48-1992 (Permanence of Paper).

10 9 8 7 6 5 4 3 2 1

Contents

Introduction

For the editing of this anthology—the first since George Bradley's version of the anthology, which ended at 1998, just as W. S. Merwin had been selected as the new judge for the series—I gave myself two guidelines, each with its potential for controversy. First, I decided that each poet would be represented by the same number of poems—three. It has been said, over the years, though not everyone is in agreement about it, that the caliber of the volumes in the Yale Series of Younger Poets was generally mediocre until Yale University Press decided to have a working, prominent poet serve as the judge, beginning in 1932 with Stephen Vincent Benét, whose selections included first books by James Agee, Muriel Rukeyser, and Margaret Walker. Overall, I agree about the caliber of earlier volumes in the series. But as I read through those volumes, so many of them by poets who had only recently graduated from college, and so many having been affected either by actual combat in World War I or by having come of age in the psychological wake of that war, it occurred to me that these poets were writing the only poems they could, in the best ways they knew how. My own sense of the poetry of that period, which pre-dates the innovations of the Modernists, is that there was not only more acceptance of sentimentality and nostalgia, but often a preference for those things, in poetry at least. One can always point to exceptions, but overall the poetry of that period seems to long for a time of innocence, which of course always comes with naïveté, as well. I don't think all of the earlier Yale poets were necessarily naive, but my sense is that they didn't yet have available to them the ways of expressing interiority, or of situating the self in relationship to such large external factors as war—also identity, also language itself—that would come later, with Modernism, confessional poetry, and such pivotal events as the Civil Rights movement, the feminist movement, the Stonewall riots, to name but a few. The early poets in the Yale series are nevertheless writing poems of their own time. They are part of the record, not just of the landscape of American poetry, but of the Yale series itself. And as such, I felt it was important that they be represented equally with other poets in the series who went on to become some of the major poets of our time.

My second decision was to select the poems I most admired by each poet. This shouldn't be controversial, given that any anthology is at some level a reflection of the editor's taste and sensibility. I suspect, though, that some readers will wonder why certain poems of John Ashbery, say, or of Adrienne Rich—poems that have since been among the most often anthologized, of those two poets—don't appear in this volume. To them I would say that popularity rarely coincides, for me, with unequivocal excellence, whatever that might be. Plus, in reading through all of these volumes, I was quite surprised by the number of wonderful poems that had not been anthologized. My hope is that, in encountering selections by some of the more well-known poets here, readers will discover something new, something surprising from an author whose work they thought they already knew well. As in poetry itself, surprise is among the rarest things to encounter in anthologies, I have found. I have sought here to offer a possible exception.

Having established those criteria, in terms of selections for the anthology, and having made the selections, I wondered what I might add, by way of an introduction, that might be helpful. In his introduction, Bradley provided readers with an eloquent and fairly exhaustive history of the Yale Series of Younger Poets. I refer readers to that introduction for such information as how Margaret Walker's book, For My People, got selected not in either of the years when Walker actually submitted a manuscript, but in the year when she decided not to send, thinking the readers for the prize simply weren't interested in the poems of an African American woman; how the rules for the prize evolved from having several Yale graduates, chosen by Yale faculty, as the winners each year to having a single winner chosen by an outside judge who had to be established enough to garner attention for the prize; how it came to be that Joan Murray's book, Poems, won the prize five years after her death; the uproar that arose when Olga Broumas came to Yale to read from her winning volume Beginning with O, with its unabashed reveling in same-sex eros; and much more. Along the way, Bradley also presented incisive portraits of the judges for the Yale prize across the years. My challenge, then, has been to determine what has happened since 1998, in terms of the judges, the prize, and even American poetry itself, as reflected in the various winners.

Besides Merwin, there have been only two subsequent judges since 1998, Louise Glück and me. Glück is the first woman to have served as judge;

I am not only the first African American, but also the only person of color at all to have served as judge. So there has been an attention to diversity—in terms of race and gender—in the selection of judges, and, as it turns out, this has resulted in increased diversity among the winners; I say "as it turns out" because it's not necessarily the case that a judge of color, say, will select a manuscript by a person of color. To put it another way, that might be an expectation of a judge of color—likewise, that a woman might select more women—but an expectation is not a requirement, nor should it be. The issue is much more complicated than that.

I'll begin by noting that there had been some diversity—not much, but some—in terms of race and gender, in the Yale series prior to 1998. Women appear fairly regularly as winners, beginning with Viola C. White's collection, *Horizons*, in 1920. Not so much can be said for racial diversity, the only two winners of color up to 1998 having been Margaret Walker, with *For My People*, and the Asian American Cathy Song, for her volume *Picture Bride* in 1982. And although there are a few volumes by openly queer writers— by which I mean openly queer at the time of publication—among them Ashbery's *Some Trees* and Daniel Hall's *Hermit with Landscape*, only Broumas's *Beginning with O* has queerness as one of its actual subjects.

How much does diversity have to do with the judges? Being a straight white man did not prevent Stephen Vincent Benét from selecting Margaret Walker as the winner in 1941, or Richard Hugo from selecting Cathy Song. Admittedly, though, these are the exceptions; the racial diversity really doesn't improve much until the two most recent judges. I believe this does have something to do with those particular judges, but it is also inextricably connected to the cultural conversation at any given time. With that in mind, I'll point to a watershed moment for the landscape of American poetry: the founding, in 1996, of Cave Canem, a writers' retreat designed exclusively for African American poets. I would argue that this is the pivotal moment at which the landscape of American poetry begins to change in the late twentieth century. There have been African American poets for centuries in this country, of course. But, even acknowledging the Harlem Renaissance and, later, the Black Arts Movement, I point to Cave Canem as the first official organization whose purpose was not only to bring black writers together but to foster a community of mutually supportive individuals. Cave Canem made it possible for a black writer to have a sense of belonging to something larger, to confirm that she wasn't writing alone; Cave Canem has also proved an opportunity for black writers to recognize the great aesthetic diversity of writing from within their community. One of the chief results has been that, through the confidence gained by sheer numbers, black poets began interrogating the poetry establishment, and specifically began insisting on the right to have their voices heard in journals that earlier had not represented them. At the same time, for many publishers of journals, Cave Canem became a resource, a place to turn if they wanted to know who some of the up-and-coming black writers might be. It seems worth mentioning, as well, that Cave Canem began only a couple of years after the Internet became available to the general public. This has meant at least two things: that there is more opportunity to discover other voices by people of color; and that there are more opportunities for people of color to publish online (and indeed to create their own publications) as an alternative to many of the print journals that had ignored racial diversity. Simply put, there's more opportunity to spread the word.

The year 2004 saw the founding of Kundiman, a similar retreat, this one for Asian American poets, and in 2009 CantoMundo, a retreat for Latinx poets, was established. These and Cave Canem have opened up poetry in the United States in exciting ways, in crucial ways, effecting positive change not just in terms of what we read in journals and what books are more readily available, but also changing, challenging, and complicating the conversation at university writing programs and at organizations ranging from the National Book Foundation to the Academy of American Poets. In addition, these organizations have deepened and enriched the pool of manuscripts available for publication. My sense is that the change in conversation had a lot to do with Yale University Press eventually choosing the first female judge and, afterward, the first African American judge. And even as the pool of manuscripts in the United States has been getting increasingly diverse, I believe the fact of diversity, at the level of the judge, has inspired more diversity among the entries. The work may be out there, but something has to get the poet to send it to this particular contest, and the identity of the judge can surely help, as it can also sometimes hinder (again, there's the example of Walker deciding to give up entering the contest, because she saw no proof that there was interest in writing by a black woman, no visible proof in the form of an earlier winner of color, or in the form of a judge of color).

What can be said, generally and in particular with respect to diversity, about the Yale Series of Younger Poets since 1998? Perhaps it's easiest, following in Bradley's footsteps, to go judge by judge. Merwin controversially chose no winner the first year he was judge, claiming not to have seen a manuscript that was worthy. While I don't doubt that Merwin didn't like any of the manuscripts he saw, I cannot believe that there wasn't a worthy winner among the submissions; I think he simply chose to look at a very limited number of them. But Merwin did go on to select five winners in the years that followed: Craig Arnold, Davis McCombs, Maurice Manning, Sean Singer, and Loren Goodman. All are men, and to my knowledge all are white (Singer was born in Guadalajara, Mexico, but I have not known him to identify as Latinx). But even though Merwin's choices don't move significantly beyond the history of racial or gender diversity, they are consistent with the wide aesthetic range the prize has presented since the time of Benét, who was the first outsider to become a judge. Although each has a decidedly distinct voice, what I find most interesting about Merwin's choices is what several of them have in common. *Ultima Thule* (McCombs) and *Lawrence Booth's Book of Visions* (Manning) are both examples of what has come to be called the "project" book, by which is meant a book of poems that cohere around— or are written *in order to* cohere around—a particular theme, often a narrative one; for McCombs, there are two narratives of life in and around Mammoth Cave, in the 1800s and 1990s, respectively, the narratives grounded in an examination of the cave's history; Manning gives us a speaker who may be real, may be allegorical, who takes us on what *Library Journal* called "a postmodernist journey through the rural Kentucky landscape of the 1970s." *Famous Americans* (Goodman) is less narrative, but it also has a project in mind, namely, to take on a wide variety of Americans, famous and otherwise, as a way of investigating fame and its relationship to the self and reality. I remember wondering, at the time, if Merwin had a penchant for this type of book-length project, but I sometimes think this kind of book was simply beginning to be more popular among young poets (not that the idea was new to the twentieth century even then, given Glück's *Ararat*, Rita Dove's *Thomas and Beulah*, or, for that matter, Berryman's *The Dream Songs*). In any event, in the time since Merwin's choices, whether coincidentally or because of them, this has become the most common type of book I encounter in American poetry.

Louise Glück served eight years as judge. Only three of the eight winners are women, which takes me back to how the identity of the judge is not an easy gauge of what she will be drawn to. Glück's choices do, however, include some significant firsts in terms of racial diversity, specifically Fady Joudah (*The Earth in the Attic*), who, as a Palestinian American, is the first winner of Arabic descent, and Ken Chen (*Juvenilia*), who is Asian American. She also chose Richard Siken's *Crush*, which is easily the most overtly queer book of poems to appear since Broumas won the prize. Again, hard to say how much these choices have to do with the racial and gender identity of the judge, or with her aesthetic proclivities, or of what she had to choose from to begin with. Which brings up again the question of the extent to which some of these manuscripts were entered only because the entrant felt that Glück might be particularly receptive to the work (though this last point is tricky, because knowing a judge's own poetry is no more a gauge of what she likes to read than is her identity). But one new factor does come into play with the arrival of Glück as judge: she is the first to have screeners outside of Yale University Press. Which is to say, from 1933, when Benét became the first external judge, until 2003, when Glück became judge, readers at the press pretty much determined which manuscripts to pass on to the judge, the number of manuscripts varying according to how many the judge was willing to read. To this extent, the judge's decision is reflective of her taste, yes, but only of what appealed to her taste out of a limited number of manuscripts that she might or might not have chosen in the first place. Another way to see it is that the decision is also reflective of the screeners' tastes. This makes it crucial, to my mind, to give some thought to the choice of screeners.

I don't know, with one exception, who Glück's screeners were, but when I took on the position of judge, and after Glück advised me to choose my screeners with care, I made a point of choosing those who represented a wide range of aesthetics and reflected how diverse poetry has become in terms of gender, sexual orientation, and race. At this point I have eight screeners, who are variously white, African American, Native American, Latinx, and Asian American. Only one is a straight male. Six of the eight are women. At least three screeners are queer, to my knowledge. I do think that this range of screeners (each of whom selects the best six or seven manuscripts to give me) has led to my having a diverse pool to choose from. My first choice, *Slow Lightning*, by Eduardo Corral, who is queer and Chicano

American, was easy. But I had to have a screener who put that manuscript in front of me in the first place. Interestingly enough, though, the screener who passed Corral's manuscript along is a straight white woman. Just as interesting is that my next two picks, Will Schutt and Eryn Green, are both straight white men, but their manuscripts were passed on to me by, respectively, a straight white woman and a queer black woman.

What all this means is hard to say, but what it has equaled during my tenure has been a steady increase in the racial diversity of the prize. Corral was the first Latinx winner, Duy Doan and Yanyi are only the second and third Asian American winners, Yanyi is the first trans winner, and Airea D. Matthews is only the second African American winner in the history of the Yale series. One thing that surprised me, as I considered all of my picks for this introduction, is that only two have been women—two out of eight. It just now occurs to me that I've in fact chosen three women for the prize, but in one of the years the first selection (by a woman) turned out to have been taken for another prize, so I went to my next choice, which happened to be by a man. In any event, I hope the ratio will be more balanced by the time of my final selection in 2020.

Our awareness, as a society, of all kinds of diversity and of a need to be more inclusive has evolved considerably since the 1950s, and that evolution has been especially swift in the last fifteen years. The Yale Series of Younger Poets has, I think, become increasingly reflective of that inclusivity. The value of diversity, for American poetry, should be obvious, I hope: we are a diverse country, and anything that wants to call itself American poetry must be reflective of that diversity—how call it American, if it represents only one voice in a choir of voices? The effect of diversity is another, subtler, and ultimately more revolutionary matter. A shared aspect of the majority of poetry written by historically marginalized people is that the poems often interrogate and trouble their relationship to a language and prosody that have been handed down by a primarily white, male, English tradition. We see this in Rich's attempt (in work subsequent to her Yale volume) to find a "common language" across genders, and in Corral's use of Spanish as, in part, a refusal to accept English as the default language. And this overall restlessness with a tradition assumed to be the "norm" has helped make American poetry less complacent, inasmuch as it challenges easy assumptions; such challenges can only be good, ultimately, for the growth of the art.

In addition, the restlessness with tradition has gotten poets of color, in particular, to come up with greater innovation, in their quest to find a language and form that speaks for them—which is to say, racial diversity often coincides with prosodic diversity, and as this diversity becomes increasingly part of the American poetry landscape, it puts a pressure on poetry to keep evolving: surely this is the ultimate responsibility of the poet, to master traditions, and at the same time to keep pushing those traditions usefully forward in such a way that tradition remains at once a relevant touchstone and an exciting point from which to leap forward into new definitions not just of how to write a poem, but of poetry itself. It comes back to inclusivity, I believe, and a desire to include more voices and more kinds of voices.

Two more recent changes in the history of the prize have made it possible to be even more inclusive. In 2015 the press decided that the series would no longer have an age limit of forty, nor would it require U.S. citizenship for eligibility. Again, these changes came about in large part as the result of changes in the cultural conversation. In the same year, the poets Javier Zamora, Christopher Soto, and Marcelo Hernandez Castillo—acting as the Undocupoets—circulated a petition to various presses and organizations, asking them to lift several contest restrictions, in particular to open the contests to those "in the U.S. with Deferred Action for Childhood Arrivals (DACA) status or Temporary Protected Status (TPS)" (*Poets & Writers*, July/August 2015). Yale University Press agreed to this, and at the same time lifted the age restriction (although the series remains, oddly enough, the Yale Series of Younger Poets). This latter decision may or may not have been spurred on by another concern that had started to arise around the subject of first-book contests: what exactly constitutes an emerging writer? To what extent is emerging necessarily connected with youth? And, for the purposes of the Yale prize, does emerging stop happening at forty?

That Airea D. Matthews was the first winner of the prize after the age limit had been lifted—she was forty-three at the time—is proof enough that exciting voices don't necessarily emerge before forty; some poets have been raising families, others have full-time jobs (Matthews was doing both), and not everyone has the luxury of time to focus exclusively on writing. Perhaps more to the point, it's my belief that any writer worth reading is continuing to surprise herself, to find new ways of deploying language and different reasons for doing so; in this sense, the committed artist is always emerging into something new. To quote one of the judges of the series, Stanley Kunitz,

Though I lack the art
to decipher it,
no doubt the next chapter
in my book of transformations
is already written.
I am not done with my changes.

I watched Kunitz read those lines (from "The Layers") at a celebration of his one hundredth birthday; he read them with a conviction that suggested he meant every word, even at one hundred.

What I've aimed for as a judge is what Glück, too, seems to have wanted: selections that have no clear or easy point of commonality—with my work or with each other's. My only instructions to the screeners have been to choose what they feel are the best manuscripts—however they define that—and not to choose what they think I might like. For myself, the chief criterion has been surprise in how the material, whatever its subject, gets handled. This might be at the formal level, though more often it has been in terms of sensibility. I want to feel as if I've been asked to see the world through a strange lens, to hear a voice whose confidence comes in part from how unaware it is of its own strangenesses—think Dickinson, think Hopkins. Their sheer weirdness. And yet that weirdness can come in the form of restraint and understatement, too.

What does the prize mean at this point, and where might it be headed? Toward the end of his introduction from 1998, Bradley offered this assessment of the state of the art:

Twentieth-century American verse has conducted several variations on the age-old dispute between Apollonian and Dionysian notions of inspiration, between the poetry of intellect and the poetry of emotion. (The debate finally presents a false choice, but it has been prosecuted with vigor nonetheless.) During the period when Auden and Fitts were Yale editors, both credos were well represented among the nation's poets. The argument is pretty much over now, at least for the time being, and a balance has been lost. With the triumph of unmediated emotion in the latter half of the century, formalism has suffered neglect. The lack of instruction, approval, and practice has had a cumulative effect, and if it is deemed worthwhile to recover the skill level of a Merrill or an Auden, it is going to take a sustained movement to effect recuperation. In the meantime, a resource has gone out of our art. [xcv]

The implication seems to be that it will be more difficult to find manuscripts that offer the combination of intellect and emotion and prosodic skill that was somehow once more abundant. I disagree. Or I suppose I would argue with any fixed definition of prosody. I have not encountered manuscripts that are strictly formal—that is, employ metrical regularity, rhyme schemes, and so on. But what I've encountered instead are poets who have mastered those particular prosodic traditions, and are pushing them forward in ways that range from Matthews deciding that tweets and text messages can be turned into prosodic tools, to the restrained, muscular sentence that Yanyi deploys in his prose poems, to the code-switching by which Spanish and Vietnamese become part of a poem's prosody, in the work of Corral and Doan, respectively. What the Yale winners since 1998 have especially shown is that the possibilities for poetry have opened up, concomitant with an opening of the conversation to allow those voices that were silenced earlier to be heard now. And what those voices most often seem to be asking is: Who decided, finally, what a poem is? Who decides who gets to write one? Meanwhile, to return to Bradley's comments, why does emotion have to lead to a lack of formal rigor, and since when is formal rigor the unmistakable mark of intellect?

The prize's history of evolution—the longest history of any existing poetry prize in the United States—toward increased inclusivity, of identity but also of content, the decision to have a female judge and, afterward, an African American judge, the flexibility that Yale University Press has shown in its ability to accommodate shifting ideas of what is meant by terms like "emerging" or "American"—these all convince me that the Yale poetry prize is not only one of the most distinctive prizes, still, but also likely to be one of the most enduring. The prize has never been a guarantee of a distinguished and lengthy career—not all winners have gone on to be Adrienne Rich, for example. But many factors go into a career. Or more exactly, a combination of many factors goes into, variously, the making or breaking or stalling or cutting forever short or immovably consolidating (as if the canon were a fixed planet markable by a flag of conquest) of a career; luck is not the least of those shifting, unpredictable factors. But the Yale prize makes a new voice known, often for the first time, and widely. That's a huge gift, as I have found it a huge gift to have the opportunity to provide that new voice its bit of time and space. The rest, as each voice included here found out, or will eventually, is anyone's guess.

. . .

It would be difficult to overestimate the debt I owe to George Bradley, for the model he provided me with his editorship of the previous iteration of *The Yale Younger Poets Anthology* (1998). Bradley's introduction to that anthology is exhaustive, a wealth of information and often very amusing anecdotes about the early history of the series. Of particular value to me was the information he was able to compile regarding the various poets' biographies. I have relied heavily on these biographical notes, adding what I could, often just rewording a bit. Other sources of information include the usual Internet sites, including Google, Wikipedia, obituaries in local papers of long ago.

I especially wish to thank Sarah Miller and Ash Lago at Yale University Press for their patience, for their unflagging energy and attention to the project, and for their assistance not only with fact finding but with the final shape of my introduction and, indeed, of the anthology overall. I am deeply grateful.

Readers will note the absence here of Michael Casey's spirited, iconoclastic poems that so unflinchingly examined the brutalities of the conflict in Vietnam. I did select poems for inclusion, but Casey, who owns the copyright to his poems, was unwilling to give permission for those selections to be included here. I regret their absence, and direct interested readers to Casey's Yale volume, *Obscenities*, from 1971. Born in 1947 in Lowell, Massachusetts, Michael Casey was drafted upon graduation from the Lowell Institute of Technology in 1968 and served as a military policeman in Vietnam. He returned to study at the State University of New York, Buffalo. He has written five books of poetry, including *There It Is: New and Selected Poems* (2017).

Two other winners of the prize had to be omitted, because the press, after several attempts, was unable to secure permission to reprint in time for production. One of these is Joy Davidman, whose *Letter to a Comrade* was the 1937 winner of the Yale prize. Joy Davidman (1915–1960) was born in New York City and studied at Hunter College and Columbia University. A Jew by birth, she became an atheist and a communist, then later converted to Christianity and wrote one of her best-known works, *Smoke on the Mountain: An Interpretation of the Ten Commandments* (1954). That book's preface was written by C. S. Lewis, whom Davidman eventually married. Davidman continued to write poetry, as well as novels and screenplays. Her marriage to Lewis was the subject of the movie *Shadowlands* (1993).

Jeremy Ingalls (1911–2000) won the 1940 Yale prize for *The Metaphysical Sword*. Born Mildred Dodge Ingalls in Gloucester, Massachusetts, she was renamed Jeremy in childhood to commemorate an ancestor. She studied at Tufts University and the University of Chicago, and became a professor of Asian studies at Rockford College in Illinois. A translator of Chinese and Japanese, Ingalls was also the author of scholarly essays, short stories, a verse play, and four subsequent volumes of poetry. Her awards include a Guggenheim Fellowship and a Ford Foundation Fellowship.

100 Years of Yale Younger Poets

Howard Buck (1884–1947) *The Tempering,* 1918

Born in Chicago, Illinois, Howard Swazey Buck earned undergraduate and graduate degrees at Yale University. For his work with the American Expeditionary Forces in France during World War I, he received the Croix de Guerre. Buck later taught at Yale University and the University of Chicago, and produced two critical works on Tobias Smollett.

Heart-Song

Beautiful, wild, with a breeze abroad
Dimpling the sunlit lake like mad,
All the bright day a gay young God,
    Showering the gems of his youth, and glad
To live and give on a day like this
When the breeze that blows on the brow's a kiss.

Beautiful so, with the thrill of life
    Awake in sunlight, a lilting song;
Blood a-leap for the exquisite strife
    Of living this day out full and strong;
And a strength that is full as the cool wind is,
And Life's full lips in one long kiss

Pressed close on yours like a bursting flower!
    Oh, a spurt of grape, a laugh, a quip,
Rain on the cheek from a thunder-shower
    Out of the North! just—life's at the lip:
Ah, drain to the dregs that dizzy draught—
What? a young satyr behind you laughed?

If It Be

It little matters that we pass within
That silent house, and never shall come forth.
Our immortality is what has been;
We, the imperfect symbols, little worth.
All great things have existed since Time's birth:
Most fortunate, if we have found one out
And given it to our time. But beyond doubt,
If we have glimpsed a truth, reached for, and failed,
Sometime the fitting warrior shall be hailed
To strike it into life, a shining link
In the armor of our immortality.

The stars live on; the rush of life flags not.
We come and open like the rose, and drink
The eternal dews—till the dank earth's forgot,
And all our babyhood's poor softnesses
Are flushed to meaning, beauty, by the flow
Of the eternal tides, and we have quaffed
The glamor of their way, yea, scoffed and laughed
Blinded Oblivion back to his haunt! Can these
Fair limbs of form, these goodly hands, this brow,
Be but as colorless clay in the rich glow
Of eternity? echoes of a dear tone
We tremble to, till it seems half our own?
Ah, no, these are but cynic-reasoned lies,
Naught, naught! Have I not seen my mother's eyes?

No wonder in the Spring we dream it so,
When the fields freshen, and birds come, and the air
Presses our lips with lips so fresh and fair.
They gave their love to Petrarch long ago;
Their beauty does not fade; they cannot die.
And oh, to hear the immemorial cry,
Out of the clouds poured down, skylark a Shelley heard,
And outsung in the morning of his prime!

The same wild notes—I hear his dizzy word!
Where now is the brave singer? Our brief time
Is but a ray of light on things that are,
And death is darkness.
                              Yet not so do I
Despair, wishing this dreaded thing afar.
Because I wake not, never stir, nor heed
Your anguished cry beyond the gray abyss,
Feel not the trembling of your dear, dear kiss,
Nor heed a voice that makes death hard indeed—
Shall I presume that Love no longer is?

Le Mort

Here on this stretcher now he coldly lies,
      A burlap sack hiding his beaten head.
      The idle hands seem heedless lumps of lead,
And the stiff fingers of abnormal size.
I almost stooped to brush away the flies,
      Musing if yet she knew that he was dead.

Gayly laughing they brought him
      Up the dusty road,
Chatting as if they thought him
      But a luckless load,
And laid him here beside this scarred old tree,
Till some death-wain should chance by luckily:
Those wagons carry back the honored dead.
But, necessarily,
On the return trip they will carry bread.

All day he lay there, and all night,
      Wrapped in the shining mists that swim
Along the ground. The sullen might
      Of thunder shaking the earth shook not him.

And strangely lightening through the mist that crept,
    Moving like some slow, luminous, foaming sea,
    Washing black shores of twisted tarn and tree,
        The flaring star-shells here
        Over his lonely bier,
White meteor-tapers, his pale vigil kept.

John Chipman Farrar (1896–1974) *Forgotten Shrines,* 1918

John Farrar was born in Burlington, Vermont. A graduate of Yale University, he served as an aviation inspector in World War I. Farrar later went into publishing, most notably helping to found Farrar and Rinehart as well as Farrar, Straus & Giroux. In addition he helped establish the Breadloaf Writer's Conference at Middlebury College in Vermont.

Yet More Than This

Have you sought beauty where night mystifies
    The loves and laughter of the cool closed flowers?
Have you learned the exquisite passion of dear eyes
    Or followed the furious path of autumn showers?

There are eyes of anguish in the thronging street,
    Made tender by a longing for the dawn.
There are lives of irony! . . . but these are sweet
    In dreams of secret gentleness, not gone,

But hiding for a space; and there are those
    Who sing the mountain heights of life along,
Stilling the world to watch a budding rose?
    And knowing these ——have you found nought but song?

These were the meadow lands of his delight,
    Far-stretching to the green hills and the sky,
And here the brook he fished in, laughing by
With benison of comfort. And the light,
Sorrowing for him, veils with graying white
The ripples and the sleepy herds that lie
Dreaming. Far overhead his wild things cry,
Swaying among the rushes after flight.

I pick a bit of beauty for his room,
A chastened branch of late October leaves
And sigh to think that he has left the whole:
The future quietness of snow, the bloom
Of sudden April—yet my heart believes
That here, in deepening beauty, dwells his soul.

I watched you as you turned and waited there,
Slim, in the darkened hall, and like a cloud
Blown to the ruddy moon, your amber hair
Clustered about your face. I cried aloud
The thoughts that harried me! Could you not love
As I love!—Like a snow-stilled stretch of plain
The silent house, with your dim face above,
Gloriously holy with unspoken pain.

There are sorrows that burn like bands of white-hot steel
And pains that lower like an angry sky!
I knelt—and in the darkness I could feel
Your dear hand stretched to comfort me. Why, why,
Did you not chide my petty love or flee!
Oh, how your tender pity tortured me.

David Osborne Hamilton (1893–1953) *Four Gardens,* 1919

Born in Detroit, Michigan, David Hamilton graduated from Yale University and served in the medical corps in France in World War I. He later published two novels, *Pale Warriors* (1924) and *Picaresque* (1930), and another volume of poems, *Hoofs and Haloes* (1941).

A Portrait

The flowing art of his desire to please
    Like magic veils the blackness of his way;
He hides in smooth agreement, and with ease
    Receives the thanks for gifts he cannot pay.
At night in his locked bedroom does he call
    The little lies that hide beneath his tongue
And feed them sweets,—or praise his hands for all
    The faith that they from trusting men have wrung?
Or does he guard himself with stern commands,
    And train his lips to curve—his eyes just so,—
        A tyrant of good servants? No:—instead,
Before his mirror I am sure he stands
    Sleek to the last! He smiles and does not know
        The devil tucks him deftly into bed.

The Black Swan

In state beside the stream the queen passed by;
    With her own hands her snow-white swans she fed;
Her pages clad in scarlet formed her train;
Each bore a golden goblet full of grain.
    Her velvet cloak was blown above her head,
And rose a purple thundercloud on high.
    "Whence came this swan as black as ebony?"

Sea-green and cold as emeralds were her eyes.
"Drive from my flock this strange, dark swan," she said;
Her pages stoned him; from the flock he fled;
Then down the stream they followed him with cries,
Until the black swan fled into the sea.

His crown like fire beneath the sunlight shone,
And weary was the queen's young son of play.
Beside the sea that morn he paused to rest;
He saw the black swan swimming on the breast
Of the cool water; down each winding way
He looked to see if he were all alone.
His crown upon a willow branch he hung;
Upon the grass his sapphire belt fell low
Like sparkling dew! His soft robes slipped away
From his small body, till at last they lay
In golden folds about his feet as though
A wreath of daffodils, unseen, had sprung!

He stood there laughing—then he swam out far:—
The queen walked in her bower beside the sea:—
She heard him laugh and call the swan to play;
Far out she saw the black swan lead the way;
And as she gazed the wind rose suddenly:
The sky turned black as night without a star!
That morn their broken nets all shining bright
Some fishermen found on the beach, flung high
By breakers in the night. "O something fair
Among the shells and weeds lies tangled there!
Is this a mermaid's sleeping child?" they cry.
"How silently he lies! How silver-white!"

The Goblin's Bride

Why should she wed a goblin king—
    She for whom tasselled princes sighed
And troubadours went wandering,
    And knights in silver armor died.

For when she rode her palfrey white
    Through tangled streets of towered towns,
Young men turned poets at the sight
    And grey-beards blinked away their frowns.

But O her heart the goblin won,
    She gave him all her silken hair;
His oafs rare carpets of it spun
    For cavern hall and secret stair.

The sparkle of her eyes he took
    To deck his crown, and made a light
For passage-way and secret nook
    With luster of her skin so white.

If villagers at evening went
    Into the hills they often spied
Against the sky jet-black and bent
    Her figure on some lone hillside.

When naked trees their arms fling high
    To clasp wet branches overhead,
And lightning cracks apart the sky
    While clouds their angry torrents shed,

Good people bar their door-ways tight
    And circle round the ingle-side;
"The goblin king," they say, "to-night
    Is sporting with his stolen bride."

Alfred Raymond Bellinger (1893–1978) *Spires and Poplars,* 1919

Both a graduate of Yale University and a World War I veteran, Alfred Bellinger became a noted numismatist, publishing many books about ancient and classical coinage, including *Essay on the Coinage of Alexander the Great* (1963). He taught at Yale, where he was a professor of classics.

O beautiful and reckless whom I loved,
    Dead while your life was strong with youth and pride!
    Were it not better had a thousand died
Than you, with all your promises unproved?
Full debonair and modest as behoved
    A gallant gentleman, as yet untried,
O beautiful and reckless whom I loved,
    Dead while your life was strong with youth and pride!
Through perils, eager, unafraid you roved
    Seeking your star and turning not aside.
    Now you are gone but still there shall abide
Sunshine about the places where you moved,
O beautiful and reckless whom I loved.

Sleep in this sacred earth, the strife is done.
    Failure and triumph both are laid to rest
    Upon the all-forgiving mother's breast
In equal peace beneath the kindly sun.
Never again shall trumpet call or gun
    Arouse you to take up the bitter quest.

Sleep in this sacred earth, the strife is done.
    Failure and triumph both are laid to rest.
Save God himself alone there now is none
    Who can divide the baser from the best
    Or weigh the worth of the unworthiest.
But they that hopeless fought and they that won
Sleep in this sacred earth. The strife is done.

C. L. W., with a Mirror

Last year, as tribute to your gallant heart,
    Our scanty best of offerings we brought
To you, and you with a surpassing art
    Made rich by your acceptance things of naught.

And I had nothing but my idle days—
    My gray and idle days to bring you there.
Yet you transformed the empty gifts in ways
    Most wonderful, to make them passing fair.

Yours was a magic to outlast the war,
    A power to be perpetually true.
And so, behold, I bring to you once more
    A gift to be made beautiful by you.

Thomas Caldecot Chubb (1899–1972) *The White God, and Other Poems,* 1919

Thomas Chubb was born in East Orange, New Jersey, and attended Yale University. He later became a reviewer for the *New York Times*. He continued to produce books of poems, and also wrote several biographies, including *The Life of Giovanni Boccaccio* (1930) and *Dante and His World* (1967), as well as books for young readers, among them *The Byzantines* (1959) and *The Venetians: Merchant Princes* (1968).

Song

I thought of song as a trivial thing,
A toy for my hand,
A glittering pendant of tinsel,
A handful of sand,
—But lo! I have striven to sing and song is a terrible brand!

I dreamed of song as a pleasaunce
To lighten the hour,
A catch of the leaves' refrain,
And earthly dower,
—Behold! The heavens fall down and the sky is cracked by its power!

I longed for song as a stream
That would splash for me,
A ripple adown the hillside,
A melody,
—And now it is one with the river and the river has flowed to the sea!

The mountains arise at its sounding,
The sky is dark'd with rain,
And the lands that were sunk in the ocean
Stand up again,
—But the heart of the singer is broken for song is more bitter than pain!

Reminiscence

So! Tonight the city is spread like a dream beneath me,
Or a dusky etching traced by the master's hand!
And the wind in the elms has a sleepy song to bequeath me,
But—it blows from the land!

It blows from the land, and I am a-weary of cities,
Weary, too, of the sunset tossed from their spires,
And their rigid outlines—their ardors, their scorns, their pities—
And the smoke in sooty gyres.

Their gold is too burnished for me, and each window flaming
Is a vague opal set on a lifeless breast.
—I have seen opals with fire beyond my naming,
Where the surf froths gold in the west!

Nay, but yonder those languid colorous clouds are turning
Idly, like dreaming barques on an enchanted mere,
And all the western towers seem to be burning
Warmly and clear;

And this is beauty you cry. . . . Ah, remember those places
Where the gray beach shows the dimmed end of the land;
And the phosphorescent wash of each wave as it races
Up on the gleaming sand;

And the moonlit sails . . . And still you laugh and deride me,
For drowsing here in the twilight so indolently.
Oh! Though the dark elms were wonderful gods beside me,
Could I forget the sea?

After Combat

Hark! Yonder elm-tree seems to pulse with singing
That fire has hardly spared. Hark! Do I hear
The mavis-note in that seared bracken ringing,
No trace of fear?

The rank grass strives to hide the hideous scourings
Of blundering man. The e'er-immortal earth
Re-flowers to life—despite unlovely lowerings—
In clearer birth.

Was it a dream—so little seems regretted,
While more, more gorgeousness comes on us soon—
That I saw spearmen, last night! silhouetted
Against the moon?

Darl MacLeod Boyle (dates unknown) *Where Lilith Dances,* 1919

Darl Boyle was the first Yale Younger Poet not to have attended Yale, having gradu-
ated from Stanford University. A veteran of World War I, he taught at the University
of California, Los Angeles.

Ere the Years Numbered Nine

In the lang, lang syne,
When the world was a toy,
Ere the years numbered nine,
I remember one joy:
'Twas to rise in the grey
Of a white winter's morn
When the low sun's red ray
Made the world forlorn,
To see on the pane
The magic Jack Frost
Had wrought once again,
And in silver embossed:

Strange seas of white spray,
That fell not nor rose;
White trees that ne'er sway
In a wind that ne'er blows;
Silver streams 'mong the hills
Of a far silver moon;
White noonday that chills,
White skies in a swoon.

Since then I have seen
Snowy range upon range
Lift its far head serene,

Vast, kingly and strange;
White sea-waves that froze
Before they could fall,
Flush of soft sunset rose
On the high snowy wall,
Mountain-clouds in the noon,
Dim, mocking the sight,
And where the white moon
Walked alone on the height;
Yet these sights never moved
Nor made my heart fain
As the grey dawns I loved,
And the frosts on the pane!

Strange seas of white spray,
That fell not nor rose;
White trees that ne'er sway
In a wind that ne'er blows;
Silver streams 'mong the hills
Of a far silver moon;
White noonday that chills,
White skies in a swoon.

But that was lang syne,
When the world was a toy,
Ere the years numbered nine,
When to live was a joy!

All Souls' Eve

The evening is dark, and the sky is misty, and the wind blows low;
O wind, cease swaying the bare, bare branches, bending them to and fro,
They look too like ghosts in the pale moonlight,
Ah, too like ghosts in the dusky night,
When ghosts glide to and fro!

O ghosts not laid, and ghosts forgotten, and ghosts of the evil dead,
Why will ye come to sear my heart, when I thought ye had gone, had fled,
Why do ye come on this night of the year,
Does it ease your pain to behold my fear,
Since all is done and said?

The Night Wind

Out in the dark sad night the wind seems fretting,
Like a sick child in pain,
As if his soul were all forgetting
The spring's soft rain.

Not as some fair girl's happy weeping,
Like April's sunny showers,
The sky, a breaking heart, when earth is sleeping,
Weeps through the hours.

Say, does the wind remember the young faces
On which he loved to blow?
And does the night-cloud think of those far places,
Where they lie low?

Grieve not! 'twas that free wind and that wide heaven,
Their mountains and their sea,
That made them men; now they their lives have given
To keep these free!

Theodore H. Banks, Jr. (1895–1969) *Wild Geese,* 1920

A World War I veteran, Theodore Banks graduated from Yale University and did postgraduate work at Harvard and Yale. He later taught English at both Yale and Wesleyan University. His other books include *Milton's Imagery* (1950), translations from Sophocles, and a rendering of Sir Gawain and the Green Knight.

The Tokens

I know by these that she cannot have died:
The woodland quiet, the sparkle of the sea,
The flutter of leaves, the flooding of the tide,
Earth's lure and loveliness and mystery;
For all these things she loved, and these abide.

Nor is her spirit, clad in gentleness,
Courage and courtliness and ancient grace,
Less than the beauty of the stars, or less
Than fading light that touched her tender face,
The twilight calm, or the low wind's caress.

The dark pine woods, secluded and secure
Against the world, the majesty that moved
On the tempestuous ocean, and the pure,
Pale light of dawning: all these that she loved
Were transient, earthly things; and these endure.

"A Sea Change"

The snow falls silently, and brings
New loveliness to common things,
And gives to every ugly place
Still forms of beauty and of grace,
Making the busy, bustling street

A solitude where phantoms meet
And dimly pass on muffled feet.

And could I to like beauty turn
The passions that within us burn,
The grief, the weariness, the strife,
The tumult of our daily life,
Then in a hushed world you would see
How strangely altered we should be,
How clothed in lasting mystery.

Winter

Harsh is the north wind's breath,
And harsh is death.
Huddled together in the searching air
The oaks stand gaunt and naked to the cold;
All things are bowed beneath a dark despair,
Are helpless, hopeless, tired and very old;
For the north wind's bitter breath
Is death.
The haggard trees are black against the west
Where a dull sunset smoulders sullenly,
While like a spent soul vainly seeking rest,
Foredoomed and fated to a fruitless quest,
Yet seeking endlessly
The wind goes by.
From bank to frozen bank
The long lake's face is blank;
And overhead
The sky is dead.

Now from the north comes the storm like a fierce wild thing that is lost,
Ruthlessly wrenching the boughs of the oaks in their agony tossed
Heavenward, writhing, imploring a respite, beseeching a rest
From the shuddering wildness of wind and the terror of tempest pressed

All but resistless against them. As bitter as death the blast
Mercilessly scourges the meadows, until like a dream that is passed,
The earth and the heavens have vanished, dead leaves in tumultuous flight,
And nothing remains but a wind that wails in a chaos of cold and night.

And now in utter silence, utter dark
The world lies stiffened, naked, stark;
No light, no sound beneath a barren sky,
Save for the black ice cracking suddenly.
All things shall come to this:
All wonder and all bliss,
All the swift passion of the hearts that beat
With sense of life unutterably sweet,
All song and laughter, all friendship and all love,
Delight in deed and dreaming, and above
The rest the rapture of creation,—all
Shall through the ages fail and fade and fall;
Until the earth, without one glowing spark
In all its livid leagues of frozen ground,
Shall whirl beneath the sky without a sound
Save for the black ice cracking in the dark.

Viola C. White (1889–1977) *Horizons,* 1920

Viola White was the first woman to be named a Yale Younger Poet. Born in Brooklyn, she studied at Wellesley College, Columbia University, and the University of North Carolina. White, who was the first scholar to produce a doctoral dissertation on Herman Melville (1934), became the Abernathy Curator at Middlebury College's library, where she built one of the more prominent collections of American literature in the country. She was also the author of a novel, *Not Faster Than a Walk* (1939).

Nocturne

We have given our hearts to the Beast, for the Beast to share,
The stealthy-footed patrol of the city street.
Custom his name, and tame all his ways and sweet,
Though blood yet drips on the chartered pavement fair.
Not as the conquered, flinging to ancient air
Hearts more free than their fiery winding-sheet,
We have given our hearts to the Beast, for the Beast to share,
The stealthy-footed patrol of the city street.
Long his hunger as an avenging prayer,
While we, crying out where the midnights meet,
Mark the pacing of those majestic feet
With the recurrence of never-evaded care.
We have given our hearts to the Beast, for the Beast to share.

The North Wind

I hear the north wind plunging to a goal
That he knows not,—
The formless one, the nameless one, the unforgot,
Beyond the arctic or antarctic pole.
I hear him howling anger up the night

Because a windowpane arrests his flight
With form, and, manifest, the journey breaks.
A stream, a cliff, a branchy wood he makes,
Clanging his wings in anger at the sight,
Detained from warfare with the infinite;
In anger and in terror from the spot
Flies to the formless one, flies to the nameless one, the unforgot,
Lessening along the night
To what is not.

Elan Vital

Some days I tend with careful sun and showers,
But hungry time demands their fruit of me,
And I alone possess my wasted hours,
Which are the children of infinity.
I dare rejoice that I have offered gifts
To many a deity of wood and clay,
And many a house have built where sea sand drifts,
And many a ship lost on the ocean-way.
I dare rejoice at trespassing and tears
And at the doomed Niagaras of the soul
That, flowing faster as the chasm nears,
Go down in thunder, knowing not their goal;
For by their depth of wastage I can tell
How deep the source, how inexhaustible.

Hervey Allen (1889–1949) *Wampum and Old Gold,* 1920

Born William Hervey Allen in Pittsburgh, Pennsylvania, Allen was a World War I veteran and a graduate of the University of Pittsburgh. In addition to publishing several volumes of poetry, he wrote a best-selling novel (*Anthony Adverse,* 1933), a biography of Poe, several historical novels, and a nonfiction book about his experiences in the war (*Toward the Flame,* 1926).

Bacchus Is Gone

Bacchus *is gone!*
I saw him leave the shore
Upon a moonless time,
And he is gone—is gone—
Forevermore.
I saw the satyrs and the bacchanals—
Bacchus is gone—is gone—
With smoking torches as at funerals
Light him across the sea at dawn.

I saw the whimpering pards
Where he had passed—
Bacchus is gone—is gone—
Sniff to the water's edge,
Where purple stained, his footprints led—
I heard the Goat-foot whisper in the hedge,
"Bacchus is dead—is dead,"
And go aghast,
Snapping the myrtle branches as he fled.

Bacchus is gone!
And with him dancing Folly—
Bacchus is dead—is dead—
Oh, Melancholy!

No! No! He is not dead; he has but fled
To kindlier lands he knew in days before
Men snatched the purple roses from his head.

He does but wanton by some liberal shore—
Sun kissed—
And wreathed with vine leaves as of old,
With spotted beasts and maidens by his car,
And sound of timbrels like a story told
Of youth and love and blood and wine and war.

The Wingless Victory

Nike of Samothrace,
Thy godlike wings
Cleft windy space
Above the ships of kings,
Fain of thy lips,
By hope made glorious,
Time kissed thy grand, Greek face
Away from us.

Our Nike has no wings;
She has not known
Clean heights, and from her lips
Comes starvèd moan.
Mints lie that coin her grace,
And Time will hate her face,
For it has turned the world's hope
Into stone.

We

We who have come back from the war,
And stand upright and draw full breath,
Seek boldly what life holds in store

And eat its whole fruit rind and core,
Before we enter through the door
To keep our rendezvous with death.

We who have walked with death in France,
When all the world with death was rife,
Who came through all that devils' dance,
When life was but a circumstance,
A sniper's whim, a bullet's glance,
We have a rendezvous with life!

With life that hurtles like a spark
From stricken steel where anvils chime,
That leaps the space from dark to dark,
A blinding, blazing, flaming arc,
As clean as fire, and frank and stark—
White life that lives while there is time.

We will not live by musty creeds,
Who learned the truth through love and war,
Who tipped the scales for right by deeds,
When old men's lies were broken reeds,
We follow where the cold fact leads
And bow our heads no more.

Deliver us from tactless kin,
And drooling bores that start "reforms,"
And unctious folk that prate of sin,
And theorists without a chin,
And politicians out to win,
And generals in uniforms.

We have come back who broke the line
The hard Hun held by bomb and knife!
All but the blind can read the sign;
The time is ours by right divine,
Who drank with Death in blood red wine,
We have a rendezvous with life!

Oscar Williams (c. 1899–1964) *Golden Darkness,* 1920

Born Oscar Kaplan to Russian parents, Williams grew up in New York City and, in response to being rejected by publishers, at his sister's suggestion took a pen name. He continued to produce books of poetry but is most well known as an influential anthologist, with books including the New Poets Series, *Immortal Poems of the English Language,* and the Little Treasure series for Scribner's.

Two Pale Hands in the Night

Framed in the blackness of a factory pane,
Two pale hands moved and stitched long day on day,
And I, who dreamed and watched across the way,
Saw joyous beauty wander by in vain:
The sky blundered over the roof; the dawn
Lit to a dull smile the window's dust and stain;
Sunset went by, twilight and the wild grey rain;
And all the time the dim white hands stitched on.

Like drowning hands they cried in that dark place;
Winters spread wide their snow, and springs their green.
One day only a black, blank pane was seen,
And they were gone, I never saw the face;
But where the waves had closed on that white cry
The darkness thundered on beneath the sky. . . .

The Reckoning

It is not that I shall never see again
    Beauty bending over the hours,
Changing and ever-present like the sky
    Feeding the crimson flames of flowers.

It is not that I shall never feel again
    The wild rain's dolorous downpour,
Or wind and sun and glamour of the earth
    When spring is at the door.

But what if after all is over and done,
    In a weird and hushed place,
What if I should come upon the darkness
    Face to face?

All the Things I Yearned to Say

All the things I yearned to say,
All the things I never said,—
Oh, are they unrecorded as
The movements of the waves?
Oh, will they vanish—vanish as
The trails of ships at sea?

I know not, but they sometimes come
Like little ghosts of things unborn,
And flutter, furtive, through my dreams,
And haunt the dusk with wistfulness,
And sometimes through the things I say
They pulse and pulse, as silent as
The ocean's heartbeats coursing through
The veins of singing leaves.

Harold Vinal (1891–1965) *White April,* 1921

Harold Vinal was born in Vinalhaven, Maine. Largely self-educated, he was a pianist and a teacher in Maine, and later founded *Voices*, a magazine of verse. Vinal's later books of poetry include *Hurricane* (1936) and *The Compass Eye* (1940).

Forgotten

How can I remember
    Autumn and pain,
When trees hold dreams
    In their arms again?

How can my heart break
    Till it cries?
The joy of summer
    Has made me wise.

I can't remember
    What hurt me so—
Autumn and winter
    Were so long ago.

Earth Lover

Old loveliness has such a way with me,
That I am close to tears when petals fall
And needs must hide my face against a wall,
When autumn trees burn red with ecstasy.
For I am haunted by a hundred things
And more that I have seen in April days;
I have held stars above my head in praise,
I have worn beauty as two costly rings.
Alas, how short a state does beauty keep,

Then let me clasp it wildly to my heart
And hurt myself until I am a part
Of all its rapture, then turn back to sleep,
Remembering through all the dusty years
What sudden wonder brought me close to tears.

Rumors

There is a rumor when each ship returns
Of ghostly harbors that it touched at dawn,
Of blue lagoons where lifted beauty burns,
Shore lines towards which its wooden spars have gone.
There is a rumor of disastrous days
And nights by quiet islands near a town,
Of wine-red hills, beyond the waterways
Where both the moon and lovely stars looked down.
Now do they dream beneath the April sky
Of olden time and golden circumstance,
Of ancient summers, ended like a dance,
And mad adventures, now a memory.
A secret flower lying on their breast
The wind dropped down upon an old, old quest.

Medora C. Addison (1890–?) *Dreams and a Sword,* 1921

Medora Addison was born in Fitchburg, Massachusetts. Under her married name of Medora Addison Nutter, she wrote a subsequent volume of poems, *Mountain Creed* (1950), continued to contribute to literary publications throughout the 1930s, and served for a time as associate editor of *House Beautiful* magazine.

Wasted Hours

There was a day I wasted long ago,
Lying upon a hillside in the sun—
An April day of wind and drifting clouds;
An idle day and all my work undone.

The little peach trees with their coral skirts
Were dancing up the hillside in the breeze;
The grey-walled meadows gleamed like bits of jade
Against the crimson bloom of maple trees.

And I could smell the warmth of trodden grass.
The coolness of a freshly harrowed field;
And I could hear a bluebird's wistful song
Of love and beauty only half revealed.

I have forgotten many April days
But one there is that comes to haunt me still—
A day of feathered trees and windy skies
And wasted hours on a sunlit hill.

Walls

I live in a garden
    Flanked by walls, high walls,
A beautiful garden
    Where the sunlight falls,

And sometimes I listen
    When the trees are still
To the song of a boy
    On a far-off hill.

. . .

I wonder if he hears,
    When his singing calls,
The beating of white hands
    Against high walls?

The Deserted Farm

With darkened windows staring down the lane
And tattered shingles clinging to its side,
    It crouches by the hill,
And waits for those who will not come again
To that scarred doorway fashioned with such pride
    By hands that lie so still.

Bernard Raymund (1891–1977) *Hidden Waters,* 1921

Bernard Raymund lived in Dublin, Ohio, and taught at Ohio State University. Subsequent poems and reviews appeared in Poetry magazine, among other publications.

Shepherd's Pipe

I sat me down on the hilltop's rim
Toward the wane of a long, slow afternoon
Where the shadows crept from the river's brim
Bringing the twilight none too soon,
And found beside me a fallen bit
Of twig that a bee had burrowed in,
Four clean-cut holes just made to fit
Four fingers, and a rounded, thin,
Most tempting mouthpiece! Quick had sought
My lips to call the spirit forth.
No sound—Mayhap have the shepherds taught
Their lays as their lambs to shun the north?
Or must I follow the selfsame way
Forgotten by men long, long ago,
That the first lone herdsman learned to play?
Sure the stubborn reed would have it so!
But try as I might I tried in vain,
The long lost way was closed—to me;
And only the ghost of a lilting strain
Came floating with airy mockery
From a land as old as melody
Where a shepherd sat on a hilltop's rim
Toward the wane of a long, slow afternoon
And the huddled sheep lay close by him
Where the shadows crept from the river's brim
Bringing the twilight none too soon . . .

Wind Flower

(To R. M. S.)

You were so little and the wind took you,
Carried you over the garden wall,
What a wonder it was that anyone found you
Who scarcely had opened at all.
Damp earth and dead leaves strewn thick about you,
How could such a fragile thing grow
So straight and unstunted, so shining and slender!
Will anyone ever know?
So little you asked for, a corner of quiet,
A glimpse of sun and a patch of sky,
A flash of wings in the gray of morning
From some bird passing by.
A corner of quiet by moss-stained maples
Tucked in under the garden wall;
What a pity the wind must whip down on you
Before it was yours at all!

Wanderer

I have come home again to meadowland and orchard,
And the dear, cool fingers of home wind fast about my own,
While broken words of love are sounding at my shoulder
Saying—You were away, and everything was lone.
—The hills you knew and meadowland and house were empty;
The cherries blossomed and the petals fell unseen,
The dark fruit rounded, ripened and was gathered,
And oh how empty was the place where you had been!
Sometimes the dogs would come, whining softly for you,
Asking for a romp across the windy fields once more,
Wondering what kept you so, worried and bewildered,
Waiting for your eager step, your whistle at the door—.

Yes, I am home again, the chimney smoke is rising
Straight against the sunset, and lo! a window gleams,
But there's no voice at my shoulder, no clasp of dear cool fingers,
Only the quiet frost and the dim-eyed sorrow of dreams.

Paul Tanaquil (1898–1972) *Attitudes,* 1921

Born Jacques Georges Clemenceau Le Clercq in Austria, Paul Tanaquil became
an American citizen and graduated from the University of California, Berkeley.
He served in the Office of War Information during World War II. As Paul Tanaquil,
he continued to write poetry, and as Le Clercq he translated Balzac, La Fontaine,
Sforza, and Giono. He was also the father of the prima ballerina Tanaquil
LeClercq.

Pour Elle

There are things of Beauty of which I never shall tire:
Moving seas and sea foam; and the blue
Sky above the tall church spire;
And the blue smoke
That rises from a hidden fire
Deep down in the valley; flowers; dew
Over the green grasses; moonlight dripping through
Sieves of silver foliage, delicately intricate as lace;
Mighty hills arising ever higher;
Long, sloping roofs and clean white houses under;
April rain; flash of lightning; crash of thunder;
Children laughing; the trill of meadowlarks; and the lithe grace
Of horses at a canter; more—-and more—all true,
Noble and good and beautiful to view.

But best of all, the wonder,
The poignancy of you
As changing shadows creep across your face. . . .

Mirage

And all of it is laughter
That moves us an hour
And vanishes after,
Or tears . . . tears . . .
Deep—without power
Over the years.

Les Cygnes

I have watched swans . . . drifting . . . languorously
Down placid pools and stirring scarce a ripple
On the smooth surface that shone glassily,
The tips of their red mouths round as a nipple
Or, opened wide, as sharp as points that stipple
Sinuous, rare designs; all-dreamily
Craning their slim necks forward in a triple
Beauty of movement, line and symmetry.

I have watched swans with such a curious care
That all their movements are become for me
Token of the eternal beautiful:
A flash of light across a silent pool,
A thing created but that it might be
For them that watch a wonder and despair.

Dean B. Lyman, Jr. (1896–1965) The Last Lutanist, 1922

Educated at New York University, Dean Lyman became treasurer of the Union and New Haven Trust Company, and wrote a history of that firm. An amateur historian of New Haven, Connecticut, he compiled *An Atlas of Old New Haven* (1929).

Fragment

     . . . through the tumult swift I ran,
The bloody sword above me in my hand.
I hacked and hewed, blood ran, shouts rang, groans answered.
The air was thick with smells and sounds of battle.
My eyes were shining with the sheer excitement
And madness of the moment. Breath was labored,
The limbs were weary, but forgotten—. Forward!
Crash helm! Stick belly! Up! Up the ladder!
Ah! Now we're over! Onward! On! Pursue them!

But after all, what pleasure in pursuing?
The lines are broken and the wall is won . . .
And nothing else remains but lassitude.
Who would have dreamed this spot was close to us—
The cool-green grove, pressed in against the wall?
How soon the fever of fury yields to color—
The calm, sweet green of grass and trees! How soon
The limbs protest, bereft of exaltation,
And ache to rest upon the inviting sward!
The hilted blade is heavy to the hand,
And suddenly the wonder comes to mind
That there should ever be an urge to battle.
For now it seems that all delight is here,
Is rampant in the wind and sky, and lies

Along the greenery on the cushioned earth
Beside this conquered wall. It's Heaven here.

Who said the Hanging Gardens were a dream?

Restless

Along the winding reaches of the river
The water-willows bend above the tide,
And through the sentient semi-darkness quiver
The broken gleams of twilight. Side by side
Upon the water, indolently glide
Two swans with dripping silver in their wings.
No motion else upon the waters is
And through the stillness not a bird-call rings.
The God of Silence to this region brings
Only the muted music which is his.
Upon the river quietly descends
The calm of evening-hour. The swans at last
Together tranquilly have floated past.
The ruffle on the river-surface ends.
And yet the tumult of my troubled heart
Beats on beneath a surface-quietude
And longings inexpressible impart
The undercurrent of a restless mood.

The Dark City

There is a dark city
Off in a far strand
Where is no love, no pity,
And no kind hand,
But dull dreams
Pass in the dark silence
Of tall grass and cool streams.

A dark city shines
In the dusk of a far strand
And the walls touch the tall pines
That grow on either hand
Where dim dreams
Pass in the dark whisper
Of tall trees and spent streams.

There is a dark city
In the depths of a mad mind
Where neither love nor pity
Shall ever be divined,
But dead dreams
Pass in the dark temple
Of thwarted hopes and memory-gleams.

Amos Niven Wilder (1895–1993) *Battle-Retrospect,* 1922

Born in Madison, Wisconsin, Amos Wilder served in World War I and later studied at Oxford University, the University of Belgium, and the Yale Divinity School. In addition to his World War I journal, *Armageddon Revisited*, which was published posthumously in 1994, Wilder wrote numerous books on theology. After teaching at the Chicago Theological Seminary and the University of Chicago, he joined Harvard University as Hollis Professor of Divinity.

Battle-Retrospect

Those sultry nights we used to pass outdoors
And through the cherry orchards to the fields
That stretched down to the floor of the Champagne,
And there that steady thunder in the west
That nightly rolled and echoed without rest
Broke on our ears with new intensity.
As those who come out suddenly upon
The sea, whose murmur reached them in the woods,
Are stunned by the loud-crashing surf that runs
In surging thunder all along the coast,
So the great breakers of this sea of sound
Broke over us when we had reached the fields,
And through the starry silences was borne
That fluctuating roar, its rise and fall
And climaxes that filled the soul with dread.

We saw the febrile flashes, hour by hour,
Incessant, over many miles of front,
Succeeding each the other instantly
As though in some fantastical pursuit,
In ever madder race. They shot their light
To the last stars; the empyrean throbbed
With man's device,—or were they men, or gods?

We saw the soaring signals flare and float,
Likewise incessant, multitudinous,
As though some city of the Vulcans lay
Across the land with flaming forges bright,
And panting furnaces that scorched the night,
Hammering out the ribs of a new earth
Or some new instrument of destiny.

A perturbation deeper far than fear
Took hold on us,
Never did man behold or hear
A thing more ominous;
So regular, so fierce, fatality
Was in its voice; no power on earth
Could halt that tempest for the briefest space,
Nor cool that mighty furnace, nor reach down
To guard the myriad souls within its blast.

Gazing upon that scene, it seemed there boiled
Red lava from the ground, some mouth of hell
Gaping, and smoking horror to the skies;
Or that some molten tide of death swept down
Beating relentlessly against the fields,
The summer fields that would not be submerged.

And I have seen, or thought I saw, the gods
(Mayhap the saints and devils of our faith)
Gather like planing eagles in the dusk
Above the battle and direct its course,
Clashing in mid-air, sweeping in great troops
To new reliefs and warring in the sky,
Whose immanence translated the dark hour
And sublimized the drama till it seemed
A war of genii and a spectre strife,
Enveloped in an Æschylean shade.

. . .

The dead are gone and we are left alive
And those incredible and awful days
Are now no more. Nay, e'en their memory
Grows faded, and the fates that gave us them
Seem jealous that we should retain so much
As of forbidden knowledge. For no doubt
In those days there moved giants on the earth,
And it were better that these secrets lie
Unhinted at to those who never knew
Lest they find faith too easy. It were bad
Were a dull generation born for trade
To know that genii showed themselves those months
Often, scaling horizons, bent on tasks
Out of proportion to these times of peace,
And that great prodigies of ministrants
In aural loveliness would brood at night,
Extraordinary comforters, come down
To cope with like extraordinary pain.
But faith and all its then ambassadors
Have passed to some far corner of the skies
And left earth to its winter of desires,
Its ebb of passions and its leafless trees.

. . .

When will that great age recommence
And all heaven's hosts in serried flights
Circle again in sudden immanence
About the earth and fill its days and nights
With lights and glooms and atmosphere intense?

When will that great age recommence
And many heroes come to birth?
When will men have again that sense
Of great things purposed on our earth
And issues toward of great significance?

When will that greater age return
And heaven draw near to earth again,
And thoughts of cosmic moment burn
Across our skies, and it grow plain
That mighty projects call to battle stern?

How are we fallen from our high estate
Who saw the dawn at Soissons that July
Rise upon pandemonium; heard, elate,
The trampling of the steeds of destiny,
And saw the flashes at the wheels of fate!

How are we fallen on another day
Whose life was a perpetual sacrament,
Supping with gods, and kneeling down to pray
In cataclysm when the world was rent,
As we strode shouting where the lightnings play!

O Marshal of the myriad souls of men,
O Marshal of the squadrons of the stars,
Lead us out to Thy battles once again,
To marches and to sufferings and scars,
Beyond the seas, beyond the sunset-bars,
Out where the air is pure and dreams remain.

O Soldier, Friend of soldiers, understand!
Call us out from the peril of our sloth,
The cheapening of our faiths. Once more, command!
And we shall rise again, repugnant, wroth
From these dark ways, to march o'er sea and land

Again to hear the trumpets of the slain,
Again to see the flares float o'er the steep,
To see the angel legions swarm again
And on before our glorying columns sweep
Down lists that lead beyond earth's sodden plain.

Unsung

Would now that we who battled were not dumb,
Who shared the dire communion of the strife
With those who died. Would there were living some
Could paint those greatest moments to the life.
Then as the page of ancient epic flames
With heroes canonized, the wise, the strong,
So these our recent days and later names
Would grow illustrious in modern song.
Surely the world is dull of heart and blind
Dismissing with so casual a glance
This bright inheritance of recent glory,
As though great deeds were to the past confined,
When Iliads yesterday were fought in France
And Odysseys that claim their place in story.

Romanesque

Imagination smote me with his glaive
In Tournay's old cathedral as I stood
With holden eyes, and Magic clapped his hood
Upon me, gazing down its vaulted nave;
I know not what impetuous angel drave
The garish phantoms thence and so renewed
The antique Reverie, and the occult Mood,
Cloaking me in the shadows of the grave—
Vistas I saw of arches without end,
The horrid labyrinths of the Middle Age,
The catacombs of life, which high desire
Taught men by paroxysms to transcend,
Who so aspiring in ecstatic rage,
Transformed this prison to yon soaring choir.

Marion M. Boyd (1894–1974) *Silver Wands,* 1922

Born in Marietta, Ohio, Marion Boyd studied at Smith College and Yale University. As Marion Boyd Havighurst she published the novels *Strange Island* (1957), *Sycamore Tree* (1960), and *Murder in the Stacks* (1934). She and her husband, Walter Havighurst, co-wrote several books about Scandinavian settlers in Wisconsin and Minnesota.

Blackberry Winter

You wonder at cool days and cooler nights
After the heat we had a week ago.
You look about you at this opening world
And wonder if white buds are really snow.
Of course the world is white. I see it too
In drooping snowball bushes, and in plumes
Of scented locust falling at our feet,
And in slow-opening syringa blooms.
But then I cannot hold with your idea
That barefoot dawn has fallen in love with May
And that all shyly in her cool, slim hands
She brings white offerings each day.

I have a friend, a brown and earthy soul,
Who sniffs these long, cool days that feel like fall,
Then crinkles up her nose and crisply says,
"Blackberry winter." That explains it all.

Gold of Beeches

The gold I love is not of dandelions,
That prick the lawn in pattern bright;
Nor of blown daffodils, tied sails of light,
That flutter vainly at their verdant moorings;

Nor of glad buttercups that streak the fields
Like gold inlay on warriors' shields.

Perhaps you have not seen the gold I love,
Nor know how permanent it is.
One has to know a beech tree to know this.
To live year round with one and know its moods;
To see the dulness of the winter bark
Transformed to silver with the melting snow;
To watch it gleaming bare where moonbeams blow,
When other trees flaunt tattered bits of green;
To wonder if the beech tree has forgot
The age-old magic of its alchemy;
And then, one day of early dawn, to see
Once more the golden miracle
Of outflung buds along a silver branch,
And to feel one with lively squirrels that leap
From tempting bud to bud where gold lies deep.
Oh, I have loved the gold of beech trees when
I could but keep the memory in my heart
Through long green months till winds had beat
A shower of burnished leaves down to my feet.

Blue Cups

Blue cups, blue plates, blue sugar-bowl and pitcher,
And blue tea-pot as well;
Strange that I remember only setting
For hands like shell.

Gray couch, gray walls, gray shadows and gray twilight,
And fog-gray eyes as well;
Strange that I remember only background
Where gold light fell.

Beatrice E. Harmon (dates unknown) *Mosaics,* 1922

Next to nothing exists in the public record or the Yale University Press archives about Beatrice E. Harmon. She lived for a time on Bestwick Street in Los Angeles.

The Woman to the Man

The dream
Is done,
And love at last departed.
Poor dream!
But one
At least, is broken-hearted!

Who'll pay
The price
Of love denied, defrauded?
You'll say,
"Suffice
That love himself applauded!"

Manlike
You smile
And shrug to speed the going;
You strike
The while
I strive and weep, not knowing.

You take,
I give,
As 'twas and ever shall be!
I break,
You live
And jest while fears appall me.

Why ask
Who'll pay?
Of us two I'm the debtor.
My task
Today—
Tomorrow I'll know better!

October

I crossed a little crooked bridge
    That leads by meadows sere;
A robin in a privet hedge
    Complained the dying year;
The flowers on the water's edge
    Dropped each a pale blue tear.

I sat down on the riverside
    To watch the maple trees;
Their banners floating far and wide
    With every vagrant breeze
Made crimson cloud and crimson tide
    And little crimson seas.

I saw a solitary bird
    Among the branches bare,
And thought I never yet had heard
    So sadly sweet an air.
I took a thought, a wish, a word,
    And made a little prayer.

Rondeau

A bluebird sings high in the white aspen tree,
    His "merry-sweet! merry-sweet! merry!" to spring;
The mavis sings soft and the robin sings free,
    And the bells of the bright heavens silverly ring.

The gray hawk swings low,
And the brown warbler cries,
And the ebony crow
Flashes down thwart the skies.
While the bluebird sings clear on his white aspen bough,
His "merry-sweet! merry-sweet! merry!" to spring,
I'll dig me a grave for my sorrow, I vow,
And I'll buy me a staff, and a rondeau I'll sing,
With a "merry-sweet! merry-sweet! merry!" to spring.

Elizabeth Jessup Blake (1894–1973) *Up and Down,* 1923

Born in Alieh, Lebanon, Elizabeth Jessup Blake graduated from Smith College, married Kingsley Blake, and raised three children in Scarsdale, New York. A privately printed volume of her poems, *Through the Years*, appeared shortly after her death.

Ode to Loneliness

They have not known you who berate you so;
    They have not chosen you as friend to know,
Sweet winsome maid that haunts the hilltop crags
    And gives the distant view a keener thrill,
Companion spirit on the wild-rose hill,
    Why do men paint you as the queen of hags,
Fit only to invest yourself in rags,
    Gifted the soul with fear and dread to fill,
Potent to drive to madness and to kill—?
    Such know you not. I seek you where the flags
Sway in the cool rush of a mountain spring.
    I find you smiling ere the sunrise stains
The soft grey wings of dawn. Your silence reigns
    At even when the mists rise from the plains.

Vainly men crowd to touch dear Beauty's dress;
    Would you know beauty, then know loneliness.

Bedouin Lullaby

The clouds sleep on the high grey hill
And the sea in silver sleeps;
An eagle soaring high and still
Watch in the noon-tide keeps;

The sun forgets that in the West
In the West is his journey done.
He sleeps aloft in the white hot sky,
Sleep too, my restless one.
Soon the winds of the afternoon
Will sing to the high grey hill,
Soon the sea will dance for thee,
Then thou shalt run at will;
But all the world must dream and rest
While the sun hangs asleep on high, —
Wait for the waking wind of the West
Then, my little bird, fly.

Memories

A Hilltop

Wind and sweet-scented sun and golden bushes,
Wind that made symphonies in sweeping rushes
Through sighing pine and tattling sassafras
O'er floes of rock adrift in seas of grass.

Dawn

A spider thread held both my hands
I was a prisoner, I knew,
Yet I was stung to nimbleness
By ice-cold pricks of trodden dew.
The breeze pulled slyly at my hair,
A sunbeam flashed across my eyes—
And all at once I was aware
That Fairyland around us lies.

Beirût—1917

The plain is still—
Down curve the slumbrous hills;
The fountain brim

With langorous music fills
The clear soft dark;
The crescent moon distills
Her magic light,
And it is night.

Dorothy E. Reid (1900–?) *Coach into Pumpkin,* 1924

Dorothy Ellen Reid studied at Ohio State University. She later worked for the American Insurance Union magazine in addition to publishing some verse for children. Reid lived in Worthington, Ohio.

Volumes

This is the agony, that we can look
    Clean to the soul of one another, see
The candid page turn backward like a book,
    And learn no more of you, no more of me.

Here are the letters, large enough and plain
    For any reading; here are words for sages;
And all their meanings, conned and conned again,
    Leave but a pleasant jumble on the pages.

You, whose bright blood leaps lightly from my heart,
    Whose every tear first kindles in my eyes,
Dwell so completely on a shelf apart
    That even commas constitute surprise.

Study in Clouds

I can never be to you a sunset
    For all you may hold me and cry
"Love, love, love"; in the evening
    You will turn again to the sky.

And there's very small comfort in knowing
    That all I can say or can do
Is less than a little chilly vapour
    With a cold sun struggling through.

Sonnet

Oh, study not to make your love so safe
That winds may never find a careless chink
Or rain anoint its portals. Never think
That love is not a wanderer and a waif.
You train the vines so carefully about
The shuttered windows and the guarded door,
You sweep the ashes from the hearth with more
Than needful care, and smooth the curtains out.
Oh, you would make of love a planted thing,
A quiet inn on some forgotten lane
Where storms will never come; but, ah my dear,
Know now love must be up and wandering
In windy weathers, and the only pain
Love does not shrink from is the pain you fear.

Eleanor Slater (1903–?) *Quest,* 1925

Eleanor Slater lived in Rochester, New York. In addition to poetry she also wrote a biography, *Charles Henry Brent: Everybody's Bishop* (1932).

Balm

Where is your heart that was full of trouble?—
And the stream so still that the swan swims double.
Where is your heart that was full of care?—
And the gold on the grass like the gold of your hair.

Because Your Heart Was Shy

Here is the breath of winter gone to waste.
Here is a perfect power lost to earth,
A mighty passion lightly, falsely placed,
So that it loses dignity and worth.
Here is the breath of summer gone astray,
Lilac where lilac never ought to be,
The ashes of a beauty swept away,
And roses blooming in obscurity,
I see your body strong in inner power;
I see your soul made radiant with beauty,
That dares to cast a shadow on its flower
And sell its freedom for a fancied duty.
My dear, what right have you each day to die
In little ways because your heart is shy?

Disillusionment

Your mind was like a primer newly bought,
Without the pages cut, with words unlearned
And lessons all untried. Now it has turned
Familiar as myself. What I had thought
Was much too deep to master, has been taught
To me each day in little ways concerned
With common things, until there has been burned
Deep in my heart the insight that I sought.
Now it is done. I find my work grown play.
I turn the pages one by one and find
Only the common words of every day.—
But I had best been ignorant and blind—
For I have found it now, in dull dismay,
An honest book, but one to leave behind.

Thomas Hornsby Ferril (1896–1988) *High Passage,* 1925

Born in Denver, Colorado, Thomas Ferril studied at Colorado College and served in World War I. He and his wife edited and published the weekly *Rocky Mountain Herald* from 1939 to 1972. Working as a press agent for the Great Western Sugar Company, Ferril also published a collection of prose sketches titled *I Hate Thursday* (1946), as well as *New and Selected Poems* (1952). He was named poet laureate of Colorado in 1979.

Mountain Rivers

Arid Channel

This is the river's skeleton,
Bone white, desert dry,
The rocks are skulls with moss for hair
That moves when the wind is high;
This is the outworn channel,
The yellow shadows slant
Through sandy crypts of oven rocks
Where pallid lizards pant.

River Gods

The river gods roam in the sweet wild mint,
Down the silver dark where the bright fish leap
At the amber moons of the faraway pools
In the hour when the willow children sleep.

Wind Flood

Sleepers who wake in the midnight roar
Of the rising wind in the pines will dream
Through the staring black of a cabin wall,
On the black flood-call of a rising stream,
But the dappled fawn where the birches quiver
Knows the roar of the pines from the roar of the river.

The Empire Sofa

They could grow used to seeing bones
Of buffalo and sometimes men,
They could grow strong on cracking dreams
Of gold to give them rest again,
They could pit happy years to come
Against the prairie's timeless length,
They had illusions that could calm
The frantic restlessness of strength.

But things like this they had to pass,
Sunk in the sand on the Arkansas,
This rosewood sofa that clutched the sun
With every foot a gryphon's claw;
They saw it shining far ahead,
They turned to see it far behind,
And dreamed of men who dared not lose
The things they dared not hope to find.

One wagon whistled *Money Musk*,
Another chattered into laughter,
But no one spoke to anyone
About what they were going after;
An hour creaked by and dreams came back,
The wagons talked with even breath
And grew secure the more they passed
The more familiar forms of death.

Missing Men

Wind River, Sweetwater, Yellowstone,
Rosebud, Powder, Green,
Where are the men who wandered away,
And never again were seen?
Where are their rifles, knives and traps?
Last night they sat around the fire,

The air was sweet with evergreen,
The air was wild with brier.

How many times did they lie down
To drink with palms crushed in the sand,
And bodies arched above that world
They clutched with either hand?
How many times did they drink so,
Before the time they did not rise,
And felt no sand in either hand,
No rushes in their eyes?

They say a man lies like a log,
So weather-beaten in the grass,
That men pay no more heed to him
Than to live men who pass;
He's like a log a little while,
And soon is vanished much the same
As others who live long enough
Quite to forget his name.

Lindley Williams Hubbell (1901–1994) *Dark Pavilion,* 1926

Lindley Hubbell was born in Hartford, Connecticut. Tutored in seven languages by a polyglot aunt, he was a reference librarian at the New York Public Library for twenty-two years. In 1954, he moved to Japan to teach English and Greek drama at Doshisha University in Kyoto. Hubbell became a Japanese citizen in 1960, taking the name Hayashi Shuseki. He published seventeen books of poetry and wrote several studies of English literature, particularly Shakespeare's plays, for a Japanese audience.

Forgive Me

Forgive me if I bring
Wraiths in my eyes;
Do not show surprise
At so slight a thing.
Which of us is not
A house with frosted windows,
With figures shifting
Behind the blurred glass
Like shadows on water?
Which of us is not
A tired vane, lifting
To show which way the wind goes?
Forgive me if I bring
Death in my eyes;
Do not show surprise,
It is a common thing.

I Remember a Hill

I remember a hill with trees growing thick at the top,
    And I remember a boy who climbed the hill
On summer evenings and looked out over the city
    And watched the city grow still.

And I remember what the boy had in his heart,
    Sitting there hour after hour with his eyes blurred
And finally laying his head on the grass and crying,
    Certain of not being heard.

The Sealed Mouth to the Baffled Heart

You said, "He is proud,
He is not lonely at all.
If he should turn his head
At my footfall,
It would be
Most casually."

You said, "He is young,
Yet if I should lay my hand
Upon him, he would not care
Nor understand;
If I should lay my hand upon his hair,"
You said, "he would neither understand nor care."

Mildred Bowers (1901–1984) *Twist o' Smoke,* 1927

Mildred Bowers was educated at Mount Holyoke College, Northwestern University, the University of Chicago, and the University of Wisconsin. While in college, she contributed poems to a Chicago newspaper under the byline Twist o' Smoke, whence the title of her book. After marrying John Armstrong, she continued to publish verse in magazines under her married name before moving to Great Neck, New York, and raising two children.

I Have Sat by Many Fires

I have sat by many fires,
Clasped many a hand,
Looked and looked into dear eyes
Trying to understand.

All I understood was this—
Love can grow with years
Though fires die
And hands are frail
And eyes are dim with tears.

Punctuation

The universe unfolds itself
In cryptic explanation.
But all that I can read of it
Is the punctuation . . .
Tendrils of the grapevine
Forever shaping, "Why?",
Exclamation-points of grass,
Periods in the sky.

We must not even think of faces known
Long years ago when I was young, and you,
Of faces and of places that have grown
Different as we are different—and new,
Strange, and but half-remembered, and unreal.
Our present life has all that it can hold;
And time must fasten memory with its seal.
Remembering will hurt less when we are old.

Ted Olson (1899–1981) *A Stranger and Afraid,* 1927

Theodore B. Olson was born in Laramie, Wyoming, studied at the University of Wyoming, served in the Office of War Information in World War II, and later worked for the State Department. As a journalist, he wrote for the *New York Herald-Tribune*, the *Denver Post*, the *San Francisco Journal*, and the *Oakland Enquirer*. His other books include the poetry collection *Hawk's Way* (1941) and a childhood memoir, *Ranch on the Laramie* (1973).

Two Unlamented

Be not afraid. There can be no ghosts here.
There are no ghosts where love has never been.
Lift the latch boldly, firmly, and go in.
Dust will companion you, but have no fear
Of shadowy hands on yours, of eyes that peer
Shyly from long-shut casements, of the thin,
Far tinkle of a ghostly mandolin
Chording the ghostly tunes of yesteryear.

No ghosts are here. No furtive shade survives
Two who were dust before their years were done,
Too pale of blood for saintliness or sin.
They lie in graves as narrow as their lives,
One with the mire, who never before were one.
There are no ghosts where love has never been.

Nocturne in Sepia

This hour is satin. Draw it round you
Prayerfully. Wear it while you may.
Let it soothe a heart too quickly
Bruised by the sackcloth garb of day.

Pity that hands as frail as pollen
Should have grown in toil so rough
They dare not fill their ache with twilight,
Fearing to rend its filmy stuff.

Be not afraid. It is your hour,
Wistful and reticent like you.
Grief has no sorcery to ravel
Its gossamer of dusk and dew.

Dip your fingers in it. Gather
Its cool fragrance to your cheek.
If your eyes are tired, close them,
And do not speak.

Silence will blow, like dead leaves, over you.
Silence, like snow, will heap you high.
Who knows? Time, returning
To claim his gift, may pass you by.

Stay-at-Home Sonnets

I. *Maps*

I had no use for mezzotint or oil
When I was younger. Maps were better far
To splash your walls with color, and uncoil
Prismatic roads to Ind and Zanzibar.
Windows may frame a dung-heap, or a line
Of laundry jigging drunkenly; but these
Were casements opening wide to winds like brine,
Cormorant-pinioned winds from perilous seas.

I have torn down my maps, and burned, or sown
Their lying colors on the lying wind.
They cannot cheat me now, since I have known
The arduous roads to Zanzibar and Ind,

And found those lands of spurious jade and flame
As drab and drear as that from which I came.

II. Lariat

Once the horizon was a lariat,
Obedient to the cunning of my wrist.
And swaggeringly, the arrogant autocrat
Of an arena world, I made it twist
A tilting wheel of sinuous necromancy
Round heels and head, while, debonair and proud,
I vaulted out or in as pleased a fancy
Half tipsy with the plaudits of the crowd.

My craft has fled me now. The stubborn rope
Snarls in mid-air, goes awkwardly asprawl.
And the horizon that my urgent hope
Claimed for its toy has grown much like a wall,
Except, reata-like, it tightens fast,
To strangle me inexorably at last.

III. Plough the Road Under

Plough the road under, and nail fast the gate.
Let there be tillage where the wheels cut deep.
Lay spur and saddle by. The year grows late,
And meager time is left to sow and reap.
The share will peel the sanded ruts asunder
Until no devious clue remains to chart
How I rode forth in quest of love and plunder,
And how returned, pauper in purse and heart.

Plough deep, and harrow well, and seed it thickly.
Earth, stubbornly remembering, may reveal
This year, perhaps, by twin rows dwarfed and sickly,
The sterile heritage of hoof and wheel.
Not long, though. Earth forgets. Her old scars swell
New harvests now. And may not mine as well?

Francis Claiborne Mason (1900–?) *The Unchanging Mask,* 1927

Francis Mason studied at Harvard University and the University of Virginia. In 1931 he was an assistant professor of English at Gettysburg College in Pennsylvania.

Prophecy at Love's End

When you are gone, the quiet of his heart
Shall be as are those ancient battlefields
Whereof, long reaped, the grim and grisly yields
Of sated wars that tore the world apart
All utterly are vanished, where the worth
Of many a mighty arm is drowsing dust,
Where the last broken bayonet is rust,
And every shattered musket under earth.

And in his soul (as, in an empty square
Where towers and gibbet and the midnight's truce
Hold silence with the swaying of the noose,
The hangman nods upon the scaffold stair)
Shall couch those very specters he defied:
Dead peace and desolation, side by side.

Crossing

Three men sat by a river
    Of twisted lights agleam.
One had shattered a halo
    And one had broken a dream

And one had scattered a treasure,
    Save one dull penny of gold,

And all were wan as waiting death,
    Wearing an age un-old.

But one went over the river,
    And one turned back his feet,
And one found still, green abysses
    Of languid waters, sweet.

Song of the Image Makers

Where worn niches edge the way
    Down a templed colonnade
Rest the years of yesterday,
    Weary gods, dusk-dim in shade.

Grim of aspect, pallid, grey,
    Lie the days that gave us breath,
Sodden images of clay
    Fashioned in the fear of death.

On some pinnacle of earth
    Sleep uncarven in the stone,
Till our chisel bring them birth,
    Stronger gods we have not known.

Frances M. Frost (1905–1959) *Hemlock Wall,* 1928

Born in Saint Albans, Vermont, Frances Frost studied at Middlebury College and
the University of Vermont. She was the author of six books of poetry, five novels,
and some children's literature. Frost's awards include the O. Henry Award, the
Golden Rose Award, and the Shelley Memorial Award.

Lullaby

Earth and I,
Earth and I
Are setting our lips to a lullaby,
For spring has come
And the sowing's over—
April, April, who was your lover?
At the full of the moon, who was your lover?

My step is slow
And my heart is slow
And the child turns in my flesh and sleeps.
Spring has gone
And the growing's past,
And the time for the harvest is here at last—
Who reaps you, Earth, who reaps?

The days are yellow,
The nights are blue,
The ripened fruit drops down from the tree.
Child-limbs wait
At my body's gate
And the sickle of pain moves over me.

Earth and I,
Earth and I
Are setting our lips to a lullaby.

A long wind glides
In the fallen clover
And Earth and I remember a lover. . . .
Sleep, baby, sleep!

Deserted Orchard

They have given the orchard back to itself again,
And left it to huddle, untended
Under the hill, companioned by only a fence
That never was mended.

The dead boughs twist and slant in the bloom of the year.
White petals drift and scatter
With no one to measure the coming yield or to think
That apples matter

In a year or a life. But the orchard puts forth its fruit,
And in time the apples tumble,
Slice open and crush on a stone or smother in grass.
A man might stumble

On meanings here, as well as on orchard hummocks.
With even the fence uncaring,
The trees will blossom and yield until petals are ended
And ended the bearing.

Hands

I have held my hands to the rain,
Cupped silver wet and cool.
Rain over, I have dipped bright water
From a mountain-shadowed pool.

I have plunged my hands in loam,
Felt the after-sunset cold

Creep through furrows, cling to fingers
Suddenly grown old.

I have cupped my heart to the earth,
Beauty has burned my eyes.
Only my hands remember the cold,
Only my hands are wise.

Henri Faust (1899?–1976?) *Half-Light and Overtones,* 1928

Henri Faust was the pen name of William E. Spencer, who lived in Los Altos, California, and worked in a "quasi-judicial capacity" for the federal government. He later disavowed his Yale book, hoping to make a fresh start as an author, but he does not seem to have published anything else.

As Autumn Fields

These autumn fields come over me as strange
As music of a minor symphony
Whose themes recur in so restricted range
I marvel at their bleak intensity.
A music of the autumn's ruin—its doom—
I hear with leaves that fall, with grass that turns
From emerald to bronze, with every bloom
That languishes . . . The ruthless sumac burns
The sedge to ash . . . Meek suppliants of the law:
The snake retreats, a shiver in the grass;
The orioles depart for Panama;
And in the bitter night the wild geese pass . . .
(My thoughts make movement in restricted range,
As autumn fields, as sorrowful, as strange . . .).

The Valley of the Muted Songbirds

Beyond all sorrow-sighing and all silences
Of those who mourn in exile
And the pale stained meadows of Nirvana
Where the flame of rapture dies—
Deep plunged in a desolate stillness
In vast windless groves
That sigh not

Nor give incense unto the night
But hallow a listening void—
Is the Valley of the Muted Songbirds.

Here are the robin and the lark,
Nightingale, bluebird, bobolink,
Woodthrush, oriole, red-eyed vireo,
Cardinal, grosbeak, yellow-throated warbler,
The wren and the jay.
Silence broods.
Tiredly they draw their beaks
Into their shrunken breasts—
Their eyes stir not
They build no nests
But sit in motley company
And dream. . . .

Dream of the lost enchanted hillsides
White rivers spinning in the spring
Bloom-foam of haw lanes in the spring
Retreats under the wide cool eaves
Of poplars shingled jade and silver
Jade and silver in censer of the spring.
What madrigals of the dawn!
What delights of the sun-drowsy noon!
They swoon at remembrance of rapture
In the azure-dim hour of twilight. . . .
Their dreams are wrung with music,
Strange, holy chords—
Whether grass or tree the nesting place,
They hear delirious flutings of the fields,
Wild, intimate cravings
Of the old loved symphony. . . .

Tiredly they draw their beaks
Into their shrunken breasts
And dream. . . .

The vast windless groves sigh not
Nor give incense unto the night
In the Valley of the Muted Songbirds.

The Amethyst Gardens

Walk softly . . . here are the amethyst gardens
Fantasy of frost traced by a wintry moon. . . .
Walk softly . . . the faintest stir
Causes the glacé leaves to crack
And the heavy pendants of amethystine fruits
To clatter upon the cool hard grass
And break. . . .

Walk softly in the amethyst gardens
Where but the reverberation of moon-birds
May quiver through the dim, silvered groves,
Beating against the frozen trees, bell-tenored;
Here are lagoons that are visionary and blue
Lost in a maze of chill hyacinth clusters
And here is a languor as of fountains—
Their motion is the flow of a frozen river
And their music threads the fiber of silences. . . .
Stir softly as moth with slow-fanning wings,
Lest the taut limbs snap and crisp leaves fall,
For these are the amethyst gardens
That sharpen the pallor of the moon—
Dreamers come here and lovers,
Their legends have been caught in music
And frozen in bleak snarls of trees. . . .

Walk softly . . . in the amethyst gardens,
But dreamers come here, and lovers;
Here is their frozen rendezvous. . . .

Louise Owen (1901–1995) *Virtuosa,* 1929

Born Louise Guyol in Concord, New Hampshire, Louise Owen graduated from
Smith College and shortly thereafter married the architect Harold Holmes Owen.
She continued to write poetry and to publish widely in journals and magazines,
while raising a family and working as an editor and proofreader. Her second book
of poems was *Song Without Words.*

Two Cinquains

I

The white
Of cherry bloom
Is the white falling foam
That tops the breaking billow of
The wood.

II

Words are
The silver notes
That ring the chord of sound
And play the colored symphony
Of speech.

Farm by the Sea

It seems that work upon a farm like this
Could never be the bitter arduous toil
That it must always be in inland places.
True, there are just as many bowlders here—
New England nearly everywhere is sown
With the same rocky crop that grows in pastures
Thicker than blueberries, and fills the fields

Till every grass blade has a little struggle
To grow up straight at all. I have seen gardens
Where the defeated plowshare had to turn
And make its furrows curve around gray rocks,
So that the rows of corn could not grow even.

Here it is little better. Stubborn acres
Yield up no more potatoes every year
Than they do stones, and those in the same place
Where all the stones were weeded out last fall.
Here a man cannot live more easily
Than any farmer can.
                        And still it seems
That labor cannot be so stern and bitter
As it must be in places farther inland.
When you can look out from the kitchen window,
Or stand up from your weeding, and can see,
Farther than eyes can reach, blue miles of ocean,
A limitless horizon stretching out
To places that you cannot even name—
It's bound to make a difference in your work.

A man will always pick up things from neighbors,
From any creatures that are near him much;
So farmers learn from earth and rock and cattle—
Patience, and hardness, tolerance, endurance.
And what would you expect with such a creature
As this great sea eternally beside you?

"Loveliest of Trees"

Her face was scarred by life and many tears,
Her bones were wrenched to crookedness and pain.
Not hers the fruitful grief of April rain,
But shattering storm of harsh and dolorous years,
I know that like her body her heart was broken,

Though from its tortured depth there never came
Complaint or anger, bitterness or blame,
But only kindness done and kind words spoken.

So have I seen a cherry tree that stood,
Holding a single mutilated limb
From its black battered trunk; but every spring,
When the sweet sap thrilled through the ancient wood,
Blossoms snowed out till all the scars were dim;
And death was life, and life a lovely thing.

Dorothy Belle Flanagan (1904–1993) *Dark Certainty,* 1930

Born in Kansas City, Missouri, Dorothy Belle Flanagan studied at the University of Missouri, Columbia University, and the University of New Mexico. She went on to work as a journalist for newspapers in Albuquerque and Los Angeles. As Dorothy B. F. Hughes she wrote ten mystery novels, including *The Cross-Eyed Bear* and the *So-Blue Marble* (both 1940). She received two Edgar Allan Poe Awards, in 1950 for criticism and in 1978 for lifetime achievement.

Document

Better than dark
Is the sting
Of a moth
On the wing.

Better than sleep
Is the spire
Of a maple's
Tasseled fire.

Better than snow
Is the note
Of a lark's
Young throat.

And far better
Is a scourge
Than a faint,
Still dirge.

Better, things that
Break and bind
Than to endure
The quiet kind.

Capriccio

Portrait Pianissimo
You have slant lips
And flimsy hair,
Your eyes hold
A gilded stare.

You have blurred legs
And a deft chin,
You wear as a boast
Each pretty sin.

Your face is the lilt
Of a flower,
You blow at the wind
By the hour.

You have rapt fingers
And a brittle laugh,
Your heart is always
Broken in half.

Portrait Forte
Who touched your mouth touched wind
And a grassy sea,
Who touched your eyelids sinned
With prideful constancy.

No lover made a net
To capture your caprice;
No lover could forget
Your domino of peace.

Who gathered stars to burn
Before your couch at dawn,
Could never hope to learn
The way that you had gone.

You were storm's bright breath
And quiet crystal skies,
They tasted life and death
Who looked into your eyes.

She Who Lies Motionless with an Arrow in Her Heart

Wrap her in linen, cool and gray,
Lay her away to rest,
Quietly at the dusk of day,
Hour that she loved best.

Search for a place where lichen grows
Under a rounded stone,
Scatter the petals of a rose
And leave her there alone.

Tenderly smooth her rumpled head,
Give her over to rest,
Let her pretend that she is dead,
Asleep on the earth's brown breast.

Paul Engle (1908–1991) *Worn Earth,* 1931

Paul Engle was born in Iowa and educated at Coe College, the University of Iowa, Columbia University, and Oxford University, where he was a Rhodes Scholar. He taught for many years at the University of Iowa and was the founder of the Iowa Writers' Workshop. Engle wrote ten volumes of poetry, two novels, an opera libretto, and a number of plays. With his second wife, Hualing Nieh Engle, he translated a collection of Mao Zedong's verse.

Road Gang

1 **We** worked in the same gang a solid year:
2   Old Jim who whistled as he shoved his spade,
3 And Gregory who said he'd been afraid
4 Of dying ever since he saw how queer
5 A fellow looked who twisted in the dirt
6 After a pickax caught him on the head
7 And split it open—how his hands were spread
8 Clutching the ground, blood running down his shirt.

9 I have not seen them since we drew our pay
10 The last week on the road and said goodbye:
11 The game-kneed cook who traveled with a jerk,
12 Old Jim who always whistled at his work,
13 And Gregory—but I heard yesterday
14 That he is dead who was afraid to die.

The Torn Leaf

1 **You** were speaking then, your voice
2   A little sad—and a bittern flying
3 Into the sunlight and the wind,
4 And the wind crying.

5 "But still, you shouldn't mind so much,
6 For all these will be here: wind falling
7 Through skies and trees, and flight of birds,
8 And the birds calling.

9 "There will be always hills where you
10 May hear the water's quiet mutter
11 On stone, and watch a willow sway
12 And a leaf flutter."

13 I have seen crying birds and wind,
14 Water on stone, and torn leaves shaking . . .
15 But now there is only the bird cry hushed
16 And the heart breaking.

One Slim Feather

1 No longer while than wind climbs up a tree
2   Or water sprawls on stone
3 Would I like you alone,
4 You said—
5 As long as crickets under rotting stumps cry out
6 Their friendly song.
7 Were you a little pleased to find
8 That you were wrong?

9 I have liked you as certainly
10 As crows fly restlessly in rainy weather,
11 As swans in moonlight on black water gliding
12 Loosen into the wind one slim white feather.

13 I will like you
14 As long as purple crocus grow
15 Quietly under snow.

Shirley Barker (1911–1965) *The Dark Hills Under,* 1932

Shirley Barker was born in Farmington, New Hampshire. After studying at the University of New Hampshire, Radcliffe College, and the Pratt Institute Library School, she went on to a career at the New York Public Library. Barker also wrote ten novels, including *Peace My Daughters* (1949) and *Swear by Apollo* (1958).

Portrait

"Which grandmother is that?" we used to say,
Standing a little back and looking up
At the calm face within the walnut frame.
She seemed no kin to anything about:
To other pictures on the parlor walls,
Or thin-lipped boys already eyeing death,
And frail young girls whose hair was never gray;
Nor to the riot of life that ran below—
Our pattering feet, the crackling of the fire,
The gossip of the neighbors come to call.

"Which grandmother is that?" we used to ask,
Nor caring much, half-curious to know
Whose was the dark looped hair, the curving mouth,
High cheek-boned face and unrevealing eyes;
Whose hands laid straight the lace about that throat.
So little that was hers came down the years;
She kept her fragile immortality
Only in those sparse words which Father said:
"My father's mother, born Maria Hayes.
Taught school at Merrill's Corner for awhile—
Quick wits, they say—I don't remember her."

Why is it, when these trees are starred with buds
Of gold and green and red on wet black bark;
When I can lift my face to this soft rain,

Be glad of life, and youth, and April night—
That all my thoughts go back through space and time
To a dead woman's picture on a wall?
All these fair things were hers, as they are mine,
Things that she knew, and loved and laughed about,
And then without a protest laid aside—
And who am I to think of keeping more?
Rise where I can, by fame, or fight, or love,
The time will come when I shall only be
A calm gray face behind a walnut frame,
To which a child will lift appraising eyes
And lightly ask, "Which grandmother is that?"

A Plea Unheard

You will not doff, for bright words or for tears
        Your stolid mask of caution, nor reveal
The cowering army crouched behind the spears,
        The heart within the mind's cool sheath of steel.

Oh I may plead until my throat is stiff,
        And you may yearn to me till heaven fall;
Your mouth remains a crevice in a cliff,
        Your eyes two shuttered windows in a wall.

Sonnet XX

I never thought to start another quest,
Having attained the ultimate in you;
Nor gleam nor grail could call me with the zest
Your kisses had to keep me. I was through
With that impetuous, eager, seeking self;
Your love had tamed it to the stolid round
That life demands of those who make their pelf
By dredging furrows in the stony ground.

But only yesterday a lost wind stirred
The goldenrod as you came up the lane.
I turned my eyes away from you and heard
A voice I never thought to hear again—
The whisper in my heart that drives me on
With discontent, with yearnings to be gone.

James Agee (1909–1955) *Permit Me Voyage,* 1933

James Agee was born in Knoxville, Tennessee, and educated at Harvard University. He wrote the text for Walker Evans's acclaimed book of documentary photographs *Let Us Now Praise Famous Men* (1941) and was a screenwriter for movies including *The African Queen* and *Night of the Hunter.* His novel *A Death in the Family,* published posthumously, won the Pulitzer Prize in 1958. Agee's *Collected Poems* appeared in 1966.

Sonnet IV

I have been fashioned on a chain of flesh
Whose backward length is broken on the dust:
Frail though the dust and small as the dew's mesh
The morning mars, it holds me to a trust:
My flesh that was, long as this flesh knew life,
Strove, and was valiant, still strove, and was naught:
Now it is mine to wage their valiant strife
And failing seek still what they ever sought.
I have been given strength they never wore.
I have been given hope they never knew.
And they were brave, who can be brave no more.
And they that live are kind as they are few.
'Tis mine to touch with deathlessness their clay:
And I shall fail, and join those I betray.

Sonnet XXII

When beyond noise of logic I shall know
And in that knowledge swear my knowledge bound
In all things constant, never more to show
Its head in any transience it has found:
When pride of knowledge, frames of government,
The wrath of justice gagged and greed in power,

Sure good, and certain ill, and high minds bent
On destiny sink deathward as this hour:
When deep beyond surmise the driven shade
Of this our earth and mind my mind confirms,
Essence and fact of all things that are made,
Nature in love in death are shown the terms:
When, through this lens, I've seen all things in one,
Then, nor before, I truly have begun.

Permit Me Voyage

From the Third Voyage of Hart Crane.

Take these who will as may be: I
Am careless now of what they fail:
My heart and mind discharted lie
And surely as the nervèd nail

Appoints all quarters on the north
So now it designates him forth
My sovereign God my princely soul
Whereon my flesh is priestly stole:

Whence forth shall my heart and mind
To God through soul entirely bow,
Therein such strong increase to find
In truth as is my fate to know:

Small though that be great God I know
I know in this gigantic day
What God is ruined and I know
How labors with Godhead this day:

How from the porches of our sky
The crested glory is declined:

And hear with what translated cry
The stridden soul is overshined:

And how this world of wildness through
True poets shall walk who herald you:
Of whom God grant me of your grace
To be, that shall preserve this race.

Permit me voyage, Love, into your hands.

Muriel Rukeyser (1913–1980) *Theory of Flight,* 1934

Born in New York City, Muriel Rukeyser studied at Vassar College and Columbia University. The author of fifteen books of poetry, as well as an influential critical collection of prose titled *The Life of Poetry* (1949), Rukeyser was a lifelong feminist and civil rights activist, on the page and off, as she investigated such issues as the Scottsboro case in Alabama, silicosis plaguing miners in West Virginia, and the Vietnam War she opposed. Her awards include a National Endowment for the Arts fellowship and a Guggenheim Fellowship.

Effort at Speech Between Two People

:   Speak to me.   Take my hand.   What are you now?
   I will tell you all.   I will conceal nothing.
   When I was three, a little child read a story about a rabbit
   who died, in the story, and I crawled under a chair   :
   a pink rabbit   :   it was my birthday, and a candle
   burnt a sore spot on my finger, and I was told to be happy.

:   Oh, grow to know me.   I am not happy.   I will be open:
   Now I am thinking of white sails against a sky like music,
   like glad horns blowing, and birds tilting, and an arm about me.
   There was one I loved, who wanted to live, sailing.

:   Speak to me.   Take my hand.   What are you now?
   When I was nine, I was fruitily sentimental,
   fluid   :   and my widowed aunt played Chopin,
   and I bent my head on the painted woodwork, and wept.
   I want now to be close to you.   I would
   link the minutes of my days close, somehow, to your days.

:   I am not happy.   I will be open.
   I have liked lamps in evening corners, and quiet poems.
   There has been fear in my life.   Sometimes I speculate
   On what a tragedy his life was, really.

:   Take my hand.   Fist my mind in your hand.   What are you now?
When I was fourteen, I had dreams of suicide,
and I stood at a steep window, at sunset, hoping toward death   :
if the light had not melted clouds and plains to beauty,
if light had not transformed that day, I would have leapt.
I am unhappy.   I am lonely.   Speak to me.

:   I will be open.   I think he never loved me:
he loved the bright beaches, the little lips of foam
that ride small waves, he loved the veer of gulls:
he said with a gay mouth: I love you.   Grow to know me.

:   What are you now?   If we could touch one another,
if these our separate entities could come to grips,
clenched like a Chinese puzzle . . . yesterday
I stood in a crowded street that was live with people,
and no one spoke a word, and the morning shone.
Everyone silent, moving. . . . Take my hand.   Speak to me.

City of Monuments

Washington 1934

Be proud   you people   of these graves
      these chiseled words   this precedent
From these blind ruins shines our monument.

Dead navies of the brain will sail
      stone celebrate its final choice
         when the air shakes, a single voice
a strong voice able to prevail   :

Entrust no hope to stone although the stone
shelter the root   :   see too-great burdens placed
with nothing certain but the risk
set on the infirm column of
the high memorial obelisk

erect in accusation sprung against
a barren sky taut over Anacostia   :
give over, Gettysburg   !   a word will shake your glory   :
blood of the starved fell thin upon this plain,
this battle is not buried with its slain.

> Gravestone and battlefield retire
> the whole green South is shadowed dark,
> the slick white domes are cast in night.
> But uneclipsed above the park

> the veteran of the Civil War
> sees havoc in the tended graves
> the midnight bugles blown to free
> still unemancipated slaves.

Blinded by chromium or transfiguration
we watch, as through a microscope, decay   :
        down the broad streets the limousines
advance in passions of display.

Air glints with diamonds, and these clavicles
emerge through orchids by whose trailing spoor
the sensitive cannot mistake
the implicit anguish of the poor.

The throats incline, the marble men rejoice
careless of torrents of despair.

Split by a tendril of revolt
stone cedes to blossom everywhere.

Metaphor to Action

Whether it is a speaker, taut on a platform,
who battles a crowd with the hammers of his words,
whether it is the crash of lips on lips

after absence and wanting   :   we must close
the circuits of ideas, now generate,
that leap in the body's action or the mind's repose.

Over us is a striking on the walls of the sky,
here are the dynamos, steel-black, harboring flame,
here is the man night-walking who derives
tomorrow's manifestoes from this midnight's meeting   ;
here we require the proof in solidarity,
iron on iron, body on body, and the large single beating.

And behind us in time are the men who second us
as we continue.   And near us is our love   :
no forced contempt, no refusal in dogma, the close
of the circuit in a fierce dazzle of purity.
And over us is night a field of pansies unfolding,
charging with heat its softness in a symbol
to weld and prepare for action our minds' intensity.

Edward Weismiller (1915–2010) *The Deer Come Down,* 1935

Edward Weismiller was born near Oshkosh, Wisconsin, and studied at Swarthmore College, Cornell College in Iowa, Oxford University, and Harvard University. A Milton scholar who taught for many years at George Washington University, Weismiller wrote two additional volumes of poetry, *The Faultless Shore* (1946) and *The Branch of Fire* (1980), as well as a novel based on his work as a counterintelligence agent for the OSS, *The Serpent Sleeping* (1962). He twice received a Guggenheim Fellowship and was also a Fulbright scholar.

Thicket

You who have heard the thrush, and seen the partridge
Gliding smoothly under a gray-white sky:
The sweetest song has never come from the forest,
Nor the softest wing gone by.

You who have reached the hemlock woods, and beeches,
And seen the fallen tree and the black slate ledge:
There is more darkness still within the thicket
Than ever came to the edge.

I Would Be Wiser

The deer that leapt from the path, and thundered down
Over the shallow roots of the echoing wood,
Heard nothing move but leaves that clattered brown
In the frosty naked trees; the fox that stood

Trembling, at the peak of the dreadful hill
Where soon the gaunt, implacable hounds would go,
Thought of no other footprint but the still
Immutable autograph he left in snow.

I would be wiser; having no kindred fear
I would be bold: and the snow is countersigned
Where I stand to watch the wary fox, and the deer—
And hear no breath, no leaf, no step behind.

Skull

The mind, and some thin longing that ensnared it,
Were outraged here. In one brief sullen thrust
The bullet tapped the skull, and so prepared it
For occupancy of dust:

And that was long ago, before this season
Wrote its precarious legend on the leaf.
Here flesh was forfeit. Simply, with adequate reason,
Waiving consent or grief,

The mind forsook its trim elaborate tower,
Its windowed room, so artfully contrived.
All beauty it controlled before that hour
The stinging lead was hived—

The vision, all the intricate ways of seeing,
The pallid flesh bemused by its own doom—
Gave over then. But the bullet remains, there being
At length, sufficient room.

Margaret Haley (1906–?) *The Gardener Mind,* 1936

Margaret Haley attended Bryn Mawr College, but little else about her life can be verified. *The Yale Younger Poets Anthology* edition of 1998 reported that Haley moved to Caracas, Venezuela, shortly after winning the Yale prize—to write suspense fiction, by her own account.

To a Columbine

You are a feather
Of wind made flower,
You are the mind
Of a bird in a bower
Of heaven. You are the
Shred of a dream
Happy and wild
Beyond redeem
Of thought; the very
Posture and scent
Of gallantry;
A dolor bent
Into petals
Flung for flying
That was born
Out of a sighing
Upon a glimpse
Of the first star—
An airiest pang,
A nicest scar.

Souvenir of Maine

Wet red mushroom
In a ragged grot
That thy small hunched shoulders broke
From the springy rot

Of the forest's secret
Dark brown floor,
And hidden by the cunning
Common ferns before,

Now I see thee peep in coral
Malice on the gloom
Like a drop of fresh blood
In a formal room.

Lost

The tap of snow,
The feet of mice
Humming in walls,
And the log's precise

Spit of resin:
Is this a dream
Of sound? Ah, does it
Only seem

This winter night
Was years ago,
That I lie under
A younger snow,

That the clawed mice
Are little bones
Like ivory spindles
Among these stones?

Reuel Denney (1913–1995) *The Connecticut River and Other Poems,* 1938

Born in New York City, Reuel Denney graduated from Dartmouth College. He later became a professor of sociology, teaching at the University of Chicago and the University of Hawaii. A Guggenheim fellow, Denney wrote three more volumes of poetry but is best known for his collaboration with David Riesman and Nathan Glazer on their landmark study of twentieth-century American society, *The Lonely Crowd* (1950).

Norwich Hill

We had all been out into the winter landscape
Among the snow-curved shadows of some wood,
And we left a track, but when we turned upon
This hill no way led back from where we stood.
We knew it was the wind, who travels everywhere
And polishes the names of honest men,
That lost us; and time that brings fat beeches down
Was there and made us tremble then.
Yet the sun's rage, co-terminous with our blood,
Kindled us there for its own reason.
We saw towns miles away, and ate the cold like bread;
We hailed the stiff fields and the bleak season.

The Albino Deer

Hunting one day in an autumn the color of Persia
When the dry woods by frost to a deeper burning were driven
And the pale clouds, like little trout in heaven,
Drew schools of glints along the wind's erasure,

O'Connor with his rifle saw suddenly the white one,
Unhardened ivory, with eyes of evening snow,

Moving like a mist congealed and brilliant moments pausing
In the white spot of a dream where many wonders flow.

Imperial as a lily, this target to his gun
Stained the wild woods that day with color colorless
And, stiff with scent as beauties blown in glass,
Kept like a china clock his child's attention.

His trigger finger opened, with justice usual,
To demonstrate its sleeplessness again,
And, what was mighty more, that cleverness of men
Which, at a mile, makes beast or hero fall.

Yet as he aimed, his gunsight seemed to send
From watching brain, besieged by many terrors,
A hubbub through the doors of such a universe
That towns might die in blizzards without end.

Kill what is common, his tendons seemed to say
Like fiddle strings of music in his hands;
Sick wives and burning barns and treacherous friends
To men who shoot what's not seen every day.

Man and mouse, the egret and the looming eagle ponder
How to live out alone an original heredity
In some sun-flashing comb or some mind-flashing eye,
Against the laws that call all odd things under;

And here where the destiny comes shining through the skin
Like a god's remorseless light beneath a river,
And every membrane there, each single standing hair,
Displays outside what must be true within,

Let other minds that are against the strange,
All wonders, chances, gamble and risky venture,
End the adventure, if they will, of all that move in matter.
So men kill love with love that will not change.

The Hammer-Throw

Now he will close the book, walk toward the window,
Stretch, shift, and turn, and saunter down
Through the afternoon that brings the leaves down slowly,
To kick those leaves before him through the town.
As he comes out he feels all loosely made,
His jaunty striding wears the very sun;
And he seems golden-jointed, and new-eyed.
Legs, arms, and lungs are all a happy one.
The wide and level field becalms the daylight
Except when airs bring in the sudden sound
Of shoutings dimmed in sleepy distances.
He rubs his hands. He walks upon the ground.
On spike, and nervy, and the nostrils sharpened,
Won by the weight as the weight is whirled by him,
He pivots!—and the nerves cry out their question,
Centrifugal to heart and every limb,
Whether the world complete might be so lifted,
Whether it could be drawn so into the dervish
Of these locked knuckles and senses tight with joy:
Until, let slip, the iron leaps from hand,
And from his throat a noise, a kind of laughter,
Follows from that spent body, robbed and trembling,
The way the ball flies, with the chain drawn after.

Norman Rosten (1914–1995) *Return Again, Traveler,* 1939

Born in New York City, Norman Rosten studied at Brooklyn College, New York University, and the University of Michigan. In addition to poetry, he also published three novels, three collections of essays, and a memoir of Marilyn Monroe, and wrote the screenplay for the Sidney Lumet film *Vu du Pont,* adapting Arthur Miller's *A View from the Bridge.* A Guggenheim fellow, Rosten also served as poet laureate of Brooklyn.

We came during those years
    when the land was free for conquerors:
remembering that dawn with the great moon
still on our sails and the gulls wailing,
the green wind coming out to us over water,
and to the shore line of birches and pines
we rode with the lift of the sea into shining harbor.

Out of an East ancient with ikons
from countries of the legendary wheat
with many winds and the speech of many peoples,
from Northern boundaries facing the Arctic
where men broke their violent horses on the plains:
from the South, southward to the islands,
from every climate we came with a new century in our eyes.

Dreaming of peace and sunlight forever
we spanned a sea by the strange rumor,
across the long horizon with the late sun burning
into its curved sky, holding our prow against the star:
Believing in a free place, believing the earth
was still free for us if we believed it!
(The rumor said: Here is your land,
come and get it, march over it,
come and take the valleys in your hands!)

Our blood was clean and we had hope;
we let fall into the water our simple clothes:
it was our wish to arrive beautiful.

Taxi mister taxi

Stranger around here, mister?

Well, in a way, yes.

How about seeing the sights?
Ride you up Broadway till you get tired.

What city's this, partner?

Look, buddy, I got an open-top cab. With a radio.
Yes or no?

Can you show me one or two of the big things . . .

Everything's big, pal. This is America, U.S.A.
Across the river don't count: that's New Jersey.
You foreigners keep your eyes open;
this is the Garden of Eden, plenty of snakes.

Suppose you ride me past the biggest thing you got,
the colossus of the country, I mean
what makes the wheels go round.

Wall Street, pal: the stock exchange.
Hop in
        (and there's a radio if you're lonely).

And everywhere
screaming from billboards
boomed from the powerful antenna
announced at the outskirts of all cities

> THIS IS THE GREATEST COUNTRY
> THIS IS THE RICHEST COUNTRY
> this is the country that's got what it takes
> the land of the free and the home of the brave

and if you don't think so, start walkin'
back where you came from all the way
and don't stop till you get there,
and that goes for Indians too.

All together now:

> America   America
> God shed his grace on thee
> and crown thy good with brotherhood . . .

Suppose we boil that down
and see what it has to do with
food
clothes
work
and while we're at it
life liberty and the pursuit of happiness.

Are you for it or against it
and everything you say is held against you
don't ask questions without safe answers
or else some committee is going to get you.

Margaret Walker (1915–1998) *For My People,* 1941

Margaret Walker was born in Birmingham, Alabama, and studied at Northwestern University and the University of Iowa. The first African American to win the Yale Series of Younger Poets, she wrote four subsequent books of poetry, as well as the influential novel *Jubilee* (1966). For many years she taught at Jackson State College in Mississippi, where she founded and eventually directed the Institute for the Study of the History, Life, and Culture of Black People.

We Have Been Believers

We have been believers believing in the black gods of an old
        land, believing in the secrets of the seeress and the
        magic of the charmers and the power of the devil's
        evil ones.

And in the white gods of a new land we have been believers
        believing in the mercy of our masters and the beauty
        of our brothers, believing in the conjure of the
        humble and the faithful and the pure.

Neither the slavers' whip nor the lynchers' rope nor the
        bayonet could kill our black belief. In our hunger we
        beheld the welcome table and in our nakedness the
        glory of a long white robe. We have been believers
        in the new Jerusalem.

We have been believers feeding greedy grinning gods, like a
        Moloch demanding our sons and our daughters, our
        strength and our wills and our spirits of pain. We
        have been believers, silent and stolid and stubborn
        and strong.

We have been believers yielding substance for the world.
        With our hands have we fed a people and out of our
        strength have they wrung the necessities of a nation.

Our song has filled the twilight and our hope has heralded the dawn.

Now we stand ready for the touch of one fiery iron, for the cleansing breath of many molten truths, that the eyes of the blind may see and the ears of the deaf may hear and the tongues of the people be filled with living fire.

Where are our gods that they leave us asleep? Surely the priests and the preachers and the powers will hear. Surely now that our hands are empty and our hearts too full to pray they will understand. Surely the sires of the people will send us a sign.

We have been believers believing in our burdens and our demigods too long. Now the needy no longer weep and pray; the long-suffering arise, and our fists bleed against the bars with a strange insistency.

Southern Song

I want my body bathed again by southern suns, my soul reclaimed again from southern land. I want to rest again in southern fields, in grass and hay and clover bloom; to lay my hand again upon the clay baked by a southern sun, to touch the rain-soaked earth and smell the smell of soil.

I want my rest unbroken in the fields of southern earth; freedom to watch the corn wave silver in the sun and mark the splashing of a brook, a pond with ducks and frogs and count the clouds.

I want no mobs to wrench me from my southern rest; no forms to take me in the night and burn my shack and make for me a nightmare full of oil and flame.

I want my careless song to strike no minor key; no fiend to
        stand between my body's southern song—the fusion
        of the South, my body's song and me.

Memory

I can remember wind-swept streets of cities
on cold and blustery nights, on rainy days;
heads under shabby felts and parasols
and shoulders hunched against a sharp concern;
seeing hurt bewilderment on poor faces,
smelling a deep and sinister unrest
these brooding people cautiously caress;
hearing ghostly marching on pavement stones
and closing fast around their squares of hate.
I can remember seeing them alone,
at work, and in their tenements at home.
I can remember hearing all they said:
their muttering protests, their whispered oaths,
and all that spells their living in distress.

William Meredith (1919–2007) *Love Letter from an Impossible Land,* 1943

Born in New York City, William Meredith studied at Princeton University. After serving in the navy during World War II and the Korean War, Meredith wrote eight more volumes of poetry, winning a Pulitzer Prize and the National Book Award. A Consultant in Poetry to the Library of Congress, he taught for many years at Connecticut College.

War Sonnet

Whom Eros' errand sends to the ends of the earth
    I envy now, having in hand no quest;
Buildings are bombed and walls fall in my path
    Pursuing the partially-wished-for; I seem to lose interest.

Rich boys' toys which once made me sick with wishing
    Are noiseless before this bursting, the want of them broken,
And I am afraid to make friends or commence rebuilding
    With everything temporary, the very town perhaps taken.

I who have slept with sack packed, eager and dressed,
    Waiting no more warning than the morning order,
Have watched the expedition's expectations quashed
    With the coming of numberless bombers and ensuing horrors.

The maps were misplaced and most of the men dispersed,
And worst perhaps of all, I have lost the wanderlust.

The Islands of My Desire

The islands of my desire
    Thrust up in a boiling bay,

They inhabit a hostile hour
    As if it were their own.

They crop when the wind is barren
    Without expense of bloom,
And when the waters anger
    Keep their wits about them.

In blight's despite and danger's
    They grow a virtuous green,
And industry is of them
    As it is not of me.

Remote and inland watcher
    Of each untoward act
I wait the weather's pleasure,
    Am not for the islands yet.

In Strange Events

If the moon set, and all the stars, and still no morning came, or
If the wise few books turned changeling on the shelf, or
If the dirty-minded enemy in such numbers came
That parleying (god forbid) seemed prudent,
Where would I then turn, oh, where would I turn then?

Men have burned hotter than stars for a lasting name, and
The books of memory are nowadays rainy-faint, and
Only the hatred of the dirty-minded enemy, only
This one face of the spinning god I always own,
(Friends can die and worse, and)
Remains white-hot and clear, so
I'd keep my very hate of this, if this or this, or
This were to come, were to come suddenly now.

Charles E. Butler (1909–1981) *Cut Is the Branch,* 1944

Born in Denver, Colorado, Charles Butler was educated at the University of Colorado and the University of Chicago Library School. After serving in World War II, he worked for the Longwood College Library in Farmville, Virginia. A Guggenheim fellow, Butler also wrote a novel, *Follow Me Ever* (1950).

There Is Something to Be Said

It is admirable to survive. It is good.
It means the strength and cunning to adjust,
Gritting the teeth and tightening the belt when there is no food,
Or eating for nourishment the stale and bitter crust.
It means running, or turning to strike the blow
At the opportune time, when the pursuer is weak:
It means silence, often, when the mind and the heart know
It is braver to speak.
It is admirable, I know: it is intelligent. This is true.
But there is something to be said for those who choose
Another victory than survival, who do what they must do,
Having lost what they could not live and lose.

George

> (For G.M., Private, U.S. Army, *who asked me to write a letter*
> *home for him: he had never learned to write.*)

I know, George: I will tell them: it will be easy.
You are not very near to California,
And this is a strange life for one used to farms,
To the welcoming cry of dogs at the sagging gate
And their smooth hair soft under your rough hands,
And the voices of the cattle, strange and familiar.

I will tell them you are all right, George:
I will write to them that everything is fine.

I will not tell them of your dark eyes cloudy with sorrow,
Nor of the long evenings you stare into the closing light,
Speechless and wondering, thinking something about tomorrow,
Or yesterday, waiting for the friendly night.
I will ask them to tell you about the flocks and the farm,
And Maris' baby, and the new and costly churn,
And the bees that followed you thundering in a swarm:
I will tell them, George: I will say that you will return.

The memories swarm after all of us like bees,
George, golden and thunderous, and the sharp faint cries
Of part of our yesterdays: we all have these.
I will write to them, George: I will tell them some little lies.
I shall not tell them your wordless memories
Stare stricken and frightened out of your young eyes.

It is more than a loneliness, a lostness, I know:
It is not wholly a fear: you are as brave as most.
It is something of the yesterdays that will not go,
That follow and ring you here, ghost after ghost.
The California farm, the evening wind,
The clustered trees, with sunlight in between,
Fire smoke, the burning things you left behind—
I will tell them for you, George: I know what you mean.

The Spell

The young men may remember; they will have
A memory of death along their veins,
Running like some dark music through their hearts
Echoing in the chambers of their brains,
Whispering, moving their hands. . .
                    The young men may
Remember, after this time, this time of death;

It surrounds them now; there is nothing else;
They hear it, they taste it with every breath.
I think they may remember it as a song
Is remembered by the young; it will have a spell,
Running along their blood, binding and shaking them,
Calling a time back they have known too well.
What will they give the world, remembering,
The world that has given them this terrible thing?

Eve Merriam (1916–1992) *Family Circle,* 1945

Eve Merriam was born in Philadelphia, Pennsylvania, and studied at Cornell University, the University of Pennsylvania, and Columbia University. She published more than fifty titles, much of it poetry designed to teach children about poetry and how to understand their lives through poetry. Merriam also wrote feminist books, including *The Double Bed, from the Feminine Side* (1958) and *Growing Up Female in America* (1971). For her play *The Club* (1977) she won an Obie Award.

My Mother Sorrow

At first like a million others
I ran to my mother Sorrow;
We played all day with Yesterday,
And bolted the door on Tomorrow.

My mother Sorrow petted me,
And fed me cakes of Yesterday;
When Tomorrow knocked on the hungry door—
We sent him starving away.

Now mother Sorrow's lavish hand
Is dry as a bony hag's;
And empty of all their candy joys
Lie Yesterday's brimful bags.

So like a million others now,
I must leave my mother Sorrow;
The only house I have to go
Is hostile hard Tomorrow . . .

He will not let me play at games,
He will beat me if I borrow
So much as a cup of memory
From Yesterday or Sorrow.

Tomorrow feeds me narrow fare,
I work here for little pay.
But I am redeemed from Sorrow the bitch,
And bastard Yesterday.

Home for the Week End

Clanned by Christmas,
And in between by the usual primitive three:
Pink christening robe, white wedding veil,
Black shroud.

Carbon conversation:
"Mary and I both fine, baby a slight cold, business fair—"
While you long for the witchcraft word to open wide
The thousand-bolted door.

Table groans,
Mother has camped out in kitchen all the waiting week
As though to conjure you back to simple childhood
With favorite chocolate cake.

And passed with the dinner plates
Never-exhausted anecdotes of you as a ten-year-old,
Your jam closet career, your pocket pirate loot
Of worthless junk.

Plot fails.
Neck would be noosed in by Buster Brown collar now,
You will not stay at home and be their little boy,
Their immortality.

Clock is your aide-de-camp.
Dam up the words of love with lateness of the hour
Kick away clear from their drowning dragging fingers,
And let them drown.

Board the impersonal train,
Taking you fast and unfettered, far from the scene of your crime.
You have a life to live, troubles enough of your own.
Futile to fret any more.

And by now they have surely drowned . . .

Delilah

It was only a job: some said a sinecure.
No intricate bullet to book-learn, no groaning weight to endure.
Merely to rise from the silken midnight sleeping;
Her cat eyes green awake, her warm hips coolly creeping,
And the gossipy scissors hush-mouthed in the table drawer . . .
What in the world was she delaying for?

No blood would annoy her delicate light nightgown,
No gutted knife to disengage, no gurgling gasp to drown;
Only the sinuous snipping, the little lip of clipping . . .

It won't even hurt him—pay check prodded her on,
He'll look neat and trim with that messy tangle gone;
Hurry! Dark will slip away; clip, snip before the judge of day . . .

He's dumb, no notion of cocktail-hour talk,
No finesse at making love, no dancer's toe in his elephant walk;
Only that hemp of hair falling over the full frank stare.
Doesn't know how to treat a girl: no candy, no flowers, so gauche;
Lithe as a leopard, you coy away from his uncouth touch:
And only a few alibi hours more—what are you waiting for?

Look, he is simple: like a champing cow,
Snorting, chortling, slupping his soup,
Leaving his napkin unknown by the dinner plate:
So why do you hesitate?

He could drape your darling neck in two,
Wipes his nose on his unpressed sleeve,

Muddies the carefully carpeted floor:
What are you halting for?

In the smoking crash of temple, uncrying and cold you will stand;
The enormous pillars nothing next to your tiny deceiving hand.

Joan Murray (1917–1942) *Poems,* 1946

Joan Murray was born in London and spent her childhood there and in Paris, Ontario, and the United States. A student of dance and acting as well as writing, she is believed to have studied at the New School for Social Research with W. H. Auden. Auden picked Murray's book for the Yale Series of Younger Poets four years after her death from complications of rheumatic fever she had suffered as a child.

Lullaby

Sleep, little architect. It is your mother's wish
That you should lave your eyes and hang them up in dreams.
Into the lowest sea swims the great sperm fish.
If I should rock you, the whole world would rock within my arms.

Your father is a greater architect than even you.
His structure falls between high Venus and far Mars.
He rubs the magic of the old and then peers through
The blueprint where lies the night, the plan the stars.

You will place mountains too, when you are grown.
The grass will not be so insignificant, the stone so dead.
You will spiral up the mansions we have sown.
Drop your lids, little architect. Admit the bats of wisdom into your head.

The Long Trail

I have been marking the long high roads.
I think it was over the trail
That angles on, riddling the mountain wood
Up and down in the cool musk valleys,
Up and up to the height, where, blue and drawn,
The reaches and the farther hills
Turned their great shadows and grave lines
To more than form, to more than opulent color.

It Is Not I Who Am Sleeping in the Rock

It is not I who am sleeping in the rock under the wood,
Nor are my limbs congested with cities or the leaves:
I am lifting and dropping night and day with a good grace,
Each after each in their immoderate halves.

I have no memory to inflict unless I may sing to you,
And the weight covering my mouth holds me back.
The valleys will repeat my secret in a few
Wordless blares, or the hunter track

Toward the hollow of the brain that I would not admit
(Being the place of fawns in the angles of the tree,
The child's bound corner, or the limit
The birds must instinctively secrete in flight, or be

Swept into the erotic sun, or the edgeless tide beneath).
It is not I who am sleeping in the rock or the wedge,
And yet I thrust back the wrinkled earth for breath,
And in the dark extend thin wind-stalked fingers to extract
The brittle ledge.

Robert Horan (1922–1981) *A Beginning,* 1947

Born in Oakland, California, Robert Horan early on became a member of the Activists, a group of poets in the Berkeley area who collected around Lawrence Hart in the 1940s. By 1947 Horan had moved to New York state, where he was associated with the composers Gian Carlo Menotti and Samuel Barber. *A Beginning* is his only book of poetry.

Twenty-One Years

Came with wind and warning this morning
the first birds. Came sun polishing
the crucifix-insect where he paused
dew-instant. I beheld here and there
spiders going in grass to a thread cathedral,
and a round serpent holding both our breaths;
saw, on the twigs, the calligraphy of snails,
and ants marching on the flower-wheels.
Chariots carried all of the living down today.

Who will know later that the light was particular,
betraying by one or many signs a place,
a time arrived at in dandelion summer
that I might stop to look at the underside
of my memories, and slip from each hand
the stitched veil of a year?

Failure follows a ship on a voyage of Sundays,
but leaving a sea-greened cross to catch or drift to.
(Shirts make flags; visitors pass and will rescue.)
Listed in the boat, we turn toward lost, resighted
and prodigal island, mirage of our miracles.
But today will whirl especial in the water, will push
to a pilgrimage. The sight of a continent breaking
over the boat fountains me forward from purgatory.

On the channel the sea returns the faces
of friends in a grey mirror, their names
in the leaves of a book, washed beneath me
on the whitening wave, their flesh flashed
through this wilderness to make my cargo.

Today, the middle of a morning, I run after
any sight or sorrow, loud to discover sun
in the weather of shadow. Narrower now
by a year, called farther away and fixed faster
to a sail, leaving father and a last look
toward the back-swelling children's horizon.
But dearer than these, I go in a bird's direction
to a holiday country, priest of a water and a world.
Over the blue edge of the map with the flying fish,
that last year may not find my future face,
my hunting or haunted image frozen toward west.

Clean, Cool, Early

Clean, cool, early,
the stones arched high and hard;
cool, calm, awake
in a light of limes.
Before the leaves melt
and the fine flow alters
the wine-flushed window,
we're held apart in dawn,
rinsed clear.
The stars are rigged for morning,
spare and even,
like the color of water hardened.
Firm, unspotted, and washed
free of its random flesh,
part-frozen, an apple of air.

As with the iceberg-center,
detail is ornament in this weather;
fixed in the flowering ice,
bird, stick, star in ether,
all taste of emptiness, salted
and bottled in cobalt together.

To be late is to miss it,
while the enemy of clarity
makes rapid revision,
reels all in an abundance of light
and drops of false radiance.
It is that light withheld,
moved forward inches in a wind,
interior, that shapes a morning.
Like porcelain or casual sculpture
in ice, this is scorched
by indiscriminate sun,
unlaced in noon.

Seven is an exact moment,
the transit from station to station
when energy has been pulled pale,
but stretched, does not waver,
but full, does not tilt nor falter.
It awakens the smallest animals first.

See yourself here the imperfect stranger
early risen and boated out in blue
mirror upon mirror back to the beginning;
an unfamiliar bird and tall intruder.
Before the leaf loosens,
and between two forms of light,
take time to raise from the frosted dust
and silk-scattered hedges,
the frame of a rose, the ashes of a room,
a fern, a small fire in dew, a paused spider.

These, though moribund in stronger light and years,
may steady memory, serve to identify
an arctic, miniature, unwrinkled world.

Soft Swimmer, Winter Swan

The sun shows thin through hail, wallpaper-pale, and falls
grey from its royal world toward colder poles.
Gone, like a grave swan gone blossoming in bone,
a white tree of feathers, blown singly down.

A last, a light, and caught in the air-ladder lark,
south-driven, climbing the indian, swift dark, and listen!
Sped by the building cold and rare in ether, birds hasten
the heart already taxed with cloud and cherubim—
fretted heaven, strained songless and flown dim.
Out from the house that held them in safe summer,
small ponds and blue counties, the chequered swimmers
in air, spring sudden through the closing vault of frost.
(The last, awakened by a late storm, are forever lost.)

But the calm swan, adamant in autumn, passes
through still willowed water, parting the yellow rushes.
His eye, like a lighted nail, sees the vast
distance of amethyst roll under him, the marble beast.

Seen from the shore, this bird but luminous boat,
so motionless in speed, quiet, will float
forward in cold time, disdaining harbor; marooned
in infinite roads of rivers, his wings wrought around
to muffle danger and battle with the wind;
safe, slow, calm, a ship with frail lights, a white swan.

But seen from beneath, the soft statue hardens; the wild feet
must wrest from this pure prison some retreat,
outdistance winter and oblivion; now, in feverish motion, foam
the careless waters, throat, wing, heart, all spotless in arched bone.

Pressed, must push farther on through lakes where winter lies
secret and dumb in shallows, building bright fields of ice
to trap the transparent fish, turn the wet world to stone,
surprise the soft swimmer and capture the winter swan.

We see, serene, this desperate passage through perfect seas;
taught to see ease in agony, see only ease.
In the battle of snow against snow and wind upon wind
the dead lie fooled in the ice, too far to find.

Rosalie Moore (1910–2001) *The Grasshopper's Man and Other Poems,* 1948

Rosalie Moore was born in Oakland, California, and graduated from the University of California, Berkeley. Like Robert Horan, whose book had been selected for the Yale Series of Younger Poets the year before, Moore became a member of the Activists. She taught communications at the College of Marin in California. A Guggenheim fellow, Moore wrote three other books of poetry, including *Gutenberg in Strasbourg* (1995).

Dirge for the Living

I am the mover of other eyes,
Of other hands than these
That hang from my tree of bones—

    (The old knights, ringing their bones for battle)

I am the mover of other hands:
They came at the pitch of dawn,
Planting their spears;
The quick shrank from their crosses.

    (Winds paling the land, blow again
    The rafters of many men!)

And one came in his iron—in the low evening;
And looking above, he saw the birds at crossbow,
And a horn sounds in his throat,
And he knew he was dead amid valleys on valleys of horns.

They are dead, they are dead in their bones
And their hands are multiplied;
Their eyes have struck; their bodies
Reel in the faceless sky.

How often, mornings, hoping to hear rise horns,
Hear—(or the antler-crashing dawn!)—no sound
But the sound of my ear's bees.

With our levy of bones and nakedness of leaves
We wake in the cold plateaus,
And the stone in the chest is there—
The crows passing and passing
In blind men's eyes by daylight.
All of the streams are flattening the birds.

How last, how loom those we imaged—
As, turning on a sky, a mountain's horn.
They are a gallery of air away; they are
An iron of cold away.

They bury their dying in us,
Under some cross-sword stars.

Prologue

This wire along sky
Stains—swings wire.
The street's long people,
And at the curb, the bunched bird.

And seeing one with bubbles rising
Out of the palms . . .
(O window-fill of sun, of sea, watching!)
And the litter of streets like lost, like separate wings—
And some of the people turning.

> How down Niraea as rocks
> Little candid streams run
> ("Springes and wood-cocks")—how,
> Out of leaves looking,

The carved eyes;
How, hitting at ankles,
Flowers.

The one, over again, in aisles, in entrances,
Coming as through glass.

Or nights, down stairs of light,
Coming—and the watchers:
I know you, they said.

Sometimes again in a wax light
And at aisle end—
Thought, seen.

In the brief, actual places—
In the clear cages.

Or in the square, the stones clear
In the lowered rain.

Ripeness Is Rapid

Ripeness is rapid as plum-drop, as invader.
Plume-fall of evening captures the Turk's East, and I wonder—
The bright-ribbed Alexander . . .

Many in the berried light, riper,
The women.
But he came with a stiffness of swan,
With a tongue thick with galleys.

As one with toads or jewels at mouth speaking,
(And the waves pounding at Cypress)
He came, left hanging in air
The shaking cliffs and carrions.

Moonlight, wilderness cover;

The small wind dries on the bush,
The sail folds in Marmora.

Oh when will he return to this wooden moonlight, when uncover
All we were ever to see—that unfilled tomb
The women murmur for.

Adrienne Rich (1929–2012) *A Change of World,* 1950

Born in Baltimore, Maryland, Adrienne Cecile Rich graduated from Radcliffe College. The author of more than twenty-five books of poetry as well as numerous collections of essays, Rich was an activist—a crucial twentieth-century voice for feminism and sexual freedom. Among her many honors are the National Book Award, the Bollingen Prize for Poetry, the Ruth Lilly Poetry Prize, and two Guggenheim Fellowships.

Storm Warnings

The glass has been falling all the afternoon,
And knowing better than the instrument
What winds are walking overhead, what zone
Of gray unrest is moving across the land,
I leave the book upon a pillowed chair
And walk from window to closed window, watching
Boughs strain against the sky

And think again, as often when the air
Moves inward toward a silent core of waiting,
How with a single purpose time has traveled
By secret currents of the undiscerned
Into this polar realm. Weather abroad
And weather in the heart alike come on
Regardless of prediction.

Between foreseeing and averting change
Lies all the mastery of elements
Which clocks and weatherglasses cannot alter.
Time in the hand is not control of time,
Nor shattered fragments of an instrument
A proof against the wind; the wind will rise,
We can only close the shutters.

I draw the curtains as the sky goes black
And set a match to candles sheathed in glass
Against the keyhole draught, the insistent whine
Of weather through the unsealed aperture.
This is our sole defense against the season;
These are the things that we have learned to do
Who live in troubled regions.

What Ghosts Can Say

When Harry Wylie saw his father's ghost,
As bearded and immense as once in life,
Bending above his bed long after midnight,
He screamed and gripped the corner of the pillow
Till aunts came hurrying white in dressing gowns
To say it was a dream. He knew they lied.
The smell of his father's leather riding crop
And stale tobacco stayed to prove it to him.
Why should there stay such tokens of a ghost
If not to prove it came on serious business?
His father always had meant serious business,
But never so wholly in his look and gesture
As when he beat the boy's uncovered thighs
Calmly and resolutely, at an hour
When Harry never had been awake before.
The man who could choose that single hour of night
Had in him the ingredients of a ghost;
Mortality would quail at such a man.

An older Harry lost his childish notion
And only sometimes wondered if events
Could echo thus long after in a dream.
If so, it surely meant they had a meaning.
But why the actual punishment had fallen,
For what offense of boyhood, he could try
For years and not unearth. What ghosts can say—

Even the ghosts of fathers—comes obscurely.
What if the terror stays without the meaning?

Unsounded

Mariner unpracticed,
In this chartless zone
Every navigator
Fares unwarned, alone.
Each his own Magellan
In tropics of sensation:
Not a fire-scorched stone
From prior habitation,
Not an archaic hull
Splintered on the beach.
These are latitudes revealed
Separate to each.

W. S. Merwin (1927–2019) *A Mask for Janus,* 1951

William Stanley Merwin was born in New York City and educated at Princeton University. The author of more than fifteen books of poetry and numerous books of prose, he also translated extensively from Latin, Russian, and various Romance languages. His honors include the Pulitzer Prize, the National Book Award, and the Bollingen Prize, among many others. Merwin was the judge of the Yale Series of Younger Poets from 1990 to 1996.

The Bones of Palinurus Pray to the North Star

Console us. The wind chooses among us.
Our whiteness is a night wake disordered.
Lone candor, be constant over
Us desolate who gleam no direction.

Song with the Eyes Closed

I am the shape in sleep
While the seasonal beasts
With petulant rough step
Forsake my random coasts.

I am the face recedes
Though the pool be constant
Whose double kingdom feeds
The sole vein's discontent.

I have seen desire, such
As a violent hand,
Murder my sleep—as much
Is suffered of the wind.

Carol of the Three Kings

How long ago we dreamed
Evening and the human
Step in the quiet groves
And the prayer we said:
Walk upon the darkness,
Words of the lord,
Contain the night, the dead
And here comfort us.
We have been a shadow
Many nights moving,
Swaying many nights
Between yes and no.
We have been blindness
Between sun and moon
Coaxing the time
For a doubtful star.
Now we cease, we forget
Our reasons, our city,
The sun, the perplexed day,
Noon, the irksome labor,
The flushed dream, the way,
Even the dark beasts,
Even our shadows.
In this night and day
All gifts are nothing:
What is frankincense
Where all sweetness is?
We that were followers
In the night's confusion
Kneel and forget our feet
Who the cold way came.
Now in the darkness
After the deep song
Walk among the branches

Angels of the lord,
Over earth and child
Quiet the boughs.
Now shall we sing or pray?
Where has the night gone?
Who remembers day?
We are breath and human
And awake have seen
All birth and burial
Merge and fall away,
Seen heaven that extends
To comfort all the night,
We have felt morning move
The grove of a few hands.

Edgar Bogardus (1927–1958) *Various Jangling Keys,* 1952

Born in Mount Vernon, Ohio, Edgar Bogardus studied at Yale University. He went on to teach at the Carnegie Institute of Technology in Pittsburgh and the University of Connecticut before joining the English faculty at Kenyon College, where he also served as managing editor of the *Kenyon Review*. His book of poems, *Last Poems*, was brought out by the *Kenyon Review* in 1960.

Sailing to Europe

Time came to come abroad, to care
For culture, and to chance
One sea craft or the other there
For England or for France.

The English and expansive boat,
Imperially right,
Capacious clumsiness afloat,
Was masculine as might.

A French ship, slenderly serene,
Its deep design so steeling
It, its seamen sad and keen,
Excited sailing feeling.

Resolved, I weathered rueful rips,
And this much I advance—
Toward England always take French ships,
And English boats toward France.

Near a Cemetery Pond

The snow faintly falls,
Falls faintly on the tombstone tops,
Spreading crisp sheets.

Butterfly skaters, their faces burned
And caked with cold, take
Advantage of the thrilling pond
And its dead water.
And I am happy.

      For what seemed years
I, finding challenges in
Blank fields,
Waded through the teeming mush
Of summer, with its indolent fans
And the high bother of
Its humming flies, sick
With consummation.

All fall long, I who warm
At histories of decay,
Waited for the fight
The frost brought on.
      And now I have glided
On hearts too chilled to break.

Skaters, your world
Flakes,
And I laugh with lust
To see your spills.
I am a man of winter—
I sympathize and do not care.
I make your freezing into fuel,
Leaping on your pain.

This is my manna,
To thrive on dearth and death,
My husky soul
Admits my crime,
I love the waste white wintertime.

In Memory of Robert Menner

I

This man, aware perhaps of dying, told
His final class of the coming rush of spring
When the overwhelming robin relieves our old
March longings, and how a scribe, lured by a wing
From his hard work, might error. This was his hold,
His strict digressive pipe would make us sing,
His tender core so sweet and white had grown,
Like marrow in that academic bone.

II

Robins and pens, poets and scribes, remain
Sweet enemies, often in the same
Witched head, and yet how many notes contain
More heart than the poetry of easy fame
They try to annotate, having cost more pain,
Having cost more pleasure. You think the scholar tame,
And yet how often has it been that he,
Unlike his poet, dealt strongly with the sea.

Daniel Hoffman (1923–2013) *An Armada of Thirty Whales,* 1953

Born in New York City, Daniel Hoffman was educated at Columbia University and served in the Army Air Corps during World War II. He was the author of more than a dozen books of poetry, as well as criticism and translations. The recipient of both a Guggenheim Fellowship and a National Endowment for the Humanities fellowship, Hoffman served as Consultant in Poetry to the Library of Congress and taught at the University of Pennsylvania.

Off Chichicastenengo

Off Chichicastenengo
I saw a green flamingo flying—

Bird-God of Guatemala,
leaf-winged, whose never-dying stems

were legs toe-rooted in
the sunlit air that nourished them.

And what delicious draughts
of light that out-thrust throat devoured

before bird-verdure soared
higher than eye could see or thought

could comprehend flamingo,
green, off Chichicastenengo.

Auricle's Oracle

Intensity, when greatest, may
Prove ludicrously small.
Who concentrates compellingly
More than the snoutish snail,

Hauling gunless turret up
Perpendicular glass,
>By muscle of mind and bodily ooze advancing,
>Atop at last the aquarium glass balancing?

Yet passion at its most intense
Consumes the minuscule.
The focus of the spirit's lens
On whatever the self may will
Like sunlight squeezed through a reading-glass
Turns trash to flame. The ooze congeals
>In a golden signature of snail-identity,
>Etched in glass by the snail's and the sun's intensity.

An Age of Fable

Petit the Panther's come to town.

With great discrimination
He places on the rude concrete
His cushioned, grass-accustomed feet.

His motions are most musical:

In subtle tempi, baton-tail
Conducts a silent clawed quartette
As foot, foot, foot, & foot, step-step.

Panther prowls through telephone booth,

Highway, subway, chromium bistro,
Video trees, spikediron hedgerow,
Skeletal wires. All lack the couth

Ferocity of jungle growth,

Lack dignity of death & birth.
Goaded onward through the maze
By burning blood between his thighs

Or by some supernatural sense,

He leaps beyond all artifice:
Blots the sickly neon solstice,
Drops with graceful violence

Beside the beauty in her trance.

Beneath her leafy counterpane,
She stirs: Catfurs she disenchants!
Now Death's enchanted by their dance.

John Ashbery (1927–2017) *Some Trees,* 1955

Born in Sodus, New York, John Ashbery studied at Harvard University and Columbia University. He was a Fulbright scholar in France, where he lived for fifteen years and worked as an art critic, editor, and frequent translator. Ashbery is widely considered one of the most influential American poets of the twentieth century. His many honors include the Pulitzer Prize, the National Book Award, the National Book Critics Circle Award, and the Bollingen Prize.

A Boy

I'll do what the raids suggest,
Dad, and that other livid window,
But the tide pushes an awful lot of monsters
And I think it's my true fate.

It had been raining but
It had not been raining.

No one could begin to mop up this particular mess.
Thunder lay down in the heart.
"My child, I love any vast electrical disturbance."
Disturbance! Could the old man, face in the rainweed,

Ask more smuttily? By night it charged over plains,
Driven from Dallas and Oregon, always *whither,*
Why not now? The boy seemed to have fallen
From shelf to shelf of someone's rage.

That night it rained on the boxcars, explaining
The thought of the pensive cabbage roses near the boxcars.
My boy. Isn't there something I asked you once?
What happened? It's also farther to the corner
Aboard the maple furniture. *He*
Couldn't lie. He'd tell 'em by their syntax.

But listen now in the flood.
They're throwing up behind the lines.
Dry fields of lightning rise to receive
The observer, the mincing flag. *An unendurable age.*

Errors

Jealousy. Whispered weather reports.
In the street we found boxes
Littered with snow, to burn at home.
What flower tolling on the waters
You stupefied me. We waxed,
Carnivores, late and alight
In the beaded winter. All was ominous, luminous.
Beyond the bed's veils the white walls danced
Some violent compunction. Promises,
We thought then of your dry portals,
Bright cornices of eavesdropping palaces,
You were painfully stitched to hours
The moon now tears up, scoffing at the unrinsed portions.
And loves adopted realm. Flees to water,
The coach dissolving in mists.
                        A wish
Refines the lines around the mouth
At these ten-year intervals. It fumed
Clear air of wars. It desired
Excess of core in all things. From all things sucked
A glossy denial. But look, pale day:
We fly hence. To return if sketched
In the prophet's silence. Who doubts it is true?

Answering a Question in the Mountains

I

I went into the mountains to interest myself
In the fabulous dinners of hosts distant and demure.

The foxes followed with endless lights.

Some day I am to build the wall
Of the box in which all angles are shown.
I shall bounce like a ball.
The towers of justice are waving
To describe the angles we describe.
Oh we have been so far
To instruct the birds in our cold ways.

Near me I heard a sound,
The line of a match struck in care.

It is late to be late.

II

Let us ascend the hearts in our hearts.
Let us ascend trees in our heads,
The dull heads of trees.

It is pain in the hand of the ungodly
To witness all the sentries,
The perfumed toque of dawn,
The hysteric evening with empty hands.
The snow creeps by; many light years pass.

We see for the first time.
We shall see for the first time.
We have seen for the first time.

The snow creeps by; many light years pass.

III

I cannot agree or seek
Since I departed in the laugh of diamonds
The hosts of my young days.

James Wright (1927–1980) *The Green Wall,* 1956

James Wright was born in Martins Ferry, Ohio, and studied at Kenyon College
and the University of Washington. A Fulbright scholar and a Guggenheim fellow,
Wright was the author of ten volumes of poetry. His *Collected Poems* (1971) won the
Pulitzer Prize.

Father

In paradise I poised my foot above the boat and said:
Who prayed for me?
                              But only the dip of an oar
In water sounded; slowly fog from some cold shore
Circled in wreaths around my head.

But who is waiting?
                              And the wind began,
Transfiguring my face from nothingness
To tiny weeping eyes. And when my voice
Grew real, there was a place
Far, far below on earth. There was a tiny man—

It was my father wandering round the waters at the wharf.
Irritably he circled and he called
Out to the marine currents up and down,
But heard only a cold unmeaning cough,
And saw the oarsman in the mist enshawled.

He drew me from the boat. I was asleep.
And we went home together.

Eleutheria

Rubbing her mouth along my mouth she lost
Illusions of the sky, the dreams it offered:
The pale cloud walking home to winter, dust
Blown to a shell of sails so far above
That autumn landscape where we lay and suffered
The fruits of summer in the fields of love.

We lay and heard the apples fall for hours,
The stripping twilight plundered trees of boughs,
The land dissolved beneath the rabbit's heels,
And far away I heard a window close,
A haying wagon heave and catch its wheels,
Some water slide and stumble and be still.
The dark began to climb the empty hill.

If dark Eleutheria turned and lay
Forever beside me, who would care for years?
The throat, the supple belly, the warm thigh
Burgeoned against the earth; I lay afraid,
For who could bear such beauty under the sky?
I would have held her loveliness in air,
Away from things that lured me to decay:
The ground's deliberate riches, fallen pears,
Bewildered apples blown to mounds of shade.

Lovers' location is the first to fade.
They wander back in winter, but there is
No comfortable grass to couch a dress.
Musicians of the yellow weeds are dead.
And she, remembering something, turns to hear
Either a milkweed float or a thistle fall.
Bodiless shadow thrown along a wall,
She glides lightly; the pale year follows her.

The moments ride away, the locust flute
Is silvered thin and lost, over and over.

She will return some evening to discover
The tree uplifted to the very root,
The leaves shouldered away, with lichen grown
Among the interlacings of the stone,
October blowing dust, and summer gone
Into a dark barn, like a hiding lover.

Autumnal

Soft, where the shadow glides,
The yellow pears fell down.
The long bough slowly rides
The air of my delight.

Air, though but nothing, air
Falls heavy down your shoulder.
You hold in burdened hair
The color of my delight.

Neither the hollow pear,
Nor leaf among the grass,
Nor wind that wails the year
Against your leaning ear,
Will alter my delight:

That holds the pear upright
And sings along the bough,
Warms to the mellow sun.
The song of my delight
Gathers about you now,
Is whispered through, and gone.

John Hollander (1929–2013) *A Crackling of Thorns,* 1957

Born in New York City, John Hollander studied at Columbia University and Indiana University. In addition to more than twenty books of poetry, Hollander wrote works of criticism and the enduring manual on prosody, *Rhyme's Reason* (1981). Among his honors are the Bollingen Prize and a MacArthur Fellowship. For most of his career, he taught at Yale University.

Carmen Ancillae

Burgundy c. 1430

Wider than winter
Lying over the river
Or the frosty sky through the window
That stretches forever
Around the white pennants
Above the battlements;
Wider than all I remember
Is the bed in my Lady's chamber.

Whiter than my Lady
Gazing along the river
At the sunny grass where lately
Her liking had led her
Away from the remnants
Of frost on the battlements;
Whiter than was December
Was the bed in my Lady's chamber.

Cold is the basin
I dip into the river
When the morning sun is blazing
Beyond the crisp weather.
With its cold contents
I cross the battlements.

My Lady's bed is colder,
Almost, than the river.
When we were younger
We warmed it together,
Warmer than the anger
She showed as she grew older.

Gold shines in the water
I carry from the river.
Gold given a king's daughter
Can only enrich the giver.
      And what of my penance
      Along the battlements?

      What I bring her looks golden:
      Will it avail me ever?
      Today she will be married,
      Clothed in gold like the river.
      I have fetched and carried:
      She will think of it seldom.

Black as the pearl she gave me
To tie among my tresses
Was her face as she bade them save me
Old robes and dresses
As parting presents.
I can see from the battlements
How she stands in a temper
Of tears and rage in her chamber.

A Word Remembered

All the young poets are writing about the seasons:
It is the summer poor Hippolyte prefers,
While his friend Phoebus despairs of winter's sadness.
The former has become extravagant,

To wallow in languorous tropes, while Phoebus' verses,
Nipped, as if with the cold, get painful and silly.
It was longer ago than I like to think that spring
Fell from their favor and became as dull
As blotters. All of which has made me think
Of the time that Mary was being very pregnant
And would take no beer, but quietly watched us drinking;
Then, mentioning some event of the past April,
She had recourse to name the general season,
But stopped suddenly, as if she had forgotten
A street address she had written down somewhere:

"It happened last—what is it comes before summer?"
And we sat there, not quite believing that this had happened,
Until she finally seemed to have remembered:
"Oh. Yes. Spring." I mention this
Only because we cannot remember now
Who, or what, we felt was being outraged.

Jefferson Valley

The tops of the spruces here have always done
Ragged things to the skies arranged behind them
Like slates at twilight; and the morning sun
Has marked out trees and hedgerows, and defined them
In various greens, until, toward night, they blur
Back into one rough palisade again,
Furred thick with dusk. No wind we know can stir
This olive blackness that surrounds us when
It becomes the boundary of what we know
By limiting the edge of what we see.
When sunlight shows several spruces in a row,
To know the green of a particular tree
  Means disbelief in darkness; and the lack
  Of a singular green is what we mean by black.

William Dickey (1928–1994) *Of the Festivity,* 1958

Born in Bellingham, Washington, William Dickey studied at Reed College, Harvard University, the Iowa Writers' Workshop, and Oxford University. For most of his career he taught at San Francisco State University. Dickey wrote fifteen books of poetry, including *More Under Saturn* (1972), winner of the Commonwealth Club of California's silver medal, and *The Rainbow Grocery* (1978), which won the Juniper Prize from the University of Massachusetts Press.

Part Song, with Concert of Recorders

I

SHE   Doctor, I did not see that you were there.

HE   Madam, I've stabbed your husband in his bed.
He now makes one with the unhoused dead.
I come to have you tell me that you care.

SHE   You know I care.

II

SHE   I did not know you when you came in there.

HE   I did not then intend that you should know,
Thought in the dark I'd have my way and go,
But love has come upon me and I care.

SHE   Tell me you care.

III

SHE   Who made you come and find the door to there?
Who made you turn that handle and come in?
What we have done, what we do, it is sin;
We shall be punished for it; have a care.

HE   I cannot care.

IV

SHE	And I, who lay so warm and quiet there—
HE	And you, who grew excited with my kiss—
SHE	Who would have thought that it would come to this?
	Let all be circumspect before they care.
HE	But let them care.

V

SHE	And he lies dead—
HE	His blood is seeping there—
SHE	Where we have kissed—
HE	Where we have done much more—
SHE	I liked it best the way it was before.
HE	You like it now.
SHE	I like it, but I care.
HE	No longer care.

VI

BOTH	For we have gone a curious way from there,
	But we have love and so we go ahead.
	It does no good to think about the dead.
	What's dead is dead, it will not ever care
	As we can care.

VII

SHE	Come, Doctor, we must fly someotherwhere.
HE	I have my bag full of essential things,
	False passports, currency, and diamond rings—
SHE	True pledge of love for those who truly care.
HE	Who live and care.

Les très riches heures

The duke rides in a green, enameled wood;
Jewels called birds elaborate his trees,
All colors meet to do him courtesies,
And intricate shadows pattern to his mood.
Is it the world we would all have if we could?
Innocent of doubt, of angularities;
Perspective here is a diligence to please
So pure it cannot be misunderstood.

Somewhere behind that picture is the court,
The palace stinking like a royal sty.
But it was the subliming counterpart
That led its dance across the painter's eye,
Whose silver boar seems to admire the sport
And the perilous, delicate huntsmen riding by.

A Vision, Caged

Over the city beneficent drugs conspire
To give the murderous one more night at large.
Their absolute senses tremble at the verge,
See the just crime, the unavoidable fire
Burning the mother of two. From ward to ward
The blanket of sedation settles in
Like generous, strangling hands. Pick any card—
Once again now the action will begin.
Punch will love Judy till he breaks her skull,
Mother hit Father with the parlor chair;
Their cup of interest completely full,
All of the watching children will be there.
Night falls. The exhibitionist displays
To his tight brain the gestures that release;
Grey in the midst of institutional greys
The alcoholic lurches into peace.

Nurses like ships' sails borne on the full breeze
Loom momentarily up and disappear.
Where disappears. All of these minds, at ease,
Congratulatory, concentrate on here,
The moment of the crime, the moment when
Suddenly a buried life broke out to flower.
The bloody children are a might-have-been
Compared to the importance of that hour,
Compared to the feeling that at least it's done—
Thank God the impetus to it can run down
And say, "Dear child, good-night," and then the one
Need is to find a corner of your own—
The corner grows enormous in their sight,
The lovely hypodermic brims and spills
Straight to the heart. Heart's engines fill the night,
Ever and again it swells, it hates, it kills.

George Starbuck (1931–1996) *Bone Thoughts,* 1959

George Edwin Starbuck was born in Columbus, Ohio. Although he attended many schools—the University of California at Berkeley, the California Institute of Technology, the University of Chicago, and Harvard University—he never obtained a degree. The author of eight books of poetry, Starbuck was an editor at Houghton Mifflin for several years, thereafter teaching at the University of Iowa and Boston University. He received the Prix de Rome and a Guggenheim Fellowship.

Technologies

On Commonwealth, on Marlborough,
the gull beaks of magnolia
were straining upward like the flocks
harnessed by kings in storybooks
who lusted for the moon. Six days
we mooned into each other's eyes
mythologies of dune and dawn—
naked to the Atlantic sun,
loving and loving, to and fro
on Commonwealth, on Marlborough,
our whole half-hours. And where our bloods
crested, we saw the bruise-red buds
tear loose the white, impeded shapes
of cries. And when our whitest hopes
tore at the wind with wings, it seemed
only a loony dream we dreamed,
such heavy machination of
cars and motels confronted love
on Commonwealth, on Marlborough.
They do the trick with rockets now—
with methodologies of steel—
with industry or not at all.
But so, sweet love, do these white trees

that dare play out their lunacies
for all they are, for all they know
on Commonwealth, on Marlborough.

A Tapestry for Bayeux

I. *Recto*

Over the
    seaworthy
cavalry
    arches a
rocketry
    wickerwork:
involute
    laceries
lacerate
    indigo
altitudes,
    making a
skywritten

filigree
    into which,
lazily,
    LCTs
sinuate,
    adjutants
next to them
    eversharp-
eyed, among
    delicate
battleship
    umbrages
twinkling an

anger as
    measured as
organdy.
    Normandy
knitted the
    eyelets and
yarn of these
    warriors'
armoring—
    ringbolt and
dungaree,
    cable and
axletree,

tanktrack and
    ammobelt
linking and
    opening
garlands and
    islands of
seafoam and
    sergeantry.
Opulent
    fretwork: on
turquoise and
    emerald,
red instants

accenting
    neatly a
dearth of red.
    Gunstations
issue it;
    vaportrails
ease into
    smoke from it—

yellow and
        ochre and
umber and
        sable and
out. Or that

man at the
        edge of the
tapestry
        holding his
inches of
        niggardly
ground and his
        trumpery
order of
        red and his
equipage
        angled and
dated. He.

II. *Verso*
Wasting no
        energy,
Time, the old
        registrar,
evenly
        adds to his
scrolls, rolling
        up in them
rampage and
        echo and
hush—in each
        influx of
surf, in each

tumble of
        raincloud at
evening,
        action of
seaswell and
        undertow
rounding an
        introvert
edge to the
        surge until,
manhandled
        over, all
surfaces,

tapestries,
        entities
veer from the
        eye like those
rings of lost
        yesteryears
pooled in the
        oak of your
memory.
        Item: one
Normandy
        Exercise.
Muscle it

over: an
        underside
rises: a
        raggedy
elegant
        mess of an
abstract: a

rip-out of
kidstuff and
    switchboards, where
amputee
    radio
elements,

unattached
    nervefibre
conduits,
    openmouthed
ureters,
    tag ends of
hamstring and
    outrigging
ripped from their
    unions and
nexuses
    jumble with
undeterred

speakingtubes
    twittering
orders as
    random and
angry as
    ddt'd
hornets. Step
    over a
moment: peer
    in through this
nutshell of
    eyeball and
man your gun.

Cora Punctuated with Strawberries

Sandra and that boy that's going to get her in trouble
one of these days were out in the garden where anyone in
Mother's sickroom could see them out the upperleft corner of the
window sitting behind the garage feeding each other
blueberries and Cherry was helping with the dishes alone in the
kitchen and
um good strawberries if we did grow them just can't can without
popping one in every so often Henry was at it again in the
attic with that whatchamacallit of his when the Big
Bomb fell smack in the MacDonalds' yard you know over on
Elm and they got into Life and the papers and all all very
well but they might have been in when it hit and it would have
been a very different story for Lucy MacDonald then I'll tell
you well they say it was right in the Geographic Center of the
country the Geographic
woody Center you could hear it just as plain I thought the
elevator had blown up and I guess you read yourself the awful
things it would have
ak another one woody I tell you I don't know what's got
into these strawberries used to be so juicy they
say they only had the one and it's all it would have took well I
always knew we could beat the enemy they made such
shoddy tricks and spring-toys and puzzles and fuses and
things and besides, it wouldn't have been right.

Alan Dugan (1923–2003) *Poems,* 1960

Alan Dugan was born in Brooklyn, New York. He attended Queens College, served in World War II, and graduated from Mexico City College in 1951. His Yale volume won both the Pulitzer Prize and the National Book Award. Other honors include the Prix de Rome, the Shelley Memorial Award from the Poetry Society of America, a Lannan Literary Award for Poetry, and a second National Book Award for *Poems Seven: New and Complete Poetry* (2001).

This Morning Here

This is this morning: all
the evils and glories of last night
are gone except for their
effects; the great world wars
I and II, the great marriage
of Edward the VII or VIII
to Wallis Warfield Simpson and
the rockets numbered like the Popes
have incandesced in flight
or broken on the moon: now
the new day with its famous
beauties to be seized at once
has started and the clerks
have swept the sidewalks
to the curb, the glass doors
are open, and the first
customers walk up and down
the supermarket alleys of their eyes
to Muzak. Every item has
been cut out of its nature,
wrapped disguised as something
else, and sold clean by fractions.
Who can multiply and conquer

by the Roman numbers? Lacking
the Arab frenzy of the zero, they
have obsolesced: the butchers
have washed up and left
after having killed and dressed
the bodies of the lambs all night,
and those who never have seen blood awake
can drink it browned
and call the past an unrepeatable mistake
because this circus of their present is all gravy.

The Mirror Perilous

I guess there is a garden named
"Garden of Love." If so, I'm in it:
I am the guesser in the garden.
There is a notice by the central pond
that reads: "Property of Narcissus.
Trespass at your own risk,"
so I went there. That is where,
having won but disdained a lady,
he fell for his own face and died,
rightly, "not having followed through,"
as the sentence read, read by the lady:
Oh you could hear her crying all about
the wilderness and wickedness of law.
I looked in that famous mirror perilous
and it wasn't much: my own face,
beautiful, and at the bottom
bone, a rusty knife, two beads
and something else I cannot name.
I drank my own lips on the dare
but could not drink the lips away.
The water was heavy, cool, and clear
but did not quench. A lady laughed

behind my back; I learned the worst:
I could take it or leave it, go or stay,
and went back to the office drunk,
possessed of an echo but not a fate.

How We Heard the Name

The river brought down
dead horses, dead men
and military debris,
indicative of war
or official acts upstream,
but it went by, it all
goes by, that is the thing
about the river. Then
a soldier on a log
went by. He seemed drunk
and we asked him Why
had he and this junk
come down to us so
from the past upstream.
"Friends," he said, "the great
Battle of Granicus
has just been won
by all of the Greeks except
the Lacedaemonians and
myself: this is a joke
between me and a man
named Alexander, whom
all of you ba-bas
will hear of as a god."

Jack Gilbert (1925–2012) *Views of Jeopardy,* 1961

Jack Gilbert was born in Pittsburgh, Pennsylvania. Although he flunked out of high school, Gilbert eventually graduated from the University of Pittsburgh and San Francisco State University. He wrote four subsequent volumes of poetry, for which he received the National Book Critics Circle Award, the Los Angeles Times Book Prize, the Stanley Kunitz Prize, and the Lannan Literary Award for Poetry, among others. Gilbert's *Collected Poems* (2012) was a finalist for the Pulitzer Prize.

Perspective He Would Mutter Going to Bed

for Robert Duncan

"Perspective," he would mutter, going to bed.
"Oh che dolce cosa è questa
Prospettiva." Uccello. Bird.

And I am as greedy of her, that the black
Horse of the literal world might come
Directly on me. Perspective. A place

To stand. To receive. A place to go
Into from. The earth by language.

Who can imagine antelope silent
Under the night rain, the Gulf
At Biloxi at night else? I remember

In Mexico a man and a boy painting
An adobe house magenta and crimson
Who thought they were painting it red. Or pretty.

So neither saw the brown mountains
Move to manage that great house.

The horse wades in the city of grammar.

The Abnormal Is Not Courage

The Poles rode out from Warsaw against the German
Tanks on horses. Rode knowing, in sunlight, with sabers.
A magnitude of beauty that allows me no peace.
And yet this poem would lessen that day. Question
The bravery. Say it's not courage. Call it a passion.
Would say courage isn't that. Not at its best.
It was impossible, and with form. They rode in sunlight.
Were mangled. But I say courage is not the abnormal.
Not the marvelous act. Not Macbeth with fine speeches.
The worthless can manage in public, or for the moment.
It is too near the whore's heart: the bounty of impulse,
And the failure to sustain even small kindness.
Not the marvelous act, but the evident conclusion of being.
Not strangeness, but a leap forward of the same quality.
Accomplishment. The even loyalty. But fresh.
Not the Prodigal Son, nor Faustus. But Penelope.
The thing steady and clear. Then the crescendo.
The real form. The culmination. And the exceeding.
Not the surprise. The amazed understanding. The marriage,
Not the month's rapture. Not the exception. The beauty
That is of many days. Steady and clear.
It is the normal excellence, of long accomplishment.

It Is Clear Why the Angels Come No More

It is clear why the angels come no more.
Standing so large in their beautiful Latin,
How could they accept being refracted
So small in another grammar, or leave
Their perfect singing for this broken speech?
Why should they stumble this alien world?

Always I have envied the angels their grace.
But I left my hope of Byzantine size

And came to this awkwardness, this stupidity.
Came finally to you washing my face
As everyone laughed, and found a forest
Opening as marriage ran in me. All

The leaves in the world turned a little
Singing: The angels are wrong.

Sandra Hochman (1936–) *Manhattan Pastures,* 1962

Sandra Hochman was born in New York City and was educated at Bennington College and Columbia University. In addition to many volumes of poetry, including *Earthworks: Poems, 1960–1970*, Hochman has written novels and essays. She directed the feminist documentary *Year of the Woman* (1973).

Inferno

Hell's a place
Where lover and beloved
Lip to lip face each other's crime. The man across my quilt
Turns quietly. I read of guilt,
I know guilt is a lie.
I dive
Into the water-bed of Charon,
Limbo dissolves my breath, Paolo and Francesca spin
Over my bed to comfort me.
When I turn against a night of restless
Sleep, my book and my beloved fall upon
The wind-stained willows of Acheron.

Hansoms

Never tame, those
Honey-speckled horses
That troupe through the streets of Manhattan
Prancing with jute saddles

Carrying dancers and opera bassos.
They lugged newspapers and dolls
To sad warehouses,
Clopped through the alleys of Broadway,
(Eyes riveted on neon meathooks)

They trotted to Harlem.
And met up with cab-drivers, blonde vegetable
Horses, and cornices, and veiled ponies
Adorned for the weddings of plazas. Then they ran
From the exile of parks
Past dummies, clothes-hooks, and pelts,
Trotting down Fifth Avenue
To the sea. They

Galloped on boats
Rode on the spokes of the tides,
Rode on Venetian gondolas,
Stayed close to the lotus sterns,
Rolled on cedarwood ships,
Returning from Thebes,
Galloped on Jason's glittering boat
Carved from the branch of Dodona,
They joined the oarsmen
Close to the axis, and sailed
With groups in the galley, sailed
Viking-ships beneath sea-masks,
Faced bulwarks and rowing benches,
Stamped hooves through gold bolts of damask. And cried
With their great yellow teeth while
Lateen sails swelled. They bit
The Roman merchants, traveled with dead-eyes,
Rammed against bulkheads.

They rode on the *Great Harry*
While leather shields were displayed,
Rode hulks and caravels, set their hinds
Against bowsprits. From Portugal
They set sail on the *Galleon*. They rode
On the *Voyage Armada*, froze on merchant's ships,
On flutes, on seventy-four gun ships, on luggers,
Bugalets, frigates, feluccas, and barques.

They leapt through their dreams on tartanes, burned
On xebecs and saïques,
Exiled on brigs, snows, brigantines until
Tamed by the sea, they came home.
Never broken. But they came home,
Home to the winter, home to saddle and crop,
Blanket, stall, and the whips
Of lovesick riders
Who drove them around and around
Central Park for a view of swans.

Divers

We have chosen the sea
Because we are lonely
And resemble
All things that go down.
Sucking the sun
In our silver-finned sea-chests,
We leave antennae touching the sky,
We plummet
In the great hives of water.
Che farà Euridice?

Go, bleed the waves
And find the blue jail of Euridice.
The sea-blades wind her fingers in the salt.

(There is no bottom chamber to the sea.)
Find on the tips of waves that drifting face.

Peter Davison (1928–2004) *The Breaking of the Day,* 1963

Born in New York City and raised in Colorado, Peter Davison studied at Harvard University and Cambridge University. He was the author of twelve books of poetry, two books of criticism, and two memoirs, including *The Fading Smile: Poets in Boston, 1955–1960, from Robert Frost to Robert Lowell to Sylvia Plath* (1994). Davison was an editor at Harcourt, Brace and served as poetry editor of the *Atlantic Monthly* for many years.

Fogged In

All afternoon the bank
Had pressed on sullenly
Up channel. Quick east winds
Butted against its flank.

It drooped beneath the blue
Like rags hung out to dry.
Sun seared its top, while sea
Supplied it from below.

Yet nightfall in its turn
Gained ground upon the sun.
This morning, under shield
Of darkness, fog has won

And blurs us deaf and blind.
Enshrouded beyond call
We tremble for the end
Of islands, echoes, all.

Summer School

These tenants of the migratory season
Were children yesterday. Adulterers today,
They settle like thievish cuckoos in such nests
As they can find furnished with a summer vacancy,
And share their sandalled quest of the absolute.

Professor P., expert in semantics,
Teases their drowsy mornings with a lecture;
But once the sun announces afternoon
They strip naked in each laboratory sublet
Among worn counterpanes and last winter's books
To dedicate each fiber of themselves
To the hot discipline of appetite.

Thus in the academy of summer
These scholars, sworn to seek the limits of self,
Enlarge their own by feeding upon others
And learn by process of elimination.
What bones will they have gnawed when they return
To the major business of the autumn
With knitted brows, to read once more of love?

The Suicide

Poor starling. Her cry was sharp enough to draw blood
As she braced her whistling head and squeezed her feet
Clamp upon her local chimney top
And glared as hard as the sky that looked her down.
Taut-muscled on the ground, she pecked and pecked
Whatever she scratched up, and never sure
Which grains were food, which grains were only gravel.
Just so her loves, random as a vine.
Curse those who kept her food from her until
She'd learnt their tricks! Her hungry eyes became
Their sentinels, on watch for where the heart

Lurked, to have it out and peck peck peck—
And yet her beak most often fell on bone
Until the day she turned it on herself
And dizzyingly sang, within her throat
The sigh of the slain, the grunt of the executioner.

Jean Valentine (1934–) *Dream Barker,* 1964

Born in Chicago, Illinois, Jean Valentine studied at Radcliffe College. She has written twelve books of poems, including *Door in the Mountain: New and Collected Poems, 1965–2003*, which won the National Book Award. Other honors include the Wallace Stevens Award from the Academy of American Poets, a Guggenheim Fellowship, and the Poetry Society of America's Shelley Memorial Prize. She lives in New York City.

Asleep over Lines from Willa Cather

Now I lay me desolate to sleep
Cold in the sound of the underground flood,
Brushed in half-sleep by the phantom plant
Pressed in the book by my bed
Blue-green leaves, large and coarse-toothed . . .
With big white blossoms like Easter lilies . . .
Latour recognized the noxious datura.
In its dead shade I lay me down to sleep.

The reins inside my head that hold my hope
When it leaps, in waking life, fall slack,
And, beyond the world of falling things,
With flesh like air, and an assumed agreement
Between my body and the way it takes,
I walk aimlessly by a green and perfect river.

The garden is here, as I knew it would be;
The garden imagined through oblique windows in paintings,
Earth's lost plantation, waiting for all, all,
All to be well: the fountain translates the sun.
I do not see but know God follows me,
And I follow, without fear of madness,
Paths and turnings that are both wild and formal,
Of all colors or none, tiger-lily and rock,

Pools dead with the weight of fallen leaves, and falls,
Follow after him I love, who waits in the garden.

Mercy, Pity, Fear and Shame
Spring in this garden, for it is earth's.
My body is not air, it casts a shadow.
At the next turning I come upon him I love
Waiting by the tree from my childhood that drops
White petals that hugely snow on the whitening ground.
He takes my arm and we walk a little way
Away from the tree towards the shining river
Running clear green through the garden.

The allegorists' arrow has struck me down.
I freeze in the noise of the flood.
When my love bends to speak, it is a language
I do not know: I answer and have no voice,
I am deaf, I am blind, I reach out to touch his face
And touch a spot of spittled clay, my eye,
Hiding the garden, the river, the tree.

Sasha and the Poet

Sasha: I dreamed you and he
Sat under a tree being interviewed
By some invisible personage. You were saying
'They sound strange because they were lonely,
The seventeenth century,
That's why the poets sound strange today:
In the hope of some strange answer.'
Then you sang '*hey nonny, nonny, no*' and cried,
And asked him to finish. '*Quoth the potato-bug,*'
He said, and stood up slowly.
'By Shakespeare.' And walked away.

Sex

All the years waiting, the whole, barren, young
Life long. The gummy yearning
All night long for the far white oval
Moving on the ceiling;
The hand on the head, the hand in hand;
The gummy pages of dirty books by flashlight,
Blank as those damaged classical groins;

Diffusion of leaves on the night sky,
The queer, sublunar walks.
And the words: the lily, the flame, the truelove knot,
Forget-me-not; coming, going,
Having, taking, lying with,
Knowing, dying;
The old king's polar sword,
The wine glass shattered on the stone floor.

And the thing itself not the thing itself,
But a metaphor.

James Tate (1943–2015) *The Lost Pilot,* 1966

Born in Kansas City, Missouri, James Vincent Tate studied at the University of Missouri, Kansas State College, and the University of Iowa. He wrote more than twenty volumes of poetry, including *Worshipful Company of Fletchers* (1994), which won the National Book Award, and *Selected Poems* (1991), which won the Pulitzer Prize and the William Carlos Williams Award. Other honors include the Dorothea Tanning Award from the Academy of American Poets and a Guggenheim Fellowship. For most of his career he taught at the University of Massachusetts in Amherst.

The Face of the Waters

Perhaps I have only remained;
stood still, beautiful, and
(as a sagacious friend once

said) with a deep yearning
for the ascetic existence.
I was reading Meister Eckhart

at the time because I wanted
my friends to think I was
beautiful and had a deep

yearning for the ascetic etcetera.
Modes of advertising changed.
Selling yourself, I said,

condescending from the bottom
of a dream. What is this
springing from the ground?

Rain? Kings and queens
donkeying through the fractured
gallery of my seasons.

At least this is not the rain
I requested. Another bad
shipment due to nevermind.

The streets are alive with
free swimming animals: fiddler
crabs, coelenterates, river

otters, venus flower baskets –
I know you are out there
but you cannot come in.

The Lost Pilot

for my father, 1922–1944

Your face did not rot
like the others – the co-pilot,
for example, I saw him

yesterday. His face is corn-
mush: his wife and daughter,
the poor ignorant people, stare

as if he will compose soon.
He was more wronged than Job.
But your face did not rot

like the others – it grew dark,
and hard like ebony;
the features progressed in their

distinction. If I could cajole
you to come back for an evening,
down from your compulsive

orbiting, I would touch you,
read your face as Dallas,
your hoodlum gunner, now,

with the blistered eyes, reads
his braille editions. I would
touch your face as a disinterested

scholar touches an original page.
However frightening, I would
discover you, and I would not

turn you in; I would not make
you face your wife, or Dallas,
or the co-pilot, Jim. You

could return to your crazy
orbiting, and I would not try
to fully understand what

it means to you. All I know
is this: when I see you,
as I have seen you at least

once every year of my life,
spin across the wilds of the sky
like a tiny, African god,

I feel dead. I feel as if I were
the residue of a stranger's life,
that I should pursue you.

My head cocked toward the sky,
I cannot get off the ground,
and, you, passing over again,

fast, perfect, and unwilling
to tell me that you are doing
well, or that it was mistake

that placed you in that world,
and me in this; or that misfortune
placed these worlds in us.

Grace

The one thing that sustained
the faces on the four
corners of the intersection

did not unite them,
did not invite others to join.
Their inner eyes as the light

changed did not change,
but focused madly precise
on the one thing until

it scared them. Then
they all went to the movies.
I was just beginning

to understand when one
who represented the desperate
shrunken state came toward

me, bisecting the whole mass
of concrete into triangles,
and handed me a package.

I carried it with me for
the rest of my life, never
opening it, telling no one.

Helen Chasin (1938–2015) *Coming Close,* 1967

Helen Chasin grew up in Brooklyn, New York, and graduated from Radcliffe College. In 1975 she published a second volume of poetry, *Casting Stones*, and in 1976 she co-founded the Writers Community in Manhattan. Her honors include a Bread Loaf Scholarship in Poetry and a fellowship at the Bunting Institute at Radcliffe College.

Among the Supermarket

Dearest, this abundance of tinned goods,
quick-frozen gourmet snacks, V-8 juice, plasti-
paks, imported tidbits in foreign grease,
megatons of detergent power
and jars of cloudy premixed cocktails
undoes me: instantly
I am kin to the national idiot
agency men count on: transfixed by canned music,
astonished in the aisles, dumbly convinced of
happiness, crazy to make meals
like making love.

My dear, it is not merely persuasion; not
coming to terms with all varieties,
each with its own use; not, stunned by choice,
compulsion to cram the cart, consuming until
even Brand X is familiar

but that I can still say, amid this ridiculous
array of food and ancillaries, displayed with super-
lunatic logic
the bounty of days and households is manifest.
Surrounded by these necessities, these
trivia, I find: love is possible. We could live
among its items. These found objects are its signs.

Joy Sonnet in a Random Universe

Sometimes I'm happy: la la la la la la la
la la la la la la la la la la la la la la la la
la la la la. Tum tum ti tum. La la la la la la
la la la la la la la la la la la la la la la la.
Hey nonny nonny. La la la la la la la la la
la la la la la la la la la la. Vo do di o do.
Poo poo pi doo. La la la la la la la la la la
la la la la la la la la la la la la la la la la la la
la la. Whack a doo. La la la la la la la. Sh-
boom, sh-boom. La la la la la la la la la la
la la la la la la la la la la la la la la la la la
la la. Dum di dum. La la la la la la la la la
la la la la la la la la la. Tra la la. Tra la la
la la la la la la la la la la. Yeah yeah yeah.

Encounters And

> *A sacred being cannot be anticipated—it must be encountered.*
> W. H. Auden

Suddenly met, unaccountably set into my hours
you are entirely here
paired with your palpable absence,
particled as air.
Without knowing you I could not imagine you
gone.

     You are a gift, a grief, a gift,
a possible final grief

         like the Chinese nests
whose diminishing answers suggest infinite loss.

Judith Johnson Sherwin (1936–) *Uranium Poems,* 1968

Judith Johnson Sherwin studied at Radcliffe College, the Juilliard School, and Barnard College. Her eight books of poetry include *Cities of Mathematics and Desire* (2005) and *The Ice Lizard* (1992). She has also written fiction. Her honors include the Poetry Society of America's Alice Faye Di Castagnola Prize and Nimrod International's Katherine Anne Porter Fiction Prize. In 1985, she stopped writing under her married name, and has since written as Judith Emlyn Johnson. Johnson is professor emerita of English and women's studies at the State University of New York at Albany.

Happy Jack's Rock

mine, better tell no man
    what a don't care deep down rock ribbed stubborn
       what a cold fish tight fisted underhanded punch
        drunk son of a butter fingered bitch you were
          let it all go for him
          wouldn't let me in

better tell no man
    you spit-tinkled me out like a beer drinking river
    slag wash down the mountainside
    of the twenty lives i dug for you

happy jack mine
better tell no man
    how you rolled right over on your rockbottom flapjack
    buttered side for those memo-dripping stickpin
    eyes in a two button suit with computer ears
       and a twenty-four carat ruby red ringtailed ass
                   and a tennis
      playing pool swimming soft corporation
      attached you could drown in and never even know it

better tell no man
    in your fat cat song purring sharpy rocktoothed
    mouth what a river pissing goldfishing underground
        played out dug up   gold gone bad
        ore washed up   copper mined out   silver snaggle
                                          teeth
        pulled out assets frozen act you put on
        for me and then came
        for his kitchen magic

                        and the drowning A-frame
houses and the fireball dustcloud burnt up world
rocking down to the toothroot shaken bones
of the flick built villages sang
    out don't hand it over don't hand
    it over baby earthworm grub-hatching rainbow grit boweled
    man-eating harbor of all of us don't
        lay it all down right on the dotted line
        high-priced spread
            out wide open for him
        in a beautiful milkwhite porcelain polished
            industry wide grin
        with a cashbox rattling stock splitting mashed
            potato dancing shiver built in.

happy jack you golden chock full of fucks
bullseye of the golden west
    no one ever tell you better to go
    down dignified
    for no man
    than this worldwide
    twitch of the limbs for death
that shuts us out most when it takes us in?

Watersong

under your fishwiggle thrust
in channel and lock to feel
    skin whispers to skin
the gold seed spill
tally of days and all
holding back a forgotten taste

in salmonleaping in-
lets scale ringing scale to hear
    skin whispers to skin
hammer the grain sheer
hands, in the still pools' measure
to see fin hairy on fin

brush, winesweat and ripe to smell
the thick fur weeds leaf loose
    skin whispers to skin
the soul from their black juice-
steeped roots, and song bruise
stagger the stone-lipped well,

goldslithering, rustle a brew
out of the still place
    skin whispers to skin
that is lost yes in your face
to touch what is not you

Buzzards' Bay

it's a still backwater
it's a hard badwater
it's a damnyankee swamp each day
the owl and the pussycat put out
what the nextdoor owls have got
the owl is a pussy, the pussy's an owl

if she doesn't know when not
to   if you marry me
          i will scratch you a baby blue
          out of each irish eye
          comb from your hair with a steel fork
          ten thousand clams to
chowder with you in the damp nights
when you limerick on down
to the fine sand and the mud black
with owl shells ripped off

          don't say
          what we both know is true
          the love in me
                    will strip you

Hugh Seidman (1940–) *Collecting Evidence,* 1969

Born in Brooklyn, New York, in 1940, Hugh Seidman has written seven books of poetry, including *Selected Poems, 1965–1995* (1995). He has taught at the University of Wisconsin, Yale University, Columbia University, and the New School for Social Research. Seidman's honors include a National Endowment for the Arts fellowship, the Green Rose Prize from New Issues Press, and the Camden Poetry Award. He lives in New York City.

Fragmenta

1

The sin of poetry continues
thruout the stain of his love.
Whatever I am, he thinks.
Whatever I am.

The bodies roll off
under the sickling crescent.
He moves in the moon radiance.
False light. False purity.
Whatever I am, he thinks;
It was not for these butchers.

My love. My horrid heart.
My unspeakable terrible love.
My dread and disfigurement.
My ghoul-like dreams that step
to the shrill of the reed.
Whatever I am, he thinks.
Whatever I am.

2

What do we know of that dead time,
but Yeats perhaps,
capturer of those passionate men.

You write beautiful poems,
she said, it is enough.

To believe that,
until I imagine the screams,
conjure the blood upon myself
where no blow has fallen.

3

They are the martyrs of the Word
under the nails of the lion.

We are the men of the furnace
nailed thru our skulls
in the agony of survival.

We hold to the hours
and number the lines of the dead.

We render our hands
and dream they will release us.

Our faces are our own.
We know what we may not know.

Poem

How the Lord of Death came to lay his moist finger at my throat
I went to the fork of the streets
But the distances were different and had lengthened
I heard the voices behind me as I ran
And awoke to the leaves which were the wind
Insane with tiredness and distant from myself

And how I had awakened beside you years ago
To fend away your touch turning in half sleep
For the loss of love does not cease in this world

Pattern

Why this lust
when there is nothing mutable
but the hope of change
in the mind that knows this.

Muscles anchored to negation.
Interminable days
in the intervals of our receivers.
The sine curves of emotion.

She left me with distortion.
She said this is where you are
and what can I do.
The subtle magnet
bending the signals out of shape.

Peter Klappert (1942–) *Lugging Vegetables to Nantucket,* 1970

Born in Rockville Centre, New York, Peter Klappert studied at Cornell University and the University of Iowa. He has written six books of poetry, including *Chokecherries: New and Selected Poems, 1966–1999* (2000). He taught at George Mason University for many years before retiring in 2006. Klappert has received grants from the National Endowment for the Arts and the Ingram Merrill Foundation.

Poem for L. C.

> I. *I have only the sound of your steps*
> *to guide me in this wilderness.*
>
> (Tagore, "The Cycle of Spring")

Honey-suckle, nightshade,
the burdock tree; the hawthorn,
the spiney hawthorn with hand branches
and rock bound roots. Mud.

Protect your face. Know how to
recognize flowers, even in gardens,
know the medicinal herbs,
sweet and rude, though they be tame.
Tread paths with dry feet, leave
careful footprints. Lead me, and follow.

I have seen these thickets before
though the meadow escapes me;
don't let them tear at your eyes,
don't look back at me now, no more
than a glance. I am lost
as you are, I am tired,
I am making a home of this wood.

Buttercup, columbine, borage,
ash green thyme of the mint family.
Remember them. The weather has not been mild
and will not be mild tonight;
tomorrow, or over that hill,
look back if you can. Frail flowers
tenacious as weeds, have mystical powers.

Love me. Show by the path you tread
you love me now. Tomorrow,
or over that hill, look back if you can.

> II. *Nothing is competent nothing is all there is.*
> (Creeley, "The Immoral Proposition")

I have brought you the wrong way, and I'm sorry.
The path you wanted is back, out of the thickets
of rhetoric; follow the trampled plants.
Metaphor began with words, and metaphor

misleads: 'buttercup' and 'columbine' are weeds,
they have no healing powers. Shallows of color,
texture and euphony make no flowers last.
The inscriptions of hawthorns cling.

And there is no truth beyond logic—surely
you have walked in circles looking.
Meadows grow into forests, and wilderness
clearings erode or strangle in neglect.

Perhaps there was a valley, and a path,
though this path ended. 'Love' is a conceit
earned in commitment; we are unintentional
liars. My figure has led you to briars.

No Turtles

For ten months now
no turtles.

Walnuts.   Clumped
like mudballs on the rug.

I've done my best.
Washed the dishes, folded up
my clothes,

even swept the porch.   No
turtles
                blooming
in the turtle trees.

Softly, at night,
I hear the walnuts breathe,
but get down on my knees
or not

        no turtle movements
interrupt my sleep.

Photographs of Ogunquit

> *Abbot Lot came to Abbot Joseph and said: Father, according as I am able,
> I keep my little rule, and my little fast, my prayer, meditation and con-
> templative silence; and according as I am able I strive to cleanse my heart
> of thoughts: now what more should I do? The elder rose up in reply and
> stretched out his hands to heaven, and his fingers became like ten lamps of
> fire. He said: why not be totally changed into fire?*
>
> (The Wisdom of the Desert, translated by Thomas Merton)

I

On the last day you would not
let me take your picture. The sun
was shattering on glass,

the stonewharf hurt my eyes. I was angry
and the sky would not cloud over.

You were only twenty. It was the beginning
of the last day. The fishermen
refused to see the air between us,
the full face of your smile, the full
mouth, spitting. They sat eyeing the sea.

The wind ignited your hair. I resisted
your flight and walked away
way down the beach. The beach was full
of families. Your eyes were bluegreen.
Your distress was wild and anonymous.

I resisted your flight, now what more
must I do? The rocks hurt my eyes.
I was angry. I turned. The beach
was full of families. The fishermen
looked at their lines. Children are singing.

II

The curtains stood up and watched us,
the swollen door was forced shut, we were
warped against each other. I could not
tell you from the humid air. I wanted
to say I will not want to take your
picture to tell the truth I wanted to say
the sheets are smothering I
wanted to refuse to sleep against
the door I wanted to say the room
is standing in the corners holding its breath.
When it was over, neither of us laughed.

III

It was one o'clock. I'm not sure
how far I walked. You walked the wharf.
We walked back.

What you've given you cannot take
out of my hands, and what I've
given is still mine to give.
I take it with me, there is sand
in the shutter. Perhaps you meant
to leave it on the chair.

                We will fight back
with anger and recriminations,
with demands and ultimatums.
The camera is set on #4. The fishermen
saw nothing.
       I hope the bus has brought you
safely to yourself.
            When you wouldn't pose
you said "Now what more must I do?"
Children were singing.

          The camera
is at the bottom of the suitcase.

Robert Hass (1941–) *Field Guide,* 1972

Robert Hass was born in San Francisco, California, and educated at Saint Mary's College and Stanford University. He has written six books of poetry (including *The Apple Trees at Olema: New and Selected Poems,* 2010), as well as several books of criticism (*Twentieth Century Pleasures: Prose on Poetry,* 1984) and translation (*The Essential Haiku: Versions of Basho, Buson, and Issa,* 1994). His many honors include the Pulitzer Prize, the National Book Award, the National Book Critics Circle Award, and a MacArthur Fellowship. From 1995 to 1997, Hass served as poet laureate of the United States.

Maps

Sourdough french bread and pinot chardonnay
• • •
Apricots—
the downy buttock shape
hard black sculpture of the limbs
on Saratoga hillsides in the rain.
• • •
These were the staples of the China trade:
sea otter, sandalwood, and bêche-de-mer
• • •
The pointillist look of laurels
their dappled pale green body stirs
down valley in the morning wind
Daphne was supple
my wife is tan, blue-rippled
pale in the dark hollows
• • •
Kit Carson in California:
it was the eyes of fish
that shivered in him the tenderness of eyes
he watched the ships come in

at Yerba Buena once, found obscene
the intelligence of crabs
their sidelong crawl, gulls
screeching for white meat
flounders in tubs, startled
• • •
Musky fall—
slime of a saffron milkcap
the mottled amanita
delicate phallic toxic
• • •
How odd
the fruity warmth of zinfandel
geometries of "rational viticulture"
• • •
    Plucked from algae sea spray
cold sun and a low rank tide
    sea cucumbers
lolling in the crevices of rock
they traded men enough
to carve old Crocker's railway out of rock
to eat these slugs
bêche-de-mer
• • •
The night they bombed Hanoi
we had been drinking red pinot
that was winter the walnut tree was bare
and the desert ironwood where waxwings
perched in spring drunk on pyracantha

squalls headwinds days gone
north on the infelicitous Pacific
• • •
The bleak intricate erosion of these cliffs

    seas grown bitter
with the salt of continents

. . .

Jerusalem artichokes
raised on sandy bluffs at San Gregorio
near reedy beaches where the steelhead ran

Coast range runoff turned salt creek
in the heat and indolence of August

. . .

That purple in the hills
    owl's clover stiffening the lupine
while the white flowers of the pollinated plant
    seep red

the eye owns what is familiar
    felt along the flesh
"an amethystine tinge"

. . .

Chants, recitations:
Olema
Tamalpais Mariposa
Mendocino Sausalito San Rafael
Emigrant Gap
Donner Pass

Of all the laws
that bind us to the past
the names of things are
stubbornest

. . .

Late summer—
red berries darken the hawthorns
curls of yellow in the laurels

your body and the undulant
sharp edges of the hills

. . .

Clams, abalones, cockles, chitons, crabs

. . .

Ishi
in San Francisco, 1911:
it was not the sea he wondered at
that inland man who saw the salmon
die to spawn and fed his dwindling people
from their rage to breed
it was the thousands of white bodies
on the beach
"Hansi saltu . . ." so many
ghosts
. . .

The long ripple in the swamp grass
is a skunk
he shuns the day

At Stinson Beach

Trompe l'oeil stillness in a steady rain

The coast road: morning glories in a drainage ditch
Pale touch-me-nots: suicide in early spring,
Its particular agony, the false note

By what name, when blossom
Falls on blossom, rain
On rain

What she brought back from that minute tranquillity
She never said

How the flower of her body
Danced her dresses into light

Fog and the early sun, an easy wind
She danced swaying in the stalled light
She danced easily without occasion

Variations in green, ferns, redwood, the rain

Two Views of Buson

1

A French scholar says he affected the Chinese manner.
When he took his friends into the countryside
To look at blossoms, they all saw Chinese blossoms.
He dressed accordingly and wept for the wild geese of Shosho.

2

One year after making love through the short midsummer night
He walked home at dawn and noticed that the river Oi
Had sunk two feet. The following year was better.
He saw bubbles of crab-froth among the river reeds.

Michael Ryan (1945–) *Threats Instead of Trees,* 1973

Born in Saint Louis, Missouri, Michael Ryan studied at the University of Notre Dame, Claremont College, and the University of Iowa. He has written four books of poems (including *New and Selected Poems,* 2004), an autobiography (*Secret Life,* 1995), and a book of essays on the craft of poetry (*A Difficult Grace,* 2000). His honors include a Whiting Award, the Kingsley Tufts Poetry Award, and the Lenore Marshall Poetry Prize. Ryan lives in California.

The Beginning of Sympathy

So close I'm defenseless,
I inhale my father's last breath:
it sticks, did I steal it,
this secret to begin myself.
Here is the secret at work:
a life fixed in its abstract immensity
that demands the usual journey:
the trees leaning close
whispering Don't worry we'll tell you something,
a big sun dropping announcements
of the unimaginable loneliness of guilt.
That is, in an otherwise normal landscape,
when you'd crawl away from your father
and have no thoughts, say to a hill
where the air's so pure it's visible,
objects become arbitrary & statements false.

Until the woman shows up
to show you origin, in a touch which shocks
like entering another person's dream,
but worth the connection to examine
the chink in yourself you stepped out of
to get here, rubbing her gently as a weapon,

this oh-so-welcome terminal salvation
I'd now compare to awakening.
Since she desires nothing, then, she's a phantom,
but finally I don't feel bad
because this ending approaches a beginning:
I've never left my father.
He's getting colder,
his voice thin as an angel's,
although his tongue is stuck in death.
Don't waste the dead, he says sympathetically,
Come sit in my mouth.

Talking About Things

for Jon Anderson

For a moment, the idiot inside me who shouts
death constantly blacks out & here I am, hobnob-
bing with objects: I ask myself, have you thanked
the pillow for muffling that bickering? And what
would I do without this fork to my hot pot pies?
Good light bulbs, I appreciate not descending
stairs in the dark . . .
Surely we all are included by objects, even if
my shirt could care more about which body slides
around inside it. From now on, let's only use
nouns: knife, widow, fume, penis, idiot. Of course
the little fellow's still unconscious. Yes I'll still call
him *Man with a past which is not his* . . .

The Blind Swimmer

for Thomas Lux

We know he's out there,
swimming slowly, searching for corners

in the sea where the dark has rubbed away.
He holds each breath like a last chance
at sleep, afraid of entering some insane
dream where voices without shapes scream
"Swim" and even the ocean is missing.
Still, he swims. The water fills his cupped hands
like breasts, a slight touch in a crowd
of waves pushing him nowhere, the blue
salt glued to his eyes like braille.
What do his dead eyes say?
The body that keeps him floating is a room,
the sun will stop if he just walks out?

On the shore, our feet planted like roots,
we watch for a sign. Some of us yell
at anything: a fat dolphin breaking the surface
for air; the edge of a seagull's wing
mistaken for a hand. The ocean doesn't stand for
our lives, calm & regular, but we still fear
drowning. So, safely together,
we wait for the blind swimmer
to walk out of the sea & say it's all right,
you can swim alone without seeing.
Some of us wait a long time.

I know he's out there.
He smells the ocean, doesn't he, that old
naked woman? She takes his tongue
in her mouth, doesn't her mouth open?
I hear him going under,
quietly as memory enters sleep, his memories
nothing I can imagine, tasting water so deep
light is terrible & fish see through their skin.

Maura Stanton (1946–) *Snow on Snow,* 1974

Born in Evanston, Illinois, Maura Stanton studied at the University of Minnesota and the University of Iowa. She has written six books of poetry, including *Immortal Sofa* (2008), as well as a novel and books of short stories. For many years she taught at Indiana University, Bloomington, before retiring. Stanton has received two National Endowment for the Arts fellowships, the Richard Sullivan Prize for Short Fiction, and the Nelson Algren Award.

Dreaming of Shells

I'm never alone now.
You rise through the silver air
of upstate New York through a dream
where each raindrop turns to a minnow.
Here is the signature of your life:
a cap pulled down over your eyes
while you speak pidgin Russian
familiarly in a blue room with women
who admire the insides of shells.

I admired the conch
for all its intricate pathways
north to the white sea I imagined
from the Midwest, on front porches
where the first kiss shocked.
The mouth is a shell.
Enter at your own risk
because I've exorcised my gentleness.
My tongue is glass in this stanza.

You find glass by the sea, too,
washed smooth as shells
who believe it's a dangerous crustacean.
I'm not afraid of dark

only of what moves within it, up
steep walls into my heart.
I'll admit it, I'm my own metaphor:
You are the grain of sand
each night I translate into pearl.

A Few Picnics in Illinois

Sometimes I hear haunted mouths
tearing at leaves or thistles
in the woods. At Starved Rock
the Indians entered their bodies
like caves, delving for rain
in the green spaces between bones.
I saw bones, later, at Dixon Mounds
where families like mine
gaped at skeletons
excavated scientifically from farmland.
At Jubilee Park, a soft fungus
licked pews in the stone church.
I couldn't grasp "a hundred years old"
& ran from a face in the wavy
glass that was me, distorted—
Once I tossed a Lincoln penny
over the tourist guardrail at a bed
in Lincoln's house, wondering
if he slept like me, legs curled
against the danger of wolves.
Oh yes I see Lincoln's ghost
down on his hands & knees
after that coin. Touching the head
like braille, he shrieks—
A Chicago woman drowned
at Starved Rock one summer:

For two weeks she made history,
the spot on the bank marked X
for children like me who imagined
her white neckbone in the weeds.
As her eye glazed, she saw
something new in the water, her body
floating away from her . . .

Going Back

The only whistle now is something odd
stuck in your brain: you haven't lived so long
you don't need ghosts. That ex-con who robbed
the mail from Cortland isn't dead, they say:
for eighty years he's combed the Erie-Lackawanna yard
for gold or rings his women never wore.
Today the rusted tracks go straight to Homer,
three miles down. No bridge blew up. No flood
wiped out the valley. The chalk red station
glowers in the sun but no train rumbles:
you kick at bits of stained-glass transom,
wondering where he sleeps. The boxcars
remind you this is home, the corset factory
making steel ball bearings, the St. Charles Hotel
crammed with old men who watch the tracks:
who won't believe in ghosts except themselves.

Maybe he sleeps in the stationmaster's
cabin. The boards peel white.
You wonder how he stands this light, grubbing for gold
that gets scarcer, that never was there.
The thing he died for burns alive.
You want it. You want a crime bigger than any
life you might waste, bigger than any hometown.
Across the tracks the bums curl up in oil drums;

no freights to jump, you wonder where they came from,
how they go. Your skull's intact, the skin
unbroken over lute-shaped bones.
You wonder if you're turning ghost yourself,
haunting your past like snow on snow.

Carolyn Forché (1950–) *Gathering the Tribes,* 1975

Forché was born Carolyn Sidlosky in Detroit, Michigan. She studied at Michigan State University and Bowling Green University. In addition to her four books of poetry, she is the editor of the highly influential anthology *Against Forgetting: Twentieth-Century Poetry of Witness* (1992). A translator and human rights activist, Forché has been awarded the Los Angeles Times Poetry Prize, the Academy of American Poets Fellowship, and the Windham-Campbell Prize, among others.

From Memory

The boar hog shovels his voice into mudslop
where corn rolls, stripped.
Come fall he will be cut: his hams,
pork links rocking in smoke.
Grandma sharpens her knife on Arkansas.
Sam bends, spits chew in the bucket,
the breeze quits.
Spiders tie nets to fruit jars,
it is boring with them in Blue Hills
when gum trees blossom.
Their thoughts are like dust in a salt box.
Boring pig blood perks below ground.

Their palsied hands like horse tails swishing flies.

Las Truchas

Adobe walls crack, rot in Las Truchas.
Sometimes a child in a doorway
or dog stretched on the road.
Always a quiet place.
Wooden wheelbarrows rest up against
boarded windows.

Not yet Semana Santa
when people of Truchas and Mora
will fill them with human bones
and walk with blood-stained eyes
in the mountains where Pecos water
flows among cork-barked fir
and foxtail grows dwarfed, gnarled.

Strangers who drive the high road
to Taos pass through Truchas.
They buy Cordova's rugs and weavings,
hear the wooden flute of the hermit.
Their minds drift to sleep in thin sky.
They hear stories about Penitentes,
that they crucify each other, whip themselves
at night screaming names of God.
Yet they return to Truchas to build
brick homes like wagons circling.
Ptarmigans fly in pines singing nothing.

Every year the village is more quiet.
The creak of wheels, whispers.
No, it is nothing.
But the village seems empty
while the smoke still winds
from sun-baked homes and the people
bless the snow.

Year at Mudstraw

Listen to the pine splits
crack in the stove.
Clouds down our roof like
burnt pine, milk.
The smell of come in the shack.

A breeze on the wall
from boiling tomatoes.
A baby snorts air
while it sucks me.

It was time to put apricots
out in the sun,
cover them with cheesecloth.

Nothing but the whine of bad mud
between the cabin logs.
I hum Cold Blew The Bliss
to the child, touch fattened dough.
I wait for the sound of his truck
hoeing a splutter of thawed ditch.

And when he comes he points his rifle
at the floor, lets the dog
smell his pants.

Soup's about done, my breasts
dropping from pot steam.
He slides a day's beard down my neck.
I open my clothes to his hands.

One buck in the woods, but too quick.
My nipples stiffen, his touch.
I want to swallow down his come,
something in his heart
freezes in a dead run.

Olga Broumas (1949–) *Beginning with O*, 1976

Born in Ermoupoli, Greece, Olga Broumas moved permanently to the United States in 1967. She was educated at the University of Pennsylvania and the University of Oregon. She has written five books of poetry, including *Rave: Poems, 1975–1999* (1999), as well as collaborative works with both Jane Miller and T. Begley. Broumas is also a noted translator of the Greek poet Odysseus Elytis. The recipient of the Lambda Poetry Award as well as fellowships from the National Endowment for the Arts and the Guggenheim Foundation, Broumas is Professor Emerita of the Practice of English at Brandeis University.

Leda and Her Swan

You have red toenails, chestnut
hair on your calves, oh let
me love you, the fathers
are lingering in the background
nodding assent.

I dream of you
shedding calico from
slow-motion breasts, I dream
of you leaving with
skinny women, I dream you know.

The fathers are nodding like
overdosed lechers, the fathers approve
with authority: Persian emperors, ordering
that the sun shall rise
every dawn, set
each dusk.   I dream.

White bathroom surfaces
rounded basins you
stand among

loosening
hair, arms, my senses.

The fathers are Dresden figurines
vestigial, anecdotal
small sculptures shaped
by the hands of nuns.   Yours

crimson tipped, take no part in that
crude abnegation.   Scarlet
liturgies shake our room, amaryllis blooms
in your upper thighs, water lily
on mine, fervent delta

the bed afloat, sheer
linen billowing
on the wind: Nile, Amazon, Mississippi.

Triple Muse

I

Three of us sat
in the early summer, our instruments
cared for, our bodies dark

and one stirred the stones on
the earthen platter, till the salt
veins aligned, and she read the cast:

Whatever is past
and has come to an end
cannot be brought back by sorrow

II

False things
we've made seem true, by charm, by music.   Faked
any trick when it pleased us

and laughed, faked
too when it didn't.   The audience couldn't tell, invoking
us absently, stroking their fragile beards, waiting

for inspiration
served up like dinner, or sex.   Past.   Here
each of us knows, herself, the mineral-bright pith.

III
It's been said, we are of one mind.
It's been said, she is happy whom
we, of the muses, love.

Spiral Mountain: the cabin
full of our tools: guitar, tapedeck, video
every night

stars we can cast the dice by.   We are
of one mind, tuning
our instruments to ourselves, by our triple light.

Snow White

> *I could never want her (my mother)*
> *until I myself had been wanted.*
> *By a woman.*

>   Sue Silvermarie

Three women
on a marriage bed, two
mothers and two daughters.
All through the war we slept
like this, grand-
mother, mother, daughter.   Each night
between you, you pushed and pulled
me, willing
from warmth to warmth.

Later we fought so
bitterly through the peace
that father blanched in his uniform,
battlelined forehead milky
beneath the khaki brim.

We fought like mad-
women till the house-
hold shuddered, crockery fell, the bed-
clothes heaved in the only passion
they were, those maddening
peacetime years,
to know.

     . . .

    A woman
    who loves a woman
    who loves a woman
    who loves a man.
                 If the circle
  be unbroken . . .
                 Three years
into my marriage I woke with this
from an unspeakable dream
about you, fingers
electric, magnetized, repelling
my husband's flesh.   Blond, clean,
miraculous, this alien
instrument I had learned to hone,
to prize, to pride myself on, instrument
for a music I couldn't dance,
cry or lose
anything to.
          A curious
music, an un-
catalogued rhyme, mother / daughter, we lay

the both of us awake
that night you straddled
two continents and the wet
opulent ocean to visit us, bringing
your gifts.
               Like two halves
of a two-colored apple—red
with discovery, green with fear—we lay
hugging the wall between us, whitewash
leaving its telltale tracks.
                   Already
some part of me had begun
the tally, dividing
the married spoils, claiming
your every gift.

. . .

Don't curse me, Mother, I couldn't bear
the bath
of your bitter spittle.
                 No salve
no ointment in a doctor's tube, no brew
in a witch's kettle, no lover's mouth, no friend
or god could heal me
if your heart
turned in anathema, grew stone
against me.
             Defenseless
and naked as the day
I slid from you
twin voices keening and the cord
pulsing our common protest, I'm coming back
back to you
woman, flesh
of your woman's flesh, your fairest, most
faithful mirror,

                    my love
transversing me like a filament
wired to the noonday sun.

Receive
me, Mother.

. . .

. . .

Bin Ramke (1947–) *The Difference Between Night and Day,* 1977

Born in Port Neches, Texas, Lloyd Binford Ramke studied at Louisiana State University, the University of New Orleans, and Ohio University. He has written eleven books of poetry, including *Theory of Mind: New and Selected Poems* (2009). Ramke teaches at the University of Denver, where he edits the *Denver Quarterly*.

The Channel Swimmer

Blackberry tangled into traps, wild rose,
a mad dream of kudzu, and passionflower's
incessant vine all surround his old age
like last living relatives.

Let us pretend that we are old
and memorize our lives. I saw
my father watch his father
stand to say he was going home;
he stood in the house he had made
fifty years before; he stood
and remembered his father's house
whose ceilings and tall walls burned
in 1922. At first we tried to tell him
who and where he was, then let him go
with sad eyes and a dog:

he stood for an hour on the green hill
(we watched from the window):
for an hour he stood
while the dog slept.
When he turned we saw his face
and had he spoken he would have said:
The world is over. You may be children

but I do not know you. I
had a father. Tomorrow
I will try again. I had brothers
whom I taught to swim. You
will learn nothing from me.

Martyrdom: A Love Poem

Each of the dozen Saints is bound
to his own stake, so like a prize
tomato. We know each death
will bear a flame red fruit.

When necessity lugs us into another year
do not be misled by calendars, a new year
begins with each tick, each time you
remember time is passing. And what a pet
you've made with a numbered dial
around time's neck, a leash
of pendulum to walk it
once around the block before you sleep.
At night time gathers itself,
a pack of neighborhood dogs
to knock over your garbage cans
to gnaw your discarded secrets
scattered for the neighbors to see if they,
bothered by the noise, will look
at your small life withering
in the dew of the backyard grass.

You and I owe nothing to sanctity,
find there no help at all, nothing
so dangerous makes us what martyrs are—
we have visions of each other
in our sleep, we know the secrets,
we have touched each other's

intimate places. We love because
it grows late and the tomatoes
are ripening. A morning glory
climbs one stake, mingles with the crude
green-and-pink-striped fruit: tomorrow
we will look at what we've done.

Certainly I would die for you:
that is the easy part, like falling
from grace or off a log.

The Green Horse

Who could be smaller than this child
on the four-horse carousel which plays
the Washington Post March
in front of the discount store?
He cares. His father
counts the time lost more than the quarter.

The child refuses distraction.
He holds tightly and watches
the neck of the yellow horse
while riding the red
in a kind of kept time.

We remember wanting to ride
in front of the supermarkets,
we all look at the child
for an embarrassed moment before
pushing the revolving door. We look
to see if he is there when we come out again.

He cannot be there. No father
will put more than two quarters in,
too much pain. I have never seen

more than two children at one time
on a four-horse carousel. I have never seen

the money removed.
What would it be like to see someone
across the room at a party,
to call out "We met once
twenty years ago,
in front of K-Mart, I was on
the blue horse, you were on the green." To call out.

Leslie Ullman (1947–) *Natural Histories,* 1978

Leslie Ullman was born in Chicago, Illinois, and studied at Skidmore College and the Iowa Writers' Workshop. She has written five books of poetry, including *Slow Work Through Sand* (1997), which won the Iowa Poetry Prize. The recipient of two fellowships from the National Endowment for the Arts, Ullman established and directed the bilingual MFA in creative writing at the University of Texas at El Paso. She now teaches in the MFA program in creative writing at the Vermont College of Fine Arts. Ullman lives in northern New Mexico.

Nostalgia

The old man who told us all he knew
has not been seen.
The shops offer thin sweaters.
The entire population
has forgotten how the bodies of its women
emerge at night before sleep.
They once strolled across the quay
or a sunlit room
and decided to stay.

• • •

Inland the lights go out
and a child's parents
call to one another
across an extra room.
Across the silence
of the house at certain hours.
The children
move into our bodies.

• • •

I heard you listening
to the murmur of her absence,
to the murmur of fame,

to the murmur of women turning in their sleep
in rooms where they'd wake alone,
to the murmur of leaves outside the house
you should have lived in.
• • •
When it rained I followed the streets
until the women leaned from windows.
The children went inside.
The men who had been away all day
went inside, and old stories
rose in me like prophecies.
• • •
At night we unpacked everything.
The marks on our skin never changed.
The warm weather returned,
the cathedral
was aired for the strangers
who would arrive in light clothing,
who would cross themselves
and peel oranges outside the gates.

His Early and Late Paintings

His first painting spoke:
the woman had forgotten many lovers

but none of the rooms in which she awoke.
He discarded the armoire and the child's hoop.

He was taken by her hands
and the clay fragments by the bed

and the way the vase left her hands.

His later paintings had no titles:
1. Did his grandchildren tell him what they dreamed?

2. Was there a dispute between peddlers outside his window?

3. Was he thinking of his death?

4. Was the woman later recognized?
At least one observer was startled

to find himself startled.

5. The woman who loved grapes.

6. The woman who spilled wine
abruptly as she left the table.

Memo

Touch was all.
Many nights of touch
and only yourself to trust.
Your hands led you
through the caverns of other hands.
You brought nothing from the journeys,
lost nothing each time the mind
took back its roots,
learned nothing
when people withdrew with pieces
of what you thought was heart.
The hands set out plates, opened cans.
Your age arrived, one corner
at a time. The familiar hungers turned
their backs. Only the hands
kept up with you,
folding the loose garments,
fingering the sheets
on the thin bed, showing more and more
of their frame, their muscle.

William Virgil Davis (1940–) *One Way to Reconstruct the Scene,* 1979

William Virgil Davis was born in Canton, Ohio, and educated at the Pittsburgh Theological Seminary and Ohio University. He has written four books of poetry, including *Dismantlements of Silence: Poems Selected and New* (2015), and several critical studies. Before retiring, Davis taught at Baylor University for many years. Among his honors are the New Criterion Poetry Prize and the Helen C. Smith Memorial Award for Poetry.

Winter Light

All night through the dark the dark
is falling. Dead limbs fill with water,
freeze in the hard light of winter.

Out walking this early morning, I stop,
stoop, stare at my own reflection,
bent like a branch is bent by water.

One Way to Reconstruct the Scene

The moon, through light snow, between the trees,
distorted by the broken glass, looked blue,
almost the color of the girl's blue dress,
or the man's eyes. The car came to rest
against the large maple forty yards from the road,
bisecting the angle of the slow curve beyond the bridge.

The girl was thrown free. She lay as if asleep
against the tree, her hands in her lap.
Perhaps she was dreaming. The man was still
behind the wheel, his hand to his head, a cup
of blood spilled over his yellow shirt. The brake
pedal was pushed all the way through the floorboard.

It was winter. A light snow fell past her window.
She had been waiting for hours. When he came
she had fallen asleep. She dreamed she was dreaming.
He whispered and she awakened. She smiled.
They sat watching snow fall through the trees,
the moon move slowly across the sky. They spoke.

He knew the road by heart. His father had helped
to build the bridge. They were speaking softly together.
The faint blue light reflected from the snow
as it fell slowly through the trees made the blue
of her dress bluer. They did not speak of the night,
no doubt they hardly noticed. There was nothing to know.

It happened without warning. There, suddenly,
outlined in the dark like an animal only visible
when it turns to let you see its eyes, a shape
of something insubstantial cut off his view
as he started to turn, beyond the bridge, just
into the long slow curve. He tried to blink it back.

The girl in the blue dress leaned against the tree.
She seemed to be sleeping. The man remained in the car,
upright, his blue eyes open. Light snow fell slowly
through the barren limbs of the tree above the car.
The moon moved across the sky. It cast a light blue
reflection on the scene, the snow, the broken glass.

In the Pit

In the pit
in the deep dark of the earth
where there is no light
where even the wind whispers
and only the oldest stones
dare to speak
blind worms

move slowly over the bones
and create
with their intricate embroidery
a moving tapestry
the model of a mind
articulately arranged

John Bensko (1949–) *Green Soldiers,* 1980

Born in Birmingham, Alabama, John Bensko studied at Saint Louis University, the University of Alabama, Auburn University, and Florida State University. He has published four volumes of poetry, including *Visitations* (2014), and a collection of short stories, *Sea Dogs* (2004). The recipient of a Fulbright professorship, Bensko teaches at the University of Memphis.

The Midnight Sun

Someone has taken him in his rocking chair
to the mountains where a cold lake
opens the snow like a blue, startled mouth.
He has forgotten her name.
So he invents one: Inga, the woman
who keeps him company for years.
This evening from the dining room
he watches the blackbirds peck the strawberries
she throws for them; the fourth day
the sun has refused to set by midnight.
The red berries sink in the snow.

Inga, what is it? The way she goes on
beyond the window, talking to the birds in sounds
that mean as little as anything. *Why are you*
throwing strawberries for blackbirds?
Who am I? An old doctor
listening to the lies of women and birds.
Inga, he remembers. Inga was his wife.
The sun is the lie she shares with him
to keep quiet about dying. The sun
in the lake is like a candle guttering
in blue wax. He waits, lost in the difference.

Rejects from the Greenhouse

The boy is bug-eyed: the duck
stands two storys tall.
How many tons of flowers?
He imagines the bodies of workers
covered with petals,
each color of the rainbow.
Who decides? Who puts them on?
A committee, the old hands . . .
Where do they get the flowers?

Heads bruised, lean stalks cut short,
they wait in cartons, lacking fragrance.

Between the beds of flowers, humming
with bees, alive with birds and crickets,
an old man with a cart
walks down the steaming aisle
of chrysanthemums. Water drips
from the top of the greenhouse,
rain from the clouds that form.

The mystery of it. He would find you
hidden in the back corner
where no one is supposed to go.
He would kill you with his spade.

How many children lie
in the long boxes sprouting?

If you are good, if you grow up
a beauty queen or famous at sports
you can join a float, smell like flowers,
wave to millions.
The wind picks up the skirts of the best.
Heroes are being made, proud veterans
are waving, thinking: when I was a kid

it seemed so large. And it is.
It is the parade in which the baton twirler steps off
a white blaze into the Western sky.

And when it is over
the boy riding the duck's back
holds on for life.
The huge carcasses, the frames
of wire and wood, are pulled apart
for charity. All those petals
are picked up and packaged by girls.

This is not the end, the boy says,
patting the duck's wing,
riding the wood frame that shakes
and threatens to fall. He whoops and spurs.
He swings into a wide arc, scattering flowers.

The Fox

Fox . . . my father said.
Where does it live, how big
is it, what does it eat besides chickens?

Tonight, one crawls
through the crack in my door.
It slides across the pillow.

I repeat God
desperately into the red fur.
Nothing has changed . . .

The fur grows beautiful.
I close my eyes
and the fox leaps inside.

David Wojahn (1953–) *Icehouse Lights,* 1981

Born in Saint Paul, Minnesota, David Wojahn was educated at the University of Minnesota and the University of Arizona. He has written eight books of poetry, including *World Tree* (2011), which won the Lenore Marshall Poetry Prize. Other honors include the O. B. Hardison Award from the Folger Shakespeare Library, the Amy Lowell Traveling Poetry Scholarship, and a Guggenheim Fellowship. Wojahn teaches at Virginia Commonwealth University.

Distance

Tonight the workmen
with red bandanas are building
a house across the street.
Light spills from the holes
they've left for windows.
They've inched across the roofbeams,
buckets of shingles in their arms.
This last man leans after
everyone's gone, his head
on a door that's propped on a tree.
I hear him singing to himself.

We both can't sleep—
his singing, and his hand
that drums a hammer again
and again into the ground.
The cats on the roof disturb him;
he stares and hammers,
hears me typing, or finds me
through the window, bent
to my lamp. I've come to admire

the distance between us,
the noises we make to ourselves

in the night, tired
as the lovers in a Japanese print
who've turned and wiped their genitals
with the blue silk scarves
they had stuffed in their mouths
while coupling.

Cold Glow: Icehouses

Because the light this morning is recondite
like figures behind curtains from a long way off,
because the morning is cold and this room is heatless,
I've gone without sleep, I brood.
The protocol of memory: the faucet dripping
into a sponge, then thinking of the way
I saw White Bear Lake freeze over
twenty years ago in Minnesota, the carp oblivious below.

I thought last night of Solomon Petrov,
a Ukrainian rabbi in my college science books
afflicted with total recall, a pathological memory
that made perspective impossible.
Once for doctors he *remembered*, running for a train
in Petersburg in winter. They recorded
his quickened pulse, body temperature plunging.
The death by fever of his first wife Tania
was not remembered, but continually relived.

And memory is not accomplishment.
Last night again you described for me
our child pulled dead from your womb. In sleep you talked
to yourself and the child, who passed unnamed
wholly into memory. Now you wanted peace,
some distance. And every memory, said Solomon Petrov,
must proceed unchanged in the mind, going on
like smoke to designate itself again

like a second floor window where I stood as a boy
to watch the fishermen park their cars
on the lake, icehouse lights in the evening below.

Or our child whose name is only ash,
is only a thought too hurtful to free.
Mornings like these, he floats at the window, waiting
and mouthing his name, there through a tangent of ice,
his face and hands ashimmer.

Another Coast

The woman singing in the house
next door draws her bath,
a country-western song—
someone's heart is broken in El Paso—
then she pulls the shades.
We've never spoken, but nights
I watch her set the table for her lover
who visits weekends and outside filets
the bluefish he's just caught.
Later, they'll tip glasses on
the balcony. Animated talk,
then such composure on their faces.

Pointless now to say
how things should have been better with us.
The way I miss you makes the days
portentous, trees not simply barren,
and I walk the tapered
streets of this seaside town,
inns all shuttered, faltering shingles.

Yesterday, a bottle-nosed dolphin
beached herself beyond the pier
and lived for hours. The cafe waiters
checkered her with tablecloths

they'd dipped in seawater
to keep her damp and breathing.
A crowd had gathered
and the next-door couple with their shiny Nikon
argued loudly about who should take the picture.

Years ago, another coast,
we fought all evening in the small apartment,
finally sleeping in separate corners.
Several times we woke, not thinking
there was more to say and later stood
a long time at the window
to watch the taverns' blurry neons—
mugs and dancing glasses—
going out in sequence before the dark,
where a man and woman stood
to batter each other haplessly,
breaking bottles on the street
but not upon themselves.
Maybe some bruises, a little blood.
Finished, they embraced
and parted, the woman shouting *call me*,

call me when you get up.

Cathy Song (1955–) *Picture Bride,* 1982

Cathy Song was born in Honolulu, Hawaii, and studied at Wellesley College and Boston University. She is the author of five collections of poetry, most recently *Cloud Moving Hands* (2007). Song is the recipient of the Shelley Memorial Award from the Poetry Society of America, a fellowship from the National Endowment for the Arts, and the Hawaii Award for Literature; she lives and teaches in Honolulu.

The Youngest Daughter

The sky has been dark
for many years.
My skin has become as damp
and pale as rice paper
and feels the way
mother's used to before the drying sun
parched it out there in the fields.

     Lately, when I touch my eyelids,
my hands react as if
I had just touched something
hot enough to burn.
My skin, aspirin colored,
tingles with migraine. Mother
has been massaging the left side of my face
especially in the evenings
when the pain flares up.

This morning
her breathing was graveled,
her voice gruff with affection
when I wheeled her into the bath.
She was in a good humor,
making jokes about her great breasts,

floating in the milky water
like two walruses,
flaccid and whiskered around the nipples.
I scrubbed them with a sour taste
in my mouth, thinking:
six children and an old man
have sucked from these brown nipples.

I was almost tender
when I came to the blue bruises
that freckle her body,
places where she has been injecting insulin
for thirty years. I soaped her slowly,
she sighed deeply, her eyes closed.
It seems it has always
been like this: the two of us
in this sunless room,
the splashing of the bathwater.

In the afternoons
when she has rested,
she prepares our ritual of tea and rice,
garnished with a shred of gingered fish,
a slice of pickled turnip,
a token for my white body.
We eat in the familiar silence.
She knows I am not to be trusted,
even now planning my escape.
As I toast to her health
with the tea she has poured,
a thousand cranes curtain the window,
fly up in a sudden breeze.

Blue Lantern

The blue lantern light
was like a full moon
swelling above the hush
of the mock orange shrubs
that separated our houses.

It was light
from your grandfather's room.

I remember the music
at night.
I dreamed the music
came in squares,
like birthday chocolate,
through the window
on a blue plate.

From his shakuhachi,
shavings of notes,
floated, and fell;
melted where the stillness
inserted itself back into night.
It was quiet then until dawn,
broken once by a single wailing:
the sound of an animal
whose hind leg is caught in a trap.

It was your grandfather
mourning his dead wife.
He played for her each night;
her absence,
the shape of his grief
funneled through the bamboo flute.
A ritual of remembrance,

keeping her memory alive
with his old breath.
He played unknowingly
to the child next door
who lay stricken by the music
transposed to her body,
waiting for the cry
that always surprised her;
like a glimpse of shadow
darting through the room
before she would drift off into sleep.

I knew you were in the room
just beyond the music.

This was something we shared.
Listening, my eyes closed
as though I were under water
in the blueness of my room;
I felt buoyant and protected.

I imagined you, his grandson,
listening and lying
in your small bed;
your head making a slight
dent in the pillow.

It was as though the weight
of his grief washed over
the two of us
each night like a tide,
leaving our bodies beached
but unbruised,
white and firm like shells.

The Seamstress

1

I work best in a difficult light,
proud of these intelligent hands
like blind fingertips pressing upon
the fine, irresistible seams.

This is my world; my work:
to occupy a lean-to of a room
with a tin roof that slants
so on one side, an entire
wall without windows.

My spine bent over the Singer
has over the years conformed
into the silhouette of a coat hanger.
If I move about, it is with the slow
descent of the spider,
attached to an invisible thread,
I let myself down off the chair.

It is my hands that take
their miraculous flight, flying
from the cloth they guide toward
the continuous drone of the needle.
Hands moist and white like lilies.
The white gloved hands of the magician.

I turn bolts of cloth into wedding dresses
like chiffon cakes in the summer.
The frayed mothers arrive with their daughters.
I pin them in the afternoon fittings,
drape the veil about their soft faces
as if it were mosquito netting.

2

Moving among the orchids this morning,
I see the straw hat and slippered feet
of my ninety-two-year-old father.
I am the second of his four unmarried daughters.

He leaves a trail of water
behind him, dragging the hose
through the grass, around the hedges.
The heavy-whiskered jackfruit are ripening.
He will pick them with a muslin sack
wired to the end of a fishing pole.

His attachment to the world
is in the daily application of a skill.
It is the cultivating of orchids,
the most highly evolved species of flowers.
For me, it is the deft turning
of a sleeve, a pleat, or a collar.

He carries a spray of the smallest
variety past the screen door, each orchid
delicately and elaborately unfurled
like the ornate headpieces
my mother would make from threads
of black silk when as a girl
she was a dollmaker's apprentice in Japan.

With her we lived in a world of miniatures.
The world got swallowed up
into the smallest square of concentration.
My sisters and I became nearsighted,
squinting in the hot, still room,
relying on our agile fingers
to duplicate with scraps of silk
a shrunken world. Ornamented dolls
no more than twelve inches high

holding musical instruments.
Looking up to meet the room
swirling as if in a cloud of insects,
there were times when we fell
to the floor from exhaustion
and the sudden readjustment of vision;
our legs still tucked, as we were taught, beneath us.

3

The dolls are encased in glass boxes
displayed like shrines around the room.
The last one was made twenty years ago
just before my mother died.
Haruko, my third sister, keeps them dusted,
plucking at the occasional termites
that squeeze through the glass corners
to gorge their amber bodies on the brocaded silk.

My eyes sting today again
as though one of my sisters
nearby were peeling onions.
We each keep to our discreet part of the house,
crossing polite paths to murmur over meals.

It seems I have always lived
in this irregular room, rarely needing
to see beyond the straight seams that fit neatly,
the snaps that fasten securely in my mind.
The world for me is the piece of cloth
I have at the moment beneath my hands.
I am not surprised
by how little the world changes.
My father carrying the green hose
across the grass, a ribbon of water
trickling down his shoulder,

staining the left pocket
of his gray, loose-fitting shirt.
The wedding dresses each white, dusty summer.
Someone very quiet once lived here.

Richard Kenney (1948–) *The Evolution of the Flightless Bird,* 1983

Born in Glen Falls, New York, Richard Kenney graduated from Dartmouth College. He has written four books of poems, most recently *One-Strand River: Poems, 1994–2007* (2008). Kenney's honors include the Lannan Award, the Rome Prize in Literature from the American Academy of Arts and Letters, and a MacArthur Fellowship. He teaches at the University of Washington.

La Brea

Early

It is very early now, no light yet, nor
sensation, apart from simple motions of waking:
discomfort in the chill air, the stiff walk
quick across cold floorboards, razor,
brushed lather and warm tap water off
my cheeks—the feel of bare wool on wrists
and throat—the hiss of the stove, and white coffee.
Alone in this house, I wonder if *tabula rasa*
ever existed at all. Lake Champlain looks flat,
black by starlight; even the sheaved winds
are flat as feathers on a sleeping raven's wing—
Later, forecast rains will toss down Smuggler's Notch
in silver skirtveils, hiss across the flatiron
lake like drops on a woodstove, into the night—

Tranquility

and hideous broom-flaps here, unfolding condors
knuckled to the vague bed rail, and hung door-
jamb anthropoid with clothes— In this appalling
light even physical objects fail, conform to older
recollection, night's La Brea, the glossy oil-pools. . . .
By breakfast all grotesques have quit their roaring,

pawing at the sky for light and release, followed
their immense tracks down sinkholes of their own
muddling until the only evidence
of dreams is gone, erratic haloes ravens
figured, just askim the water, rings, rings,
and love, your slender unstockinged feet scarcely
and always rough the nap of a newswept carpet
still, and this is not tranquility, not yet—

The Evolution of the Flightless Bird

The First Poem in Twelve Months
awkward as evolution of flight itself taxis
in the bushveldt, paddles twitching, recalling carrion
from a thousand feet, and oh, the eyes, cobalt
ice and flashing in a field of green— Careening
now, lips back, legs drive, *flap, flap,* bald
flippers slap his sides—to lift, to climb uncobbled
air, to leave his tracks. . . . But green earth still attracts
him, heavy, still, except his eyes, which feather hope
as a green point describes an arc across
a blank oscilloscope: *escape*, escape
velocity: this is the language of desire
itself, the high skywritten screech of genus *Icarus*,
whose frayed sleeves snap and leap like parting cables,
quills across his foolscap, barbed lines thick with *cire*

Perdue
and downy wool. . . . Not lost, if lost among the limbs
and stems still trembling from his passage, shallow orbit
like a feathered cannonball, a swept-winged boar-
let-off-a-bowstring six and eight feet at a bound—
Catch sight of him—again, and gone—a glimpse. . . .
We'll trace him, follow fossil footprints past the turnstile
where the Royal Garden's glass house is. Arboreal

mosses torn and swaying, stripped lianas ribboned
out behind him, crushed shoots, ferns and forest orchids
crushed, spore cases flat— note newly pollinated
flowers in a cloud of dust, where broken plants
seep milky sap, a sweet wind stirs the stale
cloud-chamber here, and ground speed is a perfect arc
in two dimensions, following the planet's

Fall Line
down— Now follow down into the dense
frond-choked chambers where the story finds its source:
this is the Orphic epic of the Age: imagine
names, time out of mind, *Phororhacos,*
or *Diatryma.* . . . Lacewings thin as oxygen
catch light where dragonflies a foot across
whirr overhead at dusk; and flying foxes,
huge fruit-eating bats, still swoop the garden's
glass walls, echoing; and see, too, pterosaurs
whose mucid wings will fold us in like eyelids,
like dream. . . . We'll cup bird calls as frail as matchlight
in our palms, and roll out fruit, and mix exotic
nectars with the dew at dawn, to try
to draw them back, attract them, *Diatryma*

Phororhacos
Horse-high carnivores bestride our dreams, their crescent
beaks curved down like the horned moon—Vanished, past
masters of the Miocene savannahs, eyes
as blue as heaven still, as still as resins
where all wings are trapped in mind. . . . Where great birds,
unbridled, saurian, renowned for their rapacity
in middle earth once raced the flat limestone horizons
underfoot, when air speed slipped on ground speed, shrieking
like asbestos burned away to nothing, to air—then burst
all bounds, bones elongate, light, antique
and delicate and wheeling, wheeling in the windy city

of the birds again. . . . Observe, though, thin shellacs
of ice begin to form, to glaze their wings—they rise,
slip sideways, slide like flat cards toward the shell-like

Earth

blue robin's egg a thousand feet below— The first
poem in twelve months faint and losing ground grinds
its passage through the stacked-stone glass-house strata
lit with history and hell's and heaven's flint-
to-tinder, tracing out the pyrotechnic line
to earth again. This is the story of the fierce
heart netted by the paralytic hand, in time,
in mind, a row of bamboo cages burst behind. . . .
Just so, these cubicles. Inside, a lint
like eiderdown, a pinfeather or two, birdlime,
the air astir—and loose bars hollow as a syrinx
whistling with it still, where the snake-necked ratite
genie of the thing's escaped, as all *errata*
do, in cursive gyres, high rings, high rings—

Colloquy at Sawmill

Diesel shut down, whining; last dust skirling
off the last log; carriage stopped; bright kerf
at rest. *Quote: One night Capt. Jos. Spaulding killed
a wolf with a cant hook, endquote, period. Go ask
her at the Town Clerk's office; she'll let you read
for yourself; it's in the book*— No doubt, and the Baskervilles'
a hound beside him! *Wolf?*—*a hundred pounds at ten or
twelve feet off let's say, an earth-to-throat
trajectory at thirty feet per second*— Parried
*with a cant hook? Gaffed him? Golfed him? Damn dinner
fork would serve as well. You wouldn't stand the whisker
of a chance, I don't care what they wrote.* . . .
This sawmill snarls all night, long carriage like an ore-
cart trembling on its rails, two silver lines receding

in a dark mind's shaft, *cry wolf!*—full moon a bright blade
whirling. . . . Who can say what feral spirit crossed
his, coursing through this yarn spun off his life line late
one night; or what man, working the seams of some old curse
swung back his peavey slick as diesel oil— And skull
crushed, torn free from the dark and snapping like a muskellunge
let's say, its story fixed for good, how was it?—red gills
beating, jaws wide, chest all pearly with saliva
silver in the moon, the thick dark coat a sky
of silver points and long gash like a wound plunged
through to dawn. . . . *Don't make me laugh, a live wolf—I've*
heard wolves are in Vermont again— That's bull shit— Coyote
in the sheep fence though, that's new, weird yodelings
all night—I've heard—I shot the skinny bastard. Goat

scot free but still I've lost six lambs— That's more
like History, a straight story here, though records
stray. What kind of men and women settled
here, what hardships shaped them so, what silted
their particular capacities among these hills? *Three sawmills*
worked here once. When Joseph Spaulding built
this house, returning home from war, was he *awarded*
fifty acres by the Colonial government for shooting a Tory
spy, just two miles down the road?— I doubt that story,
though I do believe in the wolf, I think. According
to the *Town History* (1850) *we are inferior to our*
grandfathers and mothers physically, intellectually, and morally . . .
X was a hero; Y drank whiskey; Z was a coward. . . .
Endquote. Timber wolves are returning. I doubt the story.

Pamela Alexander (1948–) *Navigable Waterways,* 1984

Born in Natick, Massachusetts, Pamela Alexander studied at Bates College and the University of Iowa. She is the author of four books of poetry, including *Slow Fire* (2007). Alexander is the recipient of the Iowa Poetry Prize and a fellowship from the Bunting Institute of Radcliffe College, and has taught at the University of Iowa, the Massachusetts Institute of Technology, and Oberlin College.

Tea Story

"that Excellente & by all Physitians approved Chinean drink"

1. Twining, Thomas. Teaman. Devereaux Court, Temple Bar

returns from the forests of Assam
in which he verified the Tea shrub to be
indigenous, abundant, and virtually
inaccessible. At noontime on the upper deck he brews
an ordinary Canton cup; salt tempers its oils, discolors
the spoon. The backs of his hands shine.
The Quaker captain
nods twice a day. Afternoons,
Thomas visits the Thibetan goat, the ten curious sheep
from Santipore; he looks for cracks or seepage in the lacquer
of oil tubs, checks the fleet of crates—cheated
of tea, they carry tortoise shell, jars of green
ginger.
        Sweet evenings,
it is not the mild vegetable infusion of his family's name
to which he turns to soothe the tick of unused muscles
before sleep, the cabin's tilt and tilt
about the hammock's axis; he downs
a glass or two, another few,
and tinkers with the fates of friends, acquaintances
he has not seen these thirteen years.

2. 9 December 1795

Stood out of the estuary, just
afternoon; junks
hoisted baskets of exploding crackers, gongs
talky at our going. The constant stir of water is
a second silence. The men are calm; sleeping
without blankets, they perfect
our vulnerability. I balance, idly, old
accounts—the Fox & Geese, Hampstead: 7 chests pekoe,
        tincture of rubarbe, sugar in loaves. &
        for Sundries Forgott.—and write odd
letters: a faster ship may pass for them.
                          Around Good Hope,
heavy weather, a hundred ducks
drown in the hold. Now
I keep to my cabin, a pint
of bitters. In all this wash it comforts me
to see sharp things, the nice
strokes about the elephant's ear
in the aquatint I have for you. I am uneasy
at whales. Algae thickens: we must be near

belled towers. Squares.
Oh solid and to be praised
stone gates, meadows, your estate.
At night an abundance: yellow, white
windows.

Primer

for Ed

Look at the birds in the tree,
you said. It sounded like a sentence
for children learning to read.
We drove toward the tree.
The starlings lifted as one
and printed, on the white sky,
a second tree beside the first.

The trees I am looking at now
are blue ones on the white china cup
warm in my hands.
The radio is tuned between stations
because the fizz helps me think,
blurs the voices that rise
through the wooden floor.
Sometimes they are children's,
cutting through wood and static
like the cries of herring gulls.
What? Why? Why?
Why do they ask so many questions?
Why do you ask such hard ones?

There were no curtains
in this small room by the sea.
A roll of glazed, white paper,
meant to wrap wedding presents,
instead protects my privacy, tacked across
the four windows. They bleach sunlight
to the color of flour.

The grove of blue trees
surrounds a pool of coffee,
black like roads in cities

and birds in wet spring trees.
It sounds like a story
children learn to read from,
words forming slowly in their minds
next to their images
of tree, road, bird.

Covered, the windows are screens.
On one of them I see us driving
under a sky streaked with birds.
You are careful of my privacy,
and your own; the questions,
infrequent anyway, stop
if you see I feel pushed.
They ask me
to make the globe in my head
a good place to live.

Words can form maps
to make the world clearer.
I care about you.
Birds hidden in the china trees
fly up in a blue stream.
When I go into the day
they color the sky.

The Vanishing Point

1

Perfectly black coffee in a white perfect cup, this
is simpler than flowered towels. The loom of course
makes its own arrangements, adding to line
histories of line, condensing
movement over time
into the short time it takes to see.

The thinking line is design.
Blooms.

Two chinese horses in a carpet.

Two chinese houses amid dim stems.

In the middle of the page is a photograph of a giraffe.
In the gazette, gazelles appear as paragraphs.

We make our rooms by hand: gestures create
the objects around them. The coffee as I mentioned.
Crockery. The stems.
A few vegetables and chairs.
The door is open a crack that is ajar.

He didn't raise hand or voice.

A stone jar smoothes with use. Useful.
An open door is empty.

A man we hadn't seen in years.
His changes made his sameness strange:
he moved us
to another room   out of doors.

A door that is opened isn't one:
a space instead.

A porch has insight like a bay window a glass boat or
bottled water. Inside
the plants consider, we sit with them;
they contain themselves. The broad
shadows of leaves make continents on the floor boards.
An english ivy; a boston fern:
we carry them off the verandah in their pots.
Wide and green, a port.

An open door is not one or two but through.
Openness brought by a stranger we knew.

Out of doors an open room.

2

A pair of donkeys on a red road.
A pair of pairs.
We think the monks are strong like geometry.

How many yellow robes
how many hours.

One in a row.

They sleep parallel like brothers like trees.
They often work in rows
in the hall
    the garden
by the fish
pond, they raise doves in a Roman ruined tower.
To what power does one raise a dove.

Doves are distinguished by pointed tails.
In the dovecote a coterie. a distinguished group.
Doux
doux
doux
the monks have a few for dinner however. A coup.

It is good that what they say disappears like food
or like a beautiful old father.
Shaping pots, weaving cloth: what they make
is plain. Their flowers are in their garden.

Foxglove. The figure of

a dove facing a fox is pointed at both ends.
They have no use for foxes; a brace
of pheasants is preferred.
They raise honey bees as well in the alcove,
the oldest part of the wall.
Their will is very old. They and we
arrange straw for bees in niches some of which are

occupied also by stone saints.
The bees are particular since
the straw creates their cloisters.

Finally we forget what we are carrying and do not
make mistakes.

George Bradley (1953–) *Terms to Be Met,* 1985

George Bradley was born in Roslyn, New York, and studied at Yale University and the University of Virginia. In addition to five volumes of poetry, including *A Few of Her Secrets* (2010), he edited *The Yale Younger Poets Anthology* (1998). Bradley's honors include the Peter I. B. Lavan Award from the Academy of American Poets, the Witter Bynner Prize from the American Academy of Arts and Letters, and a National Endowment for the Arts fellowship.

The Sound of the Sun

It makes one all right, though you hadn't thought of it,
A sound like the sound of the sky on fire, like Armageddon,
Whistling and crackling, the explosions of sunlight booming
As the huge mass of gas rages into the emptiness around it.
It isn't a sound you are often aware of, though the light speeds
To us in seconds, each dawn leaping easily across a chasm
Of space that swallows the sound of that sphere, but
If you listen closely some morning, when the sun swells
Over the horizon and the world is still and still asleep,
You might hear it, a faint noise so far inside your mind
That it must come from somewhere, from light rushing to darkness,
Energy burning towards entropy, towards a peaceful solution,
Burning brilliantly, spontaneously, in the middle of nowhere,
And you, too, must make a sound that is somewhat like it,
Though that, of course, you have no way of hearing at all.

In the Flemish Gallery

That one is wan and transparently out of this world
Does not make him less beautiful, less luminous,
And that the other is terribly still and says nothing
Does not make her reflection any less our own.

In Bruges, on a March day in 1505, each glowing instant,
Even this instant, is a chill breath away from death,
Is clothed in bright array and hides an inmost thought.
That is why the angel seems abstracted as he speaks;
That is why the woman is beside herself, imagining.
The clear bright blue that adorns the dead of winter
Still floats above mountains painted in the distance,
And the river remains frozen beneath delicate clouds.
On a March day in Bruges, spring might come at any hour,
But this angel will watch his words unravel into ages,
And the woman must pause an eternity over her reply.
It is a moment that might be lived forever, lingering
Like second thoughts or a melancholy angel, like us—
Look, the town beyond the bridge is one where we might live,
With its medieval walls and maze of interwoven streets;
See, there we are, among the crowd gathered in the square,
In Bruges, in the bitter winter of 1505.

Terms to Be Met

Of course, one way would be to resign yourself and join up,
The idea being that nobody would give it a second thought,
And that after a while it's any port in this kind of storm.
One way would be to join the Marines, to start taking orders,
To cloister yourself in a monastery and take vows of silence,
Working in God's garden while He tanned your shaved head.
You wouldn't really have to believe it, to believe anything,
That being part of the point, to have it put on a platter,
Fit conduct assigned, fit topics for thought already invented,
Your doubts all anticipated, refuted with consummate casuistry.
You could probably take pretty much the same pleasures, too,
Since the mind willfully construes conclusions out of thin air,
Since so much of inconsequence would simply be taken care of,
And thus no rationale obtains against our calm capitulation,
On some August day perhaps, in a clearing with clouds overhead.

But the rage for one's own thoughts cannot be suppressed,
The animal urge like the instinct for so much territory.
And each of us clutches his own idea through all extremity,
Though the landscape we find ourselves in isn't much support,
The sky having somehow backed off a bit, gone farther away,
Leaving us here, at the margins of the mind, where we must live.

Julie Agoos (1956–) *Above the Land,* 1986

Julie Agoos was born in Boston, Massachusetts, and studied at Harvard University and Johns Hopkins University. She is the author of four collections of poetry, most recently *Echo System* (2015). Agoos has taught at Brooklyn College since 1994, and is the recipient of the Towson State University Prize for Literature and a Robert Frost Residency fellowship.

Franklin

On this day of the week,
hardly anyone rises
up over the slope that leads
from the trees' shadows back south to the highway.
Alone on the wide street the car rocks sideways.
An old woman rocks in a green swing;
her small feet hanging
neatly crossed
swing and disappear and swing
over a low barrow of impatiens.

Next day a single shutter has come sheer
from the second story.
Green water drips from a green gutter,
missing the newsboy, who is
used to the local weather. You notice this,
in passing, from the car;   and, more noteworthy:
the naked I in the IGA;
Boats TolLet (has that one been put here?);
Cold BeerIES;
a new hole—perhaps from a bullet—
muting the Town P pulation.
An older target, always a joke, stays pinned

to the door of the Fish & Game Club:
BACK ONE TUESDAY. GONE FISHING.

Past the storefronts full of yarn and hardware,
past three sagging restaurants, the last
of South Main Street, which drew the borders
of four settlements
into a well-knit town
and paper city.
The Central Street is hidden across the bridge,
laid out by halves, in brick and plateglass, granite,
wood, and wedged into the space carved by two rivers—
its crowded neighborhood
of dams and falls,
the ruined Needle Co. and woolen mills
gone in a glance.
Past prison, Pike's Lumbers, Soeurs de Ste. Croix (set back),
dust from the gutted road cuts blows up
shimmering, bad-tasting, red
on the car seat—not any cure for it but not
any cause for worry.
Nothing stops the heart. The town clock
is funny, rather than sad or annoying.

This old meeting ground is like that.
Oh, late in the year,
when the water in Webster Lake
hardly drifts,
the wet moss reappearing everywhere
recalls with a certain loveliness
some old farmer who gave in,
and for a while the local papers raise a thousand issues
all about Loss, and there's an acute
and lovely quiet.
A barn falls,
and a beech gripping a lightning cable,

and a cake, and a prize nest,
and a man from the Merrimack Valley outpost
along with a telephone pole.
The tale comes round again,
like strike, or flood,
to Mrs. Phillip Call—scalped
by Indians, her family kidnapped
in the years of early purpose.
Someone's male cat returns
only to return small bodies
to a neighbor's doormat.
There is a long argument
over chickens, about coydogs.

But most afternoons,
hunters pull off their red jackets,
their wives pull on jackets, and from
some summer body's lakeside lawn
they might watch somebody's white canoe appear
in the round eye at the flag end
of a tall steel sculpture fixed in the ground before them;
then, sail through the eye
as if it were a hoop
actually suspended half in air,
half in water: first the bow and then the whole boat
emerging into open water towards them,
without any visible movement
or break in the lens.

This sight is a favorite illusion among the townfolk,
who view the town as somehow powerful,
just as a diver from Franklin, plunging into
the town pool, might say
that his displacement as he shoots
down into water
is not much different
from what the water feels.

Arrival

As if we had just woken later than usual,
finding only the dim light of afternoon,
and of the station lights wastefully burning
on the street that could be any other
that leads us to a small bed and breakfast
facing the water, like an old arena
outlined by green benches: a stillness, for a while
staring at the brown edges of lampposts supported
by concrete blocks in the water, catching a scent
of something we remember but cannot name.

I say we will go looking for it later
in accents that have not improved with time,
and sit trying to locate the image that brought us here
—whose past it was we wanted to enter—
when you say: anyhow, it's beautiful enough.
And I look at the boats tethered to their gold
patches of sea, and at the gold embellishment
of names along the sterns and starboard bows,
and realize that half the world is this familiar.
Then in the level water stretching between the boats,
vaguely distorting our arrival, how many
serene depths there would be;   and my desire
to stay here and claim it as a homecoming
by this time has become so elaborate,
though it started from nothing, that I do not answer.

February

In the house, without our mother in it,
spaces fill with meaning, as on those afternoons
spent waiting for the snow to fall: It's cold
for hours; breath is something new; then snow
follows like the least painful part of you.

My brothers plan a snowman for tomorrow,
and later, standing at my bedroom window,
show me, as she might have, how the lamp's a halo
throwing near-daylight on the steps up to the house.
Thinking, perhaps, that she'll forgive us now,
I vow never to forget this love I feel.
We still believe that empty space resolves itself
—like the unrenouncing fullness of the view,
for reasons inarticulate, but true.

Brigit Pegeen Kelly (1951–2016) *To the Place of Trumpets,* 1987

Born in Palo Alto, California, Brigit Pegeen Kelly studied nursing at Ivy Tech State College and writing at the University of Oregon. She published three books of poems, including *The Orchard* (2004). Kelly's many honors include a Whiting Award and fellowships from the Academy of American Poets, the Guggenheim Foundation, and the National Endowment for the Arts. She taught for many years at the University of Illinois, Urbana-Champaign.

Music School

All day long the birds lounge
on the rotting plush of the rose bush,
drunk on the rancid scent,
and play and play on their dime store instruments.
They practice so hard and never get it right.
I pound the wall but they will not stop.
They think that the whole world is chortling.
They think that my pounding is the beat of their tiny hearts.
They are dazed by the sun that presses its belly against them,
convincing them that they are their songs
and that they will never again inhabit their shabby bodies.

The White Deer

The sister was mad
and so must be forgiven,
mad as the deer
trapped in the cow field,
over and again
it threw itself at the fences,
leaping in that leaping

that is not running but flight,
bloodying its mouth,
bloodying its chest,
four blood spots
like hand prints on its neck,
frenzied by those
who helpless would yet help it,
the man and his wife
flapping like large birds
veering this way and that
to head it to the gate,
while the hawk and its thirst
flew low over the cornfield,
flew low toward the promise
of the deer hanging high,
high on the fence
with its head dropped down,
like the hand of a girl
who has given it all up,
who has looked to the sky
and to those who would help her
and has laid her soft head
on the ground.

To the Lost Child

(for Anna)

This is the field you did not come to, this
the damp November day confederate
clouds trail defeat across. The far hills
are purple as the ashes of old fires,
and black as guns or crutches the trees. But the fields
are oddly green, still, in this winter thaw.
Or perhaps it is late fall—the small
measures we find ourselves with

don't change the movement of things. We, like this crow,
passing over the cedars in lazy,
widening circles, wobbling and sliding
as it rights itself by some internal decree,
can only ride the currents that *are*,
and are not held, up and down.
                                                    I am glad
of the crows, they are like my own hands,
always here, always remembering the day
to itself, glad of the trees, of the startling
red weeds and blue pools of shale
in this field where one tulip poplar stands
brisk and tall as a good child, a bee box
at her feet, a bee box full of humming.
And this humming is the maker, the body
of the gold it broods over. This must be so.
Pollen would have no savor if it came
from colorless flowers, and silent bees,
for all their flying, would make no honey
but some watery substance, or nothing
at all. For sound does make things happen.
The cows wander and when they cry
I heave hay, rank with mold and the months
of dust that fly up in blue clouds, over
the fence; the red-hatted hunter shouts
and the deer careers into or away from
the arrow's whistling arc; planes moan,
the head rises to heaven. And, Anna,
had you called as our bull calf Moses did,
all night when he was first new, tied to a pine
under the window, bullying the thin air
he found himself in, wailing at the cows
on the other side of the fence
who would not see him for what he was
until he forgot what he was and thought
we were one of him and he a fine man

in his uniform—had you called you would
have brought the sweet milk trickling between
your lips to form its lovely, cloudy pool.
I will not be sad. I count the things
I put in a box for us, all I thought
you would see, the scrawny forsythia starters—
pulled from the mother plant that smothers
the gate and each year must be thinned—tottering
along the drive, the deer trail lined
with the yellow roses that are still foolishly
blooming, the pines that cut the gray sky,
and the brilliant burning bush that, all improbably,
Moses, then grown, ate most of
before he barrelled away through the woods
to the farmer's far barley field, where, proud and stupid,
he ate his fill until we took
him away to one whose sturdy fences
would keep him home.

                    I can sit for a long
time now. Some war is over. Below me
the bog in the woods is black
and pungent with decay and the oil from
the red cans the old tenant left, and below that,
at the base of the hill, the rushing stream
is a gathering of voices. Many voices.
Yours. Mine. It moves, we move, and hands,
these things that find and belong
to each other, also move and carry like water
more than themselves, as they fly in their bird-
like ways toward whatever small purposes
they have been given.

Thomas Bolt (1959–) *Out of the Woods,* 1988

Born in Washington, D.C., Thomas Bolt graduated from the University of Virginia.
Bolt is also a painter and a writer of fiction. His honors include the Prix de Rome
and the Peter I. B. Lavan Award from the Academy of American Poets.

After a Terrible Thing Happened

I emerged from that place
    Owning nothing
And came to this place where the path makes
    A rough mosaic
Out of the scattered gravels and busted jars,
    To find nothing more

Than what I saw wrecked black-barked in a jumble of vine,
    Its mud-spattered
Entanglement of branches strangling the creek,
    Its heart involved
In knotted roots nerved with a fine hair;
    So I walked awhile

After the intelligence at the hull of things
    Neglected not saved
And crusted with other lives than our own:
    Until I felt
My skeleton turn to old iron
    Forgotten in the mud

Edging a scrap-grounds. There were a few trees,
    Thin saplings,
Hard by a broader wood of sycamores
    Where no one looked.
My cold metals sank in the stunned-still world
    All day

As only shadows moved over the dirt
    And wreckage
And spidery nerves of root
    Where a tree
Caught between others leaned over the creek:
    All day

Sun burned on the unsalvaged metal
    And moved slowly away
Over the stubs of weeds at the woods' edge
    Until light eroded
Red in the distant emptiness of fields
    Where dismantled things

Sank in embedded mud. A loose tree propped alive
    Where only
A thicket of other limbs prevented its
    Tearing away
From the bank it held part-lifted in its roots,
    Leaned still

While the shadow of the woods crossed
    Fallen things
Strewn with broken glass, and a far scattering of nuts
    Cracked by the sun
Or rotten, bruised and buried: whatever there was stood
    While only the light moved

On my iron skeleton rusting in the mud.
    Those acorns cast
Shadows the length of oaks and the transparent
    Color of locust shells
Over the wilderness of abandoned chassis
    Where I stood

Watching the scrap-grounds darken in the shape
    Of the caught tree
Hung half-dangling; and its slow roots forgot

The tangled shape
They had displaced for years in the packed bank,
And felt for other mud.

My nerves felt for the world:
All afternoon,
With the slow burn-out of daylight on the limbs,
I watched
Things shift through the empty rungs of trees
Until I felt myself

Lurched-loose and uprooted over the strangled creek
And scrap of the world,
Restrained only in iron-gray tanglings;
But I turned
From the shock of being torn away
To move again.

I walked to the next place on a rough path
Through the shifted woods
Where that ruined metal sank in the rusting sun
All afternoon,
As its cast-off purpose blackened with other scrap
Left unclaimed

In the taste of the mineral, November air,
And its flawed ribs
Stuck from the weedless mud
Dead-still by the brown
Water of the long ditch where the shadow fell,
Wrecked and loosening

In the only world that happens.

Standing in a Clearing

What will you do, the large world
Scattered behind you, leaves a live red?
As dead branches crack under your feet
And you look across
The tilted face of a stump
At stories of orbit and eclipse
In a whorl of sawmarks,

What will you do?
In this inexpedient place,
Sun eats the heavy paint
From 55-gallon drums;
Your whirled nerves
Are worth no more than leaves, your fingernail
Is dead as the branch your foot lifts.

What will you do?
The pattern of past growth
Circles its axis of origin, hardening
In its own acids; but can still become
Whatever you want to make of every day
Of the long years
Stored in the pine stump like a battery.

Here, dialectic washes in the mud.
What, the world your wood,
Will you do with life
Explosive in the sun
In its chemical miracle,
Consumed as you are in this place,
In the moment of your hand

On the motor housing,
Fingering marks of dried gasoline?
Afoul of fall, the leaves
Are fouled with all, fluttering, falling,

Found underfoot,
A sound underfoot,
Rot under root,

Barked with the brown of days, done, down,
All ground and sand unsound underfoot;
And with your only life
Widening from a point
Of origin, and bound
By dark encircling crust, you stand
Almost autonomous,

Ringed by the fallen bronze
Of the trees
Which rise between down and none
And noun and done,
To choose whatever you can
If you can
As all the stained wood is dyed and dries.

These motley leaves
Are made the fools of fall;
Now that the air has made a fuel of all,
An unclogged ooze of days
Wrung from the trees,
A rotten ripeness looks from every pool.
Tasting fall in the fell cool of the wood, what

Are you going to do with your life?
After the caught
Noise, vibrant rasp, and rise
Of chainsaw sounds
You are
The gasoline motor shaking in your hands,
The smell of fuel,

The readiness of air.

Temporary Structure

I reflect on the buckling water
Of the cold creek
Where the present is thrown together.
The world shifts on its face, and flashes up
To move in the moment of a living mind
With all this trashy wild
Liquid and lunging forth.

I am makeshift;
Lean-to of body,
A few sticks of bone;
But my unfinished life
Is part of the world,
Part of the day
My eyes borrow.

It is a world
Of mud and meter and metal,
Stamped and seamed with sense,
A bright bucket tumbling in a creek
As my heart fills and empties, and my lungs
Give and take.
Unbroken, it is beaten back and forth

New, a booming shape
Banged and battered,
Its drum curve
Beaten by water,
Its flattened crystals blazing
Jammed between rocks,
One side in silver shadow.

Possibility
Rings in present air
With resounding sense,
But rings

Like the bucket turning over in the rocks:
Turned and overturned,
Bright zinc will wear off,

The bottom pock with rust,
Each pock
Enlarge with ruin, and,
Worn to a wafer,
The whole, punctured crust
Finally crumple under a loop
Of new water into a whorl of flakes.

What theory can contain
A muddy-metaled day
Cast from a wordless world and overturned
And turned along the rush and turbulence
Of nervous surfaces,
The cold, pictured flow
Charged with a constant change?

A theory balances,
But has to move
Unstable in a moving medium
Which can resist its equilibrium:
Clatter of day,
Sky thrown to the ground,
Light leaping up the trees.

A sounding mind
Can bang a tone of joy
Out of the bucket bouncing on the rocks,
The cold change of pebbles underwater,
Or a vessel sinking,
Clogged with bitter leaves,
And settling muffled to the hidden ooze.

This physical moment,
Circumstance of sense,

Is the living memory of having lived;
A rattling vision, thrown up from this bed,
The luscious frictions of another skin
Reshape the gathered day, and scatter out
A now of nerves and words.

Where the present is given up
Off balance
And poised between
Dangers of standing still
And risks of moving,
Running improvisation undermines
Imagined futures;

Being is being in momentum in
The unfinished business everywhere
Of verb and reverberation, galvanized
In a world of many movements
To shock-bright transitive sustained in sense;
Now is an echoing
Like the hollow of the bucket hammered on.

This living framework,
Scaffold for a life,
Will plunge into a cold scattering
Of its own accord,
Or at the world's will:
The scaffolding of my language taken down
Leave an emptiness of objects.

While I can stand,
Off-balance but alive
To punctuating rocks,
The run-on sky,
Dangling weeds and snarled clause of trees
That make the long sentence of the creek
Mean what it means,

This is the place to stand,
And let reflection fall
Unsafe in the crash of futures
And ongoing trade of surfaces and depths
Overturned and turned and turned again,
From which no thing escapes or is exempt:
This theory will also be a life.

Daniel Hall (1952–) *Hermit with Landscape,* 1989

Daniel Hall was born in Pittsfield, Massachusetts, and is largely self-educated. He is the author of three books of poetry, most recently *Under Sleep* (2007). Hall has been the recipient of a Whiting Award, the Amy Lowell Traveling Poetry Scholarship, and fellowships from the Guggenheim Foundation, the National Endowment for the Arts, and the Ingram Merrill Foundation.

Andrew's Jewelweed

One or two are past their prime
already, bruising, perishable
as the end of summer, flushed
to the spurs—mementos of the time
and pains taken to get things down
before they go. I see him still,

spotlit above the copperplate,
his fingers aching to define
the spaces memory floods
with noon, sharp sunbursts from the canopy,
grapevines and bittersweet spilling to the floor,
the rubythroats in flight, the thunderheads.

The People's Hotel

And afterwards he said please
empty your pockets: handful
of keys and small change he spent
quiet minutes sketching.
An astonishment, where instead
of one large coin the moon appeared,
familiar, rayed and bruised,
face of a loved one gone

to ruin. He pushed it toward me,
stood to go, asking for nothing
more than that we meet again.

A Sneeze on High

1
Poised in angelic
suspense at the brink
above the sound's
sun-sparked acres,
Mount Rainier's
icecap shrinking
from summer all summer,
I know the urge
to play my part
in the universal
waterworks, mindful
of a risen tonnage,
all atmospheric
reversions, rain,
cloud, snow-
melt

2
—oh:
the agreeable heat
of release, a hot
wire strung
to the heart of things,
unspooling into
oblivion.
            Memory:
the weather- and pun-
engendering mountain's

rivers drew
a shattering glaze
over anything
that wouldn't budge.
We lay sun-baked,
facedown, crosswise
on the logjam,
above a tumult
so close it gave off
cold, took in
sandgold, rocksmear.
In the shallows
minnow mimicked
and inverted silver
sky and dusky
bottom
          —but something
grazes, tickles
even now,
barely un-
forgettable, casts
a chilly shade
that day to this,
though just what
it was we why
we—

3
sphnx

4
—crash
of celestial cymbals,
a scalp-tautening
frisson, like coming

to
   —oh:
an over-doubling
pang, the plumbing
interrupted—
Better. There.
I shiver, shake
off as a gust
(or is it me?)
of gooseflesh scuffs
the sound: the sun
is gone, the mountain
going, sailboats
arcing homeward.
I linger a moment
longer, haloed
in a fume of bright
synaptic mayflies,
senseless, aimless,
already dying.

Christiane Jacox Kyle (1950–) *Bears Dancing in the Northern Air,* 1990

Christiane Jacox Kyle was born in Washington, D.C., and studied at Mount Holyoke College and Eastern Washington University. In addition to writing poetry, she has also translated Gabriela Mistral's *Poemas de Las Madres* (1996).

Oracle

I drive all night; on my right the Great Bear
wheels and winds backwards like a restless eye.
Already old, the moon slides down the sky,
a late aurora sheathes the northern air.

I think of blind seals plummeting to where
blind waters sweep the lashes from their eyes.
Measure that distance. What can sanctify
the will to wander the moon's dark side? I swear

once there were those who knew how to live
in this world, drawing great shapes on bearskin,
cave walls: huge birds with hooked wings, a deft spear
lodged in a rib, each an amulet to give
a shape to fear. I explore the sky. I begin
with the first word. I name it Fear.

Calling

Notice how quickly the rain turns,
no longer exuberant, the closed cell
of warmth surrounding the planet
gone, gone the earth surrendering,

the steady effortless rhythm of days
and drops spattering the lilacs,
pure white, thick purple in furious bloom;
gone the rain right for whispers, faces flung open
under an artless sky, wet mouths, these wet hands;
and the grass widows bobbing beneath the rain:
oh love the one world, wet and warm,
made of a single sound.

How quietly the rain turns
to sullenness, a gray sky stooped
to a gray and reticent world;
now the predictable torrents where
the eaves have been left to rot,
the red wall of the barn stunned
into silence, rain robbing the hayloft of voices,
now the absent lowing of a cow, rain
breathing down insistent as asthma,
and somewhere, a lover calling,
father, mother, child, and the calling out:
oh let fall the impenetrable wall of clouds.

The Music Box

I studied it closely, guessing at oak
or birch, although a more accomplished eye
than mine had said the only certainty
was time had been lenient. One hurried stroke
had cracked the box. It held, though forests grew
wildly along the crest of broken vines.
Patterns sketched in troubled lines
were left to fade, like something never new.

The song that rose in pieces from that wood,
did it hesitate, as if it could call

back the artist's curse, the stubborn awl
he hurled away; or had it understood
always, only the unsuspicious ear
would know the song, simple, whole, and clear?

Nicholas Samaras (1954–) *Hands of the Saddlemaker,* 1991

Nicholas Samaras was born in Foxton, Cambridgeshire, England, and later studied at Hellenic College in Brookline, Massachusetts, Columbia University, and the University of Denver. The recipient of a National Endowment for the Arts fellowship, Samaras has published a second book of poems, *American Psalm, World Psalm* (2014).

Amnesiac

No, I do not remember the rogue car
or how it rode its black metal
to the last flash of my bones.
I know only what I've woken to:
two friends bandaged, a bearded man who says he's my father.
The language on my tongue seems thick and faraway.
There is no knife for this illness,
I am a wraith in a white shift.
These are my starched legs, my hands.
This is the mirror that opens on absence.

I accept shadows in my mind.
My father's thinned lips are not mine.
Fear is a comparison and I have
no past to hold it up against.
The neurosurgeon frowns leaving the room. I stare
at the strange flowers breathing my air. The air singes me.
And all of it new! All of it, a face emptied.
I have told my told story
to the statisticians, my history
married to a white bracelet on my wrist.

Women in coarse sheaves of white
glide in to anoint: a gauzy touch
to tighten the dripping I.V.
Salved for consecration, I could
stay this pure
yet fidget for something to happen.
My father moves his lips.
Shadows wash the room, darken his features.
The room breathes in when I breathe in.
The flowers clot in their vase.

This bed drains me,
it draws like a poultice.
Yet the mirror alarms me most.
Three days of light bloomed and wilted on the wall
before they allowed one in.
Nothing there.
The world is a shock. I make a bargain with God.
My hands, untied, feel the folds of my face.
The fugue-probe hurts my brain. My hands
give up, smooth over sterile sheets, settle on nothing.

What Continues

In this village, old people kiss.
Theio crimps in from the dusk,
switches of hazel in his hands,
says I sleep the wrong hours.
When he turns to the fire,
his bristled cheeks are a glint
of silver, a field-day's face let go.
He coddles his wife in the kitchen,
folds his hands in coarse crinoline
till she pushes him away and he cackles.

The night is a scythe for the light.
The night is a burnt umber.
Theio and I go—
a man's night is spent in the tavern
with its clink of glass on tables.
A woman's night gathers on the door-stoop
as she spins the wool in her hands.
The roles are clear.

We wind back—the important
conversation done—and rake
hazel on the fire.
From the hall, we close the language.
I watch them hobble off together,
holding hands,
shadows deepening their wrinkles.
He is eighty-three, she seventy-nine.
Laid down under the thick wool flokati,

I think of the first night I knocked
on their window-shutters, introduced
myself as their nephew
and they laid their palms on me.
A life away, I think of Elaine
and a song arches in me.
Through the walls, I hear their bed
squeaking an ancient rhythm.

Amphilohios

This is the first thing you think of.
It may be the way he fills the room,
how morning light seems to flow over him
and is absorbed into his black cassock.
Immediately, this man, his
long, thick salt-and-pepper beard,

will cause you to think of little else,
will have you realize your future
is never yours
but a wind you may
only tack against.

Because you have never felt anything as
love without possession,
you could think he will want
something, eventually.
You think of everyone
who has ever wanted of you,
think of yourself
who has wanted of your life the most.
But he is simple in greeting,
muslin arms outstretched, shaking
the light from his body.

For three days, he will love you and ignore you—
something you find both appreciated and disappointing.
It is strange how you almost miss the judgment.
Into evening, he sits at a carved
table and studies; you sit
opposite, writing cards or gazing past the balcony,
learning how not to start a conversation.
Looking out to a blue vestment of sky,
you think a benign love is possible.
The weekend visit becomes an icon
burning into your sleep.

Before you are ready to give
this up, through a blue-veined wind,
the long boat at midnight leads
its ghostly wake into the harbor,
its fogbell calling.
At the wharf, you look out over the black-robed water.
Father holds you in the lightest way

goodbye, kisses your cheeks, his neutral
beard brushing you like air.
And you love the way you are
lost in the openness of his face. You love
the way you are lost.

Jody Gladding (1955–) *Stone Crop,* 1992

Born in York, Pennsylvania, Jody Gladding studied at Franklin and Marshall College and Cornell University. She has published five books of poetry, most recently *the spiders in my arms* (2018), and has translated some thirty books from French. A former Stegner fellow, she has received a Whiting Writers Award, the French-American Foundation Translation Prize, and a translation grant from the Centre National du Livre de France.

Sometimes I Went to a Dark Place

I liked it there
liked the way I could call into it
there is no light!

and it would echo back   light!
I liked the way it sounded, my voice calling
there is no light!   and the chorus back calling

light!   So I went often, stayed long
listening to my voice and the chorus
it called from the dark.

But once, after much calling and echoing, my voice
failed, and as it failed, the echo faded
and I said to myself there is no light.

No light I said again, and there was no echo.
No light I whispered because my voice had failed
and there was no echo.

So I turned whispering light
and I ran saying light
and I found my way out and called

light!   finding my voice again
in a chorus calling back
light from a dark place.

Fish Song

the heron is
my patience

my thoughtfulness
the loon

the kingfisher
my nerve

but the osprey
I am wholly

the osprey's—

Of the Many Words for Snow,

one names such scraps
melting into the embankment
where, at night, they've pitched
their box springs, rusting paint cans,
the carcass of a deer.

Of the many words for sex,
one describes a woman
taking off her clothes
and arching back like petals
into the whole spectrum of desire.

One names a bank,
prismed in March sun,

so as to reflect the way white
contains every color—here,
where the red and yellow columbine
will blossom.

And one refers to blood,
pubic bone, and the dark hairs,
coiling—what a woman
means sometimes,
undressing.

Valerie Wohlfeld (1956–) *Thinking the World Visible,* 1993

Born in Sacramento, California, Valerie Wohlfeld studied at American University in Washington, D.C., as well as Sarah Lawrence College and Vermont College. Her second collection of poems is *Woman with Wing Removed* (2010).

Season's End

1. *A Voice from Arid Riverbeds*
The body is its disappearing
universe of chemicals; seven-tenths
always water, the longing to have been
the impenetrable stone caught and turned
in a lapidary's felicitous hands.

A dowser's bough may stir so violently
the fists will strip the bark.
Like the body—in its hazel,
peach and willow—savage and closed,
wresting towards known water.

2. *Clove Lime Fruit Glass*
Let the body be taken
as spices are taken
and crushed between the fingers coarsely—
a cipher of darkness, impervious shades
of cinnamon, clove, anise: the inviolate
release of sting and aroma: cayenne, ginger
and saffron set down on the tongue—
exhalation of smoke from out of the tiny, clouded jar.

Where was my body's lime before
offered to the glassmaker?
In strands of multicolored jewels
smuggled out of Syria in Egyptian bones.

I hasten toward the egress
of rain: saturation, vicissitude, melisma.
I hold the wild linum
to my breath, unswallowed.

Now I am like a fruit
indiscernible to itself
if it is ripe or unripe.

3. Sand Verbena, Sea Lily

The thighs are multifarious,
awaiting pure note. Perianth, wafer,
foil, leaf: floriferous
moment praising itself as it dies,
glass in the euphonious voice.

I found my body in the fossil
of a shell. In sand verbena, in the sea lily.
A fish lay down in clay:
it was the beginnings of my own skeleton.
Seeded by the wind, I rose
as roots, flowers from shoals
of sand. Slowly, a sea anemone
parted; my thighs, echoing,
could not contain their ornamental sting.
The sea's on my tongue like a sugar
pill, a thorn, a salt-smell, a hook I take down.

This is why I've put the sea in a bric-a-brac box.
This is why I do not mean to let it out.

That Which Is Fugitive, That Which Is Medicinally Sweet or Alterable to Gold, That Which Is Substantiated by Unscientific Means

Earth, *Ephemera.*
Womb, *Elixir.*
Subject to its laws of development,
experience, observation and verification
of salted, borrowed blood: the given
name for the fetus must be *Empirical.*

Beaker of the body's warmth: pinprick,
secret ruby, transient blossom, Empirical.
The womb catches life like a well
harboring pennies, whatever's sent to it,
the water wise but untelling.

I lay on the table, my puerile
dress folded on a chair. Brought
with me a thesaurus, its outer covers lost.
My body moored, I watched the ceiling's white,
starless firmament and began my recitation
out of the injured book.

Cinnabar, cochineal, ponceau
Annatto, madder, ruddle, rouge
Scarlet, cardinal, vermilion
Claret-colored, flame-colored, rust-colored
Auburn, sandy, bay, sorrel, chestnut.
Again I was dark, green water
for the copper coins to hurry down to.

Lyric Task

I've seen the farm boy
splitting a crow's
tongue to coax
uncertain speech.

Wings opened—
a seedy lampblack umbrella
blown inside out.
Resigned to rummaged
corn or learned, ungraceful
note: the farm boy knows.

Along ropy mudflats, I breached
muscular mire. I hurried to meet
crows with their bolted beaks
threaded in cockles and amphipods.
I pursued guttural whipcracks,
emerged on tiptoe out of sulfureous
marsh to see (studded in violet
mud as if a whole childhood's
thumbprinted, patent leather shoes) the sky
converged to the crows' sooty umbra.

I followed gutters in their crazed
glaze of rivulets, back to meadows.
I met the farm boy's gaze,
with thistles and wild roses
gathered burning in my fists.
He wielded pocket knife to lyric task.
I tasted of the sacrifice of wild
rose. Sometimes his crows
refused the grafted voice.
Not all unmeasured song rises to its tutor.

T. Crunk (1956–) *Living in the Resurrection,* 1994

Tony Crunk was born in Hopkinsville, Kentucky, and educated at Centre College of Kentucky, the University of Kentucky, and the University of Virginia. He has written several books of poetry, most recently *To His Son* (2016), as well as books for children.

August

Twilight sifts down
into the peach trees in the yard

and the roses stir
at the hint of rain in a dry month.

My mother and father
are repotting plants on the back steps—

the dumb cane and peace lily
job's tears and pennyroyal.

A handful of bats
folds and unfolds around a hemlock

on the hill
where the wind is whispering itself to sleep.

Nothing is redeemed
except by accident.

Objects of Belief

Lying awake, watching the moon heal over,
counting all that is mine, but not my own—
breath, and the shapes my pale hands
turn in the air, and the things of my father

I still carry with me: a tin box
of foreign coins, a leather hunting coat . . .

White mist rising from the pond,
cows bawling in the distance
like angels moving slowly across the fields,
fireflies tapping out around them
the five laws of darkness:
desire . . . atomistic . . . return . . .

Constellations

the caravan of exiles
has camped in the valley
of cenobitic blue spruce

among the tents and wagons
a few gods
tending the fires
reading the ashes
• • •
angel wings
flashing

is what my grandmother

called heat lightning
• • •
tongue of flame—

the lucent
yellow parabola
on
the wall above my lamp
• • •
the last load of empty hoppers
on its way back

walks Mannington trestle
at midnight

shaving sparks of rust
off the rails

then flattens it out across the Barrens
and up into the south Peabody fields

like
ladders striding out of a whirlwind
• • •
the nails
of the cross of Jesus

    burning
are ~~rusting~~
• • •
the moon is
a chip from a bone handled knife

the moon is called
Orphan's Torch

the moon in its phases
is a musical notation

a shape note hymn
that goes:

listen
I will come for you

by rushlight

Ellen Hinsey (1960–) *Cities of Memory,* 1995

Born in Boston, Massachusetts, Ellen Hinsey was educated at Tufts University and the Université de Paris VII. She has written four books of poems, most recently *The Illegal Age* (2018), as well as essays, dialogues, and literary translations. Hinsey's honors include a Rona Jaffe Foundation Writer's Award, the Berlin Prize fellowship from the American Academy in Berlin, and a Lannan Foundation Award. The international correspondent for the *New England Review,* Hinsey lives in Paris.

The Body in Youth

After rain, in the darkened room, the body
reed-like, marked by mysteries, hungered
to escape the rhythm of change, observed
nightly in the narrow bed.

Shadowless, the washed walls receded,
though benignly, in triptych, caught the
occasional beam's passing: such
the simple Annunciations

that taught limbs to reach, as if in passion,
into the near vagaries of space. Each part
resolutely delivered its tidings: ears
fanned and thickened like

muscular flowers, that thrive in the shade
of the water's edge; birthmarks, hidden,
spread, then darkened, inspected by fingers
for their singular shape.

Ribs betrayed the pulse's quickening pace.
Only dreams cradled imperfections—
rationalized the humidity of desires;
by day the body crept

to the mirror and under its scrutiny,
waited for change like an unseen horizon.
Just before rain it seemed the body
lingered transparent,

had carried one out under the firs, set
one free under the rotating spheres.
Now flesh was a constant breath
at one's ear, intoning

its litany of limitations. Yet how far the body
had to travel—when finally, after its shape
was fixed, and became one's signature
in the world of forms,

then faithlessly, like a ship tide-persuaded,
it drifted, abandoning what it sought
to become, the body in youth lingering
only a moment in its own folds.

Planisféria, Map of the World, Lisbon, 1554

Space was easier then, and time slower—
One faced the white of distance with purpose.
            The unknown beckoned, like the polar caps,
            or stilled one, like an awkward moment:

beyond the horizon, trees stirred like birds;
heedless of latitude, temperatures rose,
            fir trees bent, their needles uncalculated.
            This desire to possess, to flatten space

was dwarfed by waves that the astrolabe could
not settle. Yet, the mapmaker took sides:
            Africa would be veined with great water
            arteries, but the Amazon would diminish

halfway across the *Mundus Novus.*
Other rivers were silenced, though needed:
>to be known, land must be entered
>by those green arched passageways

above which birds in formal plumage
led the way to inland knowledge. Still,
>whole continents slid off: passed up and cast
>into the corner of the mapmaker's dark.

The Sermon to Fishes

He was struck with awe at the sight of them:
a shoal lifting above the water's surface;
each head trained to his voice's timbre,
each spine anchored for the moment's purpose.

For the sea-dark flock, he fixed his words,
he the shepherd above them.
In the distance the itinerant waves obeyed
by ritual motion. Words flew from him —

How he had rehearsed such a miracle!
Before the silver of their scales, and
the heads in seeming infinite number,
he was great and gathered them in his hunger.

Yet, once lulled, how quiet this multitude —
that like quarter notes broke the water's line
as if hovering above the stillness where the lowest
staff separates music from endless silence.

Though his words had touched their hearing
and their heads above the water were tamed
he was pinned by his eye in water.
Arms outstretched, his figure remained

rooted, and would never master what, in one
movement turning round, they did, descending
guiltless into water, which glimmered darkly
as they fanned out, flying downward.

Talvikki Ansel (1964–) *My Shining Archipelago,* 1996

Talvikki Ansel was born in Madison, Wisconsin, and studied at Mount Holyoke College and Indiana University. Her honors include a Stegner Fellowship, a Lannan Foundation residency, and a Pushcart Prize. Ansel has written four books of poems, most recently *Somewhere in Space* (2015).

Flemish Beauty

Yesterday, all winter,
I had not thought of pears, considered:
pear. The tear-shaped, papery core,
precise seeds. This one channelled
through with worm tunnels.
Bruises, a rotten half—
sometimes there's nothing left
to drop into the pot.

              That phrase
I could have said: "you still
have us . . ."
         The knife
slides easily beneath the skins,
top to base, spiralling
them away.

The insubstantial us.
It could as well be the pear
talking to the river, turning to
the grass ("you still have us").
Besides, it's just *me*
a pear in my hand (the slop bucket full
of peels) — and sometimes, yes, that
seems enough: a pear—

              this larger one,
yellow-green, turning to red:
"Duchess" maybe, "Devoe,"
or what I want to call it: "Flemish
Beauty."
            When I can't sleep,
I'll hold my hand as if I held
a pear, my fingers mimicking
the curve. The same curve
as the newel post
I've used for years, swinging
myself up to the landing, always
throwing my weight back. And always
nails loosening, mid-bound.

Conversation with the Sun Bittern

    It preens on a root at the edge of the *igarapo.*
Light lights its lower mandible and brick-red eye.

    I say, "why am I talking to you?"
    "I don't know," it says, and spears a snail. Its head
is striped, its back mottled.

    I tell it about the drawer with the false bottom in
my mother's desk.

    I tell it about the letter I haven't finished, to a
person who gave me some diamonds.

    "I know all that," it says, and watches a minnow in among
the mangrove roots.

    "You know what you must do," it says, "you must stop . . ."
    "Breeding miniature horses," I say.
    "They are useless," it says.

I watch it lift one foot, and then the other. A drop
of water glistens on the tip of its bill.

"I know," I say, "but sometimes I am afraid."

From Stone

Coming into an empty room I find
you crying, you want
the green chair, the chair
you remember being born on. What
can I do to console you?
I would do anything for you. Today

I thought of Senefelder
discovering lithography:
the door open
to the cobbled yard, the laundress
sticks in her head, asks
for a list; he scribbles
on a piece of limestone: two shirts
three trousers, a waistcoat and hose—

why should the swish
of water on a flat rock,
a leather roller matted with ink
express anything I feel now?
Untouching, four birds
on a neighbor's chimney—

autumn: an overcast sky,
from the bluff only the sound
of waves on sand;
a distant pole, a bird, a swallow
wrapped around its heart.

In the 16th century,
it was thought that swallows

spent winters in the bottoms
of lakes. Who wouldn't
reach for that? Solace
of blood and feathers, ensconced
in clay.

Craig Arnold (1967–2009) *Shells,* 1998

Craig Arnold earned a B.A. from Yale University and a Ph.D. from the University of Utah. He was also the author of a second book of poems, *Made Flesh* (2008). The recipient of honors including the Amy Lowell Traveling Poetry Scholarship, the Hodder Fellowship from Princeton University, a National Endowment for the Arts fellowship, and a Fulbright scholarship, Arnold disappeared while hiking on the volcanic island of Kuchinoerabu-jima. He is presumed to have died from a fall while exploring an active volcano.

Hermit crab

A drifter, or a permanent house-guest,
he scrabbles through the stones, and can even scale
the flaked palm-bark, towing along his latest
lodging, a cast-off periwinkle shell.
Isn't he weighed down? Does his house not pinch?
The sea urchin, a distant relative,
must haul his spiny armor each slow inch
by tooth only—sometimes, it's best to live
nowhere, and yet be anywhere at home.

That's the riddle of his weird housekeeping
—does he remember how he wears each welcome
out in its turn, and turns himself out creeping
unbodied through the sand, grinding and rude,
and does he feel a kind of gratitude?

Great dark man

At quarter past midnight I meet
the great dark man. His hat is wet
—he wears a hat—and drips, as if
he's only just come off the street

into the bar out of the rain
although I know he's been here half
an hour already. He takes a stiff
drink, something masculine,

gin or whiskey double straight.
He doesn't look at me—he has
nothing to talk about. The broad
back of his hand around the glass

is dark with fur. Across the bar
I grapple with my shoe, the lace
knotted double and clenched tight
as a fist. My fingernails are chewed

too short, the lace is too wet
with rain to grip, half an hour
I've clawed at a knot as hard and grim
as ever. I turn, at last, to him.

He shakes his head silently *no*
at something I can't hear or see.
One hand closes around the throat
of the glass, the other tilts his hat

over his eyes, a helmet shut.
Tucked away in his dark greatcoat
somewhere, maybe, he has a knife.
What can't be untied must be cut.

Shore

For Don Platt

On the last night of our weekend getaway
        in the beachfront house
that smells of your father's white clay meerschaum pipes,

stems broken
after each smoke, of your mother's tennis whites
 packed in mothballs,

I lose it. When you bring to the table soup
 opaque but quickly
settling to powdery clouds, circling in the bowl's

 slow currents,
bringing up slick green squares of seaweed, cubes
 of pale bean curd,

I say, It's as if we're drinking cups of ocean.
 You can't drink
salt water, you reply. *You'd get sick,*

 see things,
not even angry, only matter-of-fact.
 When, by way

of explanation, I say the earth's surface
 and the human body
both are three-fifths water, say that blood

 was as much salt
as the sea itself, your answer then is even
 simpler: *So?*

I follow you on an after-dinner walk
 along the beach
in bare feet, sinking ankle-deep in the slough

 of shoreline
churned and turned, reordered and replaced,
 earth over a grave,

to watch the sandpipers steering to
 and fro, skirting
the sheets of foam that slither up, at times

even sliding across
each other, scissorblades shearing the beach,
          and try to guess

how far each wave will reach, based on its height,
          speed, fierceness
—there's no pattern, at least not one that I

          can see, this one
falters, that one stretches its margin clear
          to the high-tide mark,

a shoal of bladder-wrack and spat-up shells,
          straw and driftwood,
bits of feather, dead crabs. When I find what I think

          is a mermaid's purse,
a clutch of shark eggs, leather-tough and black,
          and take it to you

to verify, you laugh, call it a shred
          of rubber from
a semi. *It's the same with everything,*

          you say. You make it
something that it isn't. Why can't you let things be
          themselves?

Because the sea makes all these things the same,
          wearing away
the nap of the cloth, the points of the conch, the knot

          in the gray branch,
the hurtful jagged shard of glass, the cheekbones
          of a seagull skull,

grinds them all down to the tiny grains
          we're letting wash
over our feet, that we're sinking ankle-deep

into, losing
height, that rasp away the soles of our feet.
        I try to listen

past this, past the insistence of a voice,
        to make it mean
less, to hear only the hiss of white noise

        in a seashell,
and maybe it's just the tide's suck and settle
        dragging sand

out from under my feet, that makes me lose
        my balance, pitch
forward and fall, as if some swollen thought

        under the sand
has tried to shrug me off, as if I've put
        too much weight

on its shoulders. Why did you invite me here?
        I scream.
Why do you want me around? I can't see things

        the way you do,
I can't just stand around and wait for you
        to die. *You're not*

standing, you say, holding out your arm,
        braced, leaning
away to pull me up—that's all you need,

        another body
to need pulling up. In the evening
        out of the light

the scars show up paler against your skin,
        elbow to wrist,
a constellation, twenty, though I don't count:

        the day you knew,
you went and bought a pack of Lucky Strikes,
        the first in years,

on your way to lunch with me, and after you told me
        what was what,
you sat and smoked each one down to its last

        tarred and limp
pinch of tobacco, and stubbed it out in your arm,
        and I let you.

Davis McCombs (1969–) *Ultima Thule,* 1999

Davis McCombs was born in Louisville, Kentucky, and studied at Harvard University, the University of Virginia, and Stanford University. He worked for ten years as a park ranger at Mammoth Cave National Park, and now teaches at the University of Arkansas. His awards include a National Endowment for the Arts fellowship, the Dorset Prize for his second book of poems, Dismal Rock (2007), and the Agha Shahid Ali Prize for his third collection, Lore (2016).

Cave Wind

Knowing it is shaped by
the size of the passage
it unwinds through (thus its
particular form and flue), we
are not deceived when, on
summer afternoons, it stiffens into
fog, clusters in the vines
and scrub brush littering the
entrance sink — no cough or
eructation, it is a constant
velocity we read or clock
(no need to vane it)
for the scope and girth
of the cavern, asking *does
it go or siphon?* knowing
its speed portends the cave
we'll discover, whether we will
walk or crawl, the breadth
of its breath, its given,
how, listening, we step into
the fricative, enter the socket
and proceed toward the lung

or bellows one half expects,
and, breathless, creep through the
throat of the longwinded earth.

Floyd's Lost Passage

February 1925
Backlit and nervy, he bends at the cave mouth,
descends from the light past humps of moss
that tick inaudibly in the inverted skullcap
of the sink. Nothing moves in his wake.
Beancans knobbing the pockets of his coveralls,
small sustenance for the afterworld, he turns,
determined, from this one, feels his way
along splintery walls that rip at him, chafe
and paw him, the tight coil of his lank
loosens to their lusts and turns. Calloused hand
to limestone scallop, he crawls into the hollow
of a river's skeleton, and the muck wants him,
comes sweating to his touch. A switchback
and a siphon. The cave pinches down
to a sloping, narrow chute, and feet first,
the scuffed tip of his boot catches the rock that pins
his leg in the mud — a terminal breakdown
though the cave slinks on through the hills'
inhuman ribcage holding now
his looked for, soon-to-be-famous heart.

February 1995
I know they laid you out, waxen
and defaced, in the cave's first chamber,
and for a tip, they'd crack the lid —
high cheekbone, a rat-nibbled nose
in the lantern's slatted light.
One night the river took your stolen body

like a log, and still they hawked you
on the main road, ink-slung your inky end.
Complicit, I gape from greater distance
and worse light. Midnight spraddled
on your latest grave and I went looking
and felt nothing there — no disintegration,
no rest nor rekindling, just the great Flint Ridge,
white-knuckled in the half moon.

Floyd, you are the fox in its stump den,
you are the rattle in my wall.
I underestimate how close some nights
the cedars whittle on their Girkin shelves.
I want to think you're out there, if anywhere.
Nothing I can point to, nothing I can name.
What hole do you tend toward now,
what hard-won grave?

The River and Under the River

At dusk every day, our cattle leave the river,
single-file, trundling their weight to the upper pastures.
And every night, the river is left to itself, infertile
and self-loathing, most beautiful when it comes close
to absence; its grooves and grottoes hum
with the noise of a landscape's slow consumption.
If I put my ear to the ground
could I hear the drag of the river turning
limestone into silt? Would it tell of Carlos pulled
through water on a slim and muscly night at Turnhole Bend?
I want to know the missing part of his story
that ends with the flush of foxfire on a grave —
as if from the body's heat fading out.
Tonight the river is at work dissolving, solving

over and over the riddle of its loosening.
I want to know how to hear it, and what it might teach me:
how to inhabit this thing of bone, gut, and blood,
this part of me that would not vanish if I vanished.

Maurice Manning (1966–) *Lawrence Booth's Book of Visions,* 2000

Maurice Manning, born in Danville, Kentucky, studied at Earlham College and the University of Alabama at Tuscaloosa and now teaches at Transylvania University in Lexington, Kentucky. Among his awards are a Guggenheim Fellowship and a fellowship from the Fine Arts Work Center in Provincetown, Massachusetts. Manning has written five subsequent books of poetry, including *Bucolics* (2007) and *The Common Man* (2010), which was a finalist for the Pulitzer Prize.

A Prayer Against Forgetting Boys

The boy with the burned up face.
The boy walking across the railroad bridge.
The boy who saw everything.
The boy who ran to the hills and hid in a cave.
The boy racking balls at the pool hall and sweeping up ashes.
The boy from his own country.
The boy painting a fence.
The boy with the brains God gave a goose.
The boy who took thirteen rabies shots in the belly.
The boy with the horse somebody shot.
The boy with pneumonia and salve on his chest, long ago in a dim log house.
The shoeshine boy popping a rag.
The boy with one eye.
The boy with a memory shaped like a tree.
The boy who threw rocks at a train.
The boy who kept dreaming of flames.
The boy digging a trench.
The boy who never flinched.
The boy climbing a silo to send out a plea.
The boy with his hand on the neck of a snake.
The boy on a wagon covered with hay.
The boy swooping across the plain of time.

The boy who learned how to be a boy
thanks to an infinite dog.

Pegasus

An exceptional dream, a long moment
of half-sleep, the century slowly grinding
to a halt: he feels like a royal Arabian horse
with black eyes is pouncing—two hooves—
on his chest, then, the desire for featherweightiness
or a ribcage made of tempered steel, plus the cucumber
smell of a snake in a ditch; everything very ticklish now
and the horse is thirsty, hopping like a primitive
firewalker, white mane turned to leaping flames.
So Booth leads him to the river, water running
over blue rocks, a mouth exhaling, water weeds
waving on a rocky tongue and Booth sweeps his hand
like a salesman around the riverland scene: Looky!—
(two honey locust logs, a toy tractor, scrap iron scatterings,
hemlock boughs, a spooky house, a sunken barn;
the bleak hand of a man, the hem of a woman's
yellow dress, a boy's scabby knee, a girlchild's hair
blown back by the breath of God) and, finally,
the horse stops jumping. Booth's lungs uncollapse.
He thought he was drowning, but then he surfaced.

Like a Tree

The boy stood in the shadows with a makeshift
travois rig, hitched it to his Red Dog's back and looked
out at the far woods like a trapper. He would cross
the river and the railroad tracks and keep on going.
A list of his supplies: a hatchet, some fishing line
wrapped onto a spool, a pair of hooks;
the makings of a teepee, sixteen biscuits, a canteen,

and his great-grandmother's hope-chest quilt.
He was tired of algebra and inclined planes—he cried
out against The Very Heavy Vector which creates
the terrible pattern of falling apart; he was determined
to look for The Mighty Force Which Pushes Back:
he might have to steal a poor man's coal, he might
need to sneak into a widow's kitchen for a cup of coffee;
there could be long nights of keeping watch,
no telling how long he would be gone; so he made
a secret note— ⊙ + M 🐝 + ing 💗 , Law—
and put it on his mother's pillow; he had his scoutknife and
a book—*The Ways of the Indians*, copyright 1923. He sent forth
a four-letter word to curse the threat of winter and skunks,
winked at his daddy's dark horse, tapped the dog
with a willow switch, spit through his teeth, and left.

Sean Singer (1974–) *Discography,* 2001

Sean Singer was born in Guadalajara, Mexico, and studied at Indiana University, Washington University in Saint Louis, and Rutgers University. *Discography* won the Norma Farber Book Award from the Poetry Society of America. A recipient of a National Endowment for the Arts fellowship, Singer is the author of a second volume of poems, *Honey and Smoke* (2015). He lives in New York City.

The Old Record

rolled out   of the hot machine
        the Scully Automated Lathe,
              covered in   oil,
rigged to the metal   ends,
                dying of spin,
meta   on black,
          back to back thimble weights, diamond
              and rinsed
        to a new shine,
lunge and pull into   circles,
            100 grooves to the centimeter,
     calling it vinyl, midnight candle,
      drops onto the place
with the push of the nidifugous chirping needle,
         a bell crank leadplant,
     resting in a red scissor over
            the lumps of steel,
      then rising
         with
    throstle
   smoke,
jazz dust,
         rumbly with the Blues,
      the old rumormonger taking us

> to the juke,
>   (the Bambara word that is
> wicked
>
> !)
>
> bouncing resin polymer   lost to the racy sough
>   of "*Baby she got a phonograph,*
>   *and it won't say a lonesome word*
>   *Baby she got a phonograph*
>   *and it won't say a lonesome word*
>   *What evil have I done*
>   *what evil has the poor girl heard?*"

False Love

1

My hair is black and glossy but I am not Bessie Smith. Belting
out pink sequins in the shithouse night, dying for sweet conversation
or a gesture. Who left this light on?
When, perjuring yourself and hating, a loom of moon,
you break, you are a smooth ballast in a ship belly. . . . You swagger
around, fat astral minion, a green parrot, soft emerald, trying
to right yourself. When you laugh, your eyes narrow into a prism.

2

She was Sean herself ere evensong time.

3

I don't care which part of the triangle I am. Each corner
blesses. Eventually, an edge, a gene, a sparkle dwindles
me down to a bone. I enter you—your corner—ready.
Poles of morals switch charges, losing clarity. A bear trained
to a gypsy's flute, sober & tearful. Out there forcing a field
of fire, a half-human sucking. The field glistens.
You have seen it, black as shelves.

The Sweet Obsession Bleeds from Singer

Singer is dead today and in the ground forever.
How astonishing, his blue vapor
is seeping, not consuming itself, outward
from his honey and body. He is buried
in fine linen, in the old style,
and his saxophone is engraved as a tiger
lily. There was love in him.
His love was not *a wild stag*,
nor *fragrant oils*, nor *hills of cinnamon*.
It was a light through the ocean,
cool and content. He handed this poem to me
and was gone, sifting up to the surface:

> All the passions of my organs
> Are soft doorways. The garden
> Turns inside out. One dream
> Is white as a sky, one black
> And crowded as trees. Each
> With a door, a rude odor, a reed.

Remember him, darkest eyes,
playing like hell in the mountains,
love like that blue, making up
in depth for what it lacked
in brightness . . . We will not speak
of love with him again.

Loren Goodman (1968–) *Famous Americans,* 2002

A native of Wichita, Kansas, Loren Goodman is an associate professor of creative writing and English literature at Yonsei University/Underwood International College in Seoul, South Korea. He is also the author of the poetry collections *Suppository Writing* (2008) and *New Products* (2010).

The Prize

I don't win the prize—
I call up Charles and we decide to meet
Charles also fails to win the prize. I get together
Some poetry and get on the train. When I get to 168th street
I get off and walk up to 179th and Charles
"Hi Charles"
Charles says hi. "Can I get you a drink?"
"Sure, I'll have a glass of Coke. Would you like
Some of my orange juice?" Charles politely refuses
Charles' room is very nice, the walls are covered
With colorful and witty collages he himself makes
"I like them," I say
"Thank you," he replies
"So who wants to go first?"
"I'll go first," says Charles
Charles reads a good short piece in a mellow voice
"That was good"
"Really?"
"Yes—I like the blue magnets," I tell him
"Yeah" Charles smiled, "Now you read"
"O.K."
I read a long poem in a mellow voice
"Wow" says Charles, shaking his head
"That was good"
"Oh yeah?"

"Yeah. Was that 'neurofelons'?"
"Yeah" I chuckle, "neurofelons"
"Hey listen to this"
Then Charles reads another poem
"Good stuff"
'You like it?"
"Yeah, I like it. That's very good how you use colors,
Colors and images and sounds"
"Thanks. Now you read"
"O.K. buddy"
I read a poem
I look up and Charles is on the edge
Of his bed, looking off nowhere
Nodding his head, he waits and murmurs
"Very good, very good. That was a good poem"
"You serious?"
"Yeah, I'm serious. There's something about the way
You use sounds and images, it's good"
After more we get tired of reading
I just put on my scarf and I put on my hat
And leave. I finally find someone on the street
Who will tell me where the subway is. I get there
And wait for the elevator to take me to track level
The elevator pulls up and I get in and there is only
Me and the elevator man and a woman pressed up against him
They whisper without moving their lips
And tilt their heads infinitesimally

There is no sound as she crinkles her hand
Around his blue uniform and he tells her goodbye
The woman is very black, parched, small next to him
She looks too attractive for a fat guy like him
He moves the lever down and tilts his cap
"This city no good." I look up. "No, this city
Is no place for a man"
"Tell me about it," I say

"There are too many women here and not enough men,
They wear a man out, you know?"
"Right on, man"
He picks at grey frizz on his scalp—"and violence,
Dirt and violence"
"Yeah" I say
"You go to college?"
"Yeah"
"I used to go, but the money ran out
The money's good here, but it's no place,
Nowhere for a man to be"
"Yeah"
"Every day more violence
More violence and more dirt,
I'm gonna leave, no place for a man to be"
The elevator door opens. I shake his hand
His eyes are half-closed and watery
"Yeah" I say, "yeah, yeah, yeah"

Interviews

(1)

A: What disturbs you?

B: The fact that I have a skeleton inside.

A: May your anxiety be applicable to other forms of art?

B: First, it should be noted that anxiety itself is a form of art, and that
    I am not concerned with forms.

A: You have developed a reputation in your interviews for becoming
    evasive—how do you respond?

B: Would you rather I become a vase? Or jump in a pond? I feel that I
    am as necessary as my face.

A: What are your thoughts on control and merit?

B: Merit has its badges, while control is another form of emptiness.

A: Scholars have wrangled over whether you are a nationalist or a sensationalist . . .

A: What do you think of the weak?

B: Five days is never enough—five teeth cannot fill a mouth—let us have 20–28 day weeks.

(2)

Q: What would you do if you got $10,000?

A: I dunno. Maybe I go somewhere else.

Q: Where?

A: Puerto Rico—you know—it's been twenty years. Twenty years, never been there.

Q: What is that you're eating?

A: Lot a stuff.

Q: Yeah, but what?

A: Mac and cheese. Potato. Spinach. Chicken. Rolls.

Q: Where'd you get it?

A: Julio said he's hungry. He calls on the phone. Mike said fix him up too. So hey, I said Julio fix me up too.

Q: They fixed you up, huh.

A: Yeah (smiles).

Q: Would you do that (bunji jumping)?

A: No-o-o-o.

Q: No? Why not? Would you do it for money?

A: (Pause) Yeah.

Q: How much?

A: I dunno . . . a hundred, two hundred dollars.

Q: What about an airplane, how much to jump out of an airplane?

A: No, I don't do that.

Q: Not for a thousand?

A: Huh-uh.

Q: Ten-thousand?

A: No way, no.

(3)

A: What kind of music do you listen to?

B: Philosophy.

A: You've mentioned, in other interviews, having studied with those who believe, quote, "there is only one story." What implication, if any, has this so-called "literary monotheism" for your work and religious politics?

B: Yes.

A: How does the way you speak relate to words?

B: I cherish words. This affects my voice. It's not usage. Sometimes I am speakless. Logic. Mimicry. Imitation. Outcry.

A: Would you say this is systematic?

B: Nothing could be further from the truth. After I wrote *Boogaloo Volts* some students approached me—this was during the 60s when such systematic approaches were widely denigrated—and I told them I was concerned only with truth in its manifold forms. This incident, you may recall, was the basis for my stained-glass piece "Vinny."

A: This is another facet—would you say you have been accepted by the community of fine artists?

B :   There is a mutual lack of disrespect.

A: Say something about your children's works.

B: All of us, we are children.

Exploded

I got a ton of vibes from Jennifer and Yun-Su
But I didn't really get any vibes from Christine
But that's O.K. cause I was giving a lot of vibes
To Jennifer. It's funny, I got a call from Ricardo
It's very subtle, how I approach the entire evening
I was trying to show myself off in a certain light
And they were getting into it. In the bagel shop
There were two policemen and I turned to Christine
And said, there's something to—then she put her
Hand over my mouth and said I love the way you talk—
I was thinking maybe. It wasn't so easy, we just

Peter Streckfus (1969–) *Cuckoo,* 2003

Born in San Antonio, Texas, Peter Streckfus studied at the University of Texas
at Austin and George Mason University, where he is now an associate professor
and teaches in the creative writing program. Among his honors are the Brodsky
Rome Prize Fellowship in Literature from the American Academy in Rome and the
Fordham University Poets Out Loud (POL) Editor's Prize for his second collection,
Errings.

Memories Are Nothing, Today Is Important

Trust the moth that flutters in your shirt. Its branch
is nearby. Secondly, you must fix your guitar.
For this you would need knife, glue and string. The hand
is like the head—keep the fingers moving or they stiffen.
You are a fisherman. Cast from the edge of this pond
your hook, snelled to this line with a bit of gut. Cleave
the water below. Lastly, you must name the lights
that line your constellation—how else can you eat?
Call a star *work,* call another cardinal light
my house. You may name the others. Surrounded
by these points, you must keep the balance, lively fish
in this pond of stars, cleaving the waters below.

After Words

Here is a wall. The strange empty space above the wall . . . what is it for?
Here, a little boat, a canopy of silver plastic rattling above it.

Listen to the babe-scare cry of the wind. You are in the unsteady boat and this
poem is a lake.

It's too late now. You are in the boat my little skipperoo, my kitzie koodle.
Look. In the other boat, your son. All the rest, the other sons, the boy you

blinded and the daughter you maimed, the weapons and the armor, is film, a thin and punctured membrane, a fictitious hymen.

There's no place for that weapon here. Come on now, you have no choice. Trust me.

I'll speak nonsense. You speak truth. We'll see what comes of it.

Pilgrim's Progress

Hsüan-tsang and his party traveled fourteen days from Ait Aein to Wansgelt. Look. On the eighth day. Here they come:

His little monkey companion rattles its collar bell;
And the piglet requires more water than they can afford.
The little monkey's bell sounds loudly in the silent heat,
Disharmonious to the company's foot falls;
The piglet requires drink! Oh, the poor foundling piglet
Wants its paddock. Why was it taken from its mama's ninny?
At midday they lunch on tea and cookies;
                                         they nap in wait
For the day's cooler hours. The toothless horse farts, shading
Beneath the locust tree:
                        How could this nag be a long
Whiskered dragon? And this piglet, drinking all my water—
        an immortal?
The monkey jingles its bell, and points its tiny member west.

Richard Siken (1967–) *Crush,* 2004

Richard Siken was born in New York City and studied at the University of Arizona. He is also a social worker and an editor at Spork Press, which he co-founded. A painter, filmmaker, and photographer, Siken has received a National Endowment for the Arts fellowship and a Pushcart Prize. His second collection, *The War of the Foxes,* appeared in 2015.

Dirty Valentine

There are so many things I'm not allowed to tell you.
         I touch myself, I dream.
Wearing your clothes or standing in the shower for over an hour, pretending
        that this skin is your skin, these hands your hands,
            these shins, these soapy flanks.
    The musicians start the overture while I hide behind the microphone,
trying to match the dubbing
          to the big lips shining down from the screen.
    We're filming the movie called *Planet of Love*—
there's sex of course, and ballroom dancing,
      fancy clothes and waterlilies in the pond, and half the night you're
a dependable chap, mounting the stairs in lamplight to the bath, but then
        the too white teeth all night,
    all over the American sky, too much to bear, this constant fingering,
      your hands a river gesture, the birds in flight, the birds still singing
outside the greasy window, in the trees.
               There's a part in the movie
where you can see right through the acting,
      where you can tell that I'm about to burst into tears,
   right before I burst into tears
        and flee to the slimy moonlit riverbed
           canopied with devastated clouds.
We're shooting the scene where I swallow your heart and you make me

spit it up again. I swallow your heart and it crawls

right out of my mouth.

You swallow my heart and flee, but I want it back now, baby. I want it back.

Lying on the sofa with my eyes closed, I didn't want to see it this way,
everything eating everything in the end.

We know how the light works,

we know where the sound is coming from.

Verse. Chorus. Verse.

I'm sorry. We know how it works. The world is no longer mysterious.

Wishbone

You saved my life he says. I owe you, I owe you everything.
You don't, I say, you don't owe me squat, let's just get going, let's just
get gone, but he's relentless,
keeps saying I owe you, says Your shoes are filling with your own
damn blood, you must want something, just tell me, and it's yours.

But I can't look at him, can hardly speak:
I took the bullet for all the wrong reasons, I'd just as soon kill you myself,
I say. You keep saying I owe you, I owe . . . but you say the same thing
every time. Let's not talk about it, let's just not talk.

Not because I don't believe it, not because I want it any different, but I'm
always saving and you're always owing and I'm tired of asking to settle
the debt. Don't bother. You never mean it
anyway, not really, and it only makes me that much more ashamed.

There's only one thing I want, don't make me say it, just get me bandages,
I'm bleeding, I'm not just making conversation.

There's smashed glass glittering everywhere like stars. It's a Western,
Henry. It's a downright shoot-em-up. We've made a graveyard
out of the bone white afternoon.

It's another wrong-man-dies scenario, and we keep doing it Henry,
keep saying until we get it right . . . but we always win and we never quit.

See, we've won again,
here we are at the place where I get to beg for it, where I get to say Please,

for just one night, will you lie down next to me, we can leave our clothes on,
        we can stay all buttoned up . . .
But we both know how it goes—I say *I want you inside me* and you hold
my head underwater, I say *I want you inside me* and you split me open
        with a knife.
I'm battling monsters, I'm pulling you out of the burning buildings
and you say *I'll give you anything* but you never come through.
        Even when you're standing up
you look like you're lying down, but will you let me kiss your neck, baby?
Do I have to tie your arms down? Do I have to stick my tongue in your
        mouth like the hand of a thief,
like a burglary, like it's just another petty theft? It makes me tired,
Henry. Do you see what I mean? Do you see what I'm getting at?
        I swear, I end up
feeling empty, like you've taken something out of me, and I have to search
my body for the scars, thinking *Did he find that one last tender place to*
        sink his teeth in?
I know you want me to say it, Henry, it's in the script, you want me to say
Lie down on the bed, you're all I ever wanted and worth dying for, too . . .
        but I think I'd rather keep the bullet.
It's mine, see, I'm not giving it up. This way you still owe me, and that's
as good as anything. You can't get out of this one, Henry, you can't get it
        out of me, and with this bullet lodged in my chest,
covered with your name, I will turn myself into a gun, because I'm hungry
and hollow and just want something to call my own. I'll be your
        slaughterhouse, your killing floor, your morgue
and final resting, walking around with this bullet inside me like the bullet
was already there, like it's been waiting inside me the whole time.
        Do you want it? Do you want anything I have?
Will you throw me to the ground like you mean it, reach inside and wrestle
it out with your bare hands? If you love me, Henry, you don't love me
        in a way I understand.
Do you know how it ends? Do you feel lucky? Do you want to go home
now? There's a bottle of whiskey in the trunk of the Chevy and a
        dead man at our feet

staring up at us like we're something interesting. This is where the evening
splits in half, Henry, love or death. Grab an end, pull hard,
        and make a wish.

Road Music

1

The eye stretches to the horizon and then must continue up.
                                     Anything past the horizon
     is invisible, it can only be imagined. You want to see the future but
you only see the sky. Fluffy clouds.
                            Look—white fluffy clouds.
          Looking back is easy for a while and then looking back gets
murky. There is the road, and there is the story of where the road goes,
     and then more road,
the roar of the freeway, the roar of the city sheening across the city.
                        There should be a place.
At the rest stop, in the restaurant, the overpass, the water's edge . . .

2

He was not dead yet, not exactly—
     parts of him were dead already, certainly other parts were still only
         waiting
for something to happen, something grand, but it isn't
                         always about me,
he keeps saying, though he's talking about the only heart he knows—

     He could build a city. Has a certain capacity. There's a niche in his chest
where a heart would fit perfectly
        and he thinks if he could just maneuver one into place—
                        well then, game over.

3

You wonder what he's thinking when he shivers like that.
               What can you tell me, what could you possibly

tell me? Sure, it's good to feel things, and if it hurts, we're doing it
    to ourselves, or so the saying goes, but there should be
        a different music here. There should be just one safe place
              in the world, I mean
this world. People get hurt here. People fall down and stay down and I don't
    like
      the way the song goes.
        You, the moon. You, the road. You, the little flowers
by the side of the road. You keep singing along to that song I hate. Stop
    singing.

Jay Hopler (1970–) *Green Squall,* 2005

Born in San Juan, Puerto Rico, Jay Hopler earned degrees from New York University, Johns Hopkins University Writing Seminars, the Iowa Writers' Workshop, and Purdue University. His second collection, *The Abridged History of Rainfall,* was a finalist for the National Book Award in 2016. Other honors include a Whiting Award, the Rome Prize in Literature, and a fellowship from the Lannan Foundation. He is professor of English at the University of South Florida in Tampa.

Nothing to Do Now but Sit and Wait

1

A pair of African parakeets lands in the backyard
And vanishes, or seems to, because their feathers

Are a green that matches the grass almost exactly
And because the light by which the lawn is being

Lit is weaker than it used to be —

2

                                   Last-legged,

A little closer to ghostly; a little closer to October
Than to April, actually—, though it's not quite as

Visibly bristled or as sharply defined. April's got
A way of doing that, slumming about in autumn's

Ragged clothes, throwing long, funereal shadows,
Taking shallow breaths —

3

                         The parakeets are preening,
Plucking feathers from their breasts. The wind is

Bearing them away so quickly—, so quietly. It's
Like they were never here.

And the Sunflower Weeps for the Sun, Its Flower

1

There is a hole in the garden. It is empty. I envy it.

Emptiness: the only freedom there is
In a fallen world.

2

Father Sunflower, forgive me —. I have been so preoccupied with
    my backaches and my headaches,
With my sore back and my headaches and my beat-skipping heart,

I have ignored the subtle huzzah of the date palms and daisies, of
    the blue daze and the date palms —

3

                              Or don't forgive me, what do I care?
I am tired of asking for forgiveness; I am tired of being frightened
    all the time.
I want to run down the street with a vicious erection,
Impaling everything, screaming obscenities
And flapping my arms; *fuck the date palms,*
Fuck the daisies —

4

As a man, I am a disappointment, I know that.
Is it my fault I was born in shadow? Through the banyan trees,

An entourage of slovenly blondes
Comes naked and begging—

5

My days fly from me as though from a murderer.
Can you blame them?
Behind us, the house is empty and quiet as light.

What have I done, Mother,
That I should spend my life
Alone?

Aubade

1

Standing next to a large white pot
Filled to overflowing with orange

And yellow snapdragons, my old
Coonhound looks across the dew-

Strewn lawn at the magnolia tree.
Suddenly, from somewhere deep

Within the squall of all those big
And sloppy blossoms, a desolate

Call rings out.

2

                    This morning, still
And warm, heavy with the smells

Of gardenia and Chinese wisteria,
The first few beams of spring sun-

Light filtering through the flower-
Crowded boughs of the magnolia,

I cannot conceive a more genuine,
More merciful, form of happiness

Than solitude.

3

In a single, black and ragged line,
The shadow of the magnolia tree

Draws nearer to the flower pots.
The coonhound lowers her snout

To its dark edge —. What was it
We heard call out so mournfully?

To what heartbreak would a call
Like that be heir? The air is still,

But differently.

Jessica Fisher (1976–) *Frail-Craft,* 2006

Jessica Fisher was born in Claremont, California, and studied at Swarthmore College and the University of California, Berkeley. A recipient of the Brodsky Rome Prize Fellowship in Literature from the American Academy of Arts and Letters, Fisher teaches at Williams College in Williamstown, Massachusetts. Her second book, Inmost, won the Nightboat Books Poetry Prize and appeared in 2012.

Nonsight

1. Spiral Jetty

Light on water isn't a thing

though it lures the fragile eye
toward blindness

glints along the line that links
body to the disembodied—

The jetty begins underwater, reaches
the unfortunate, unseen ground;

the jetty is underwater—

we followed the shimmer of mica
because the account of their camp
had mentioned a quarry;
waist-deep in water, we swore we felt
the mounded stones.

What the jetty is like—
gone, because the beloved is gone—

What would you see, if you saw it? a stone, stones,
desire's dizzy spiral, that leads from ground
into the groundless, the deep, the windy water.

2. Sun Tunnels

Site: where the particular falls—

but it was not here
he fell—

nothing
to recommend
this place

nothing here—

a ghost town

down the road, a bar,
the one motel

and yet here's as good as any
since *site* first meant sorrow,
grief, trouble of any kind—

here's all kinds:
heat and wind and cold,
land parched until the floods

but how to frame the view
on nothing—

a concrete channel

apertures for the sun—
and for the eye

a lens to pry it open—

3. Canal

Because, despite the eye's illusion, parallel lines do not converge: so it was
that we walked the canal in tandem, you on the north side, I on the south. I
watched as you stooped to fix your shoe, as you took off your jacket, then put
it back on again; I knew you were cold, too, when the wind came, and the

rains, and then snow, sleet, hail—such offense taken, though there never
was a crime, never the imagined tryst in the summer canal, our bodies pale
against the nightblack reeds. But if the eye can love—and it can, it does—
then I held you and was held.

Tide

. . .

In your absence there was a flower, an iris there by the sea,
and so I was for once not thinking that any minute it might
drag you under. Because of the flower, the sea was backdrop only,
dusky gray to set its violet burning. You were of course
always in my heart, but it was in my eye, was its very color.
. . .

Deep water, sorrow, and why?

But even for the prisoner shackled where seawater washes
twice a day at high tide, the torture is not, I think,
in the fact of the tide, since its rising and falling
is sign of nothing but movement without determination,
of a course that is set and so is run, for no other reason.
. . .

Nothing changed, but when you came to me and traced along my shoulders
until the lines of your tracing met at mid-spine, there was so clearly then
a dress of black shimmering feathers, in straps that widened to cover
the breasts, to cover the blades that sprang as wings there, and I was then
sorrow's blossoming, abundant as nighttime, radiant in mourning.

The Hunger for Form

Sidewinder's trail in the windswept desert, that's how I saw

the snaking hairs leading down—

I'd not yet been there, I did not know how makeshift the rim.

If you sit in the front row

then you are on stage

if you see blood on the glass
then you have chosen blood

and because matter hungers for form, from form into form it passed—

Dragon of Love, love's devourer
hunger has an end:

here it is

the winding path
come full stop

what sand conceals it will reveal, in the wind

Fady Joudah (1971–) *The Earth in the Attic,* 2007

Fady Joudah was born in Austin, Texas, to Palestinian refugee parents and grew up in Libya and Saudi Arabia. He studied at the University of Georgia, the Medical College of Georgia, and the University of Texas Health Sciences in Houston, where he is now a physician. Joudah's other collections are *Alight* (2013), *Textu* (2014), and *Footnotes in the Order of Disappearance* (2018). He won a Guggenheim Fellowship and, for his translations of Darwish and Zaqtan, the PEN Center USA award and the Griffin International Poetry Prize, respectively.

Proposal

I think of god as a little bird who takes
To staying close to the earth,
The destiny of little wings
To exaggerate the wind
And peck the ground.

I see Haifa
By my father and your father's sea,
The sea with little living in it,
Fished out like a land.

I think of a little song and
How there must be a tree.

I choose the sycamore
I saw split in two
Minaret trunks on the way
To a stone village, in a stone-thrower mountain.

Were the villagers wrong to love
Their donkeys and wheat for so long,
To sing to the good stranger
Their departure song?

I think of the tree that is a circle
In a straight line, future and past.
I wait for the wind to send
God down, I become ready for song.

I sing, in a tongue not my own:
We left our shoes behind and fled.
We left our scent in them
Then bled out our soles.
We left our mice and lizards

There in our kitchens and on the walls.
But they crossed the desert after us,
Some found our feet in the sand and slept,
Some homed in on us like pigeons,
Then built their towers in a city coffin for us . . .

I will probably visit you there after Haifa.
A little bird to exaggerate the wind
And lick the salt off the sea of my wings. I think

God reels the earth in when the sky rains
Like fish on a wire.

And the sea, each time it reaches the shore,
Becomes a bird to see of the land
What it otherwise wouldn't.
And the wind through the trees
Is the sea coming home.

Morning Ritual

Every morning, after the roosters
Crow back whatever prayers were passed
Down to them that dawn
From the keeper of their order up in heaven,

I drink my coffee
To the sound of squealing pigs
Being bled to death
In the market up the road —the same market

Where I buy my fresh bread
For my peanut butter and jam. The pigs
Are bled through an armpit wound.
You can see it coming throughout the day before,

Hogs tied sideways to the backs of bicycles,
Tight as a spine, going as far as the border
Where the price is right. You will pass them
On the asphalt to the town I get

The peanut butter and jam from. They know
The bikeways out of nowhere
And suddenly they're alongside your jeep.
I lie: only goats are taken to the border.

The goats are bled differently,
And skinning is harmless after slaughter:
All you do is a vertical skin-slit
Between the shinbone and Achilles tendon,

Stick a thin metal rod
Through it, up the thigh, pull it out
Then blow, mouth to hole,
Until your breath dehisces

Fascia and dermis, reaching the belly:
Your hands
Should even out the trapped air.
Between blowing and tapping

The animal is tight as a drum.
Now the knife that slit the throat.
Who knows
What you'll need skin for.

Additional Notes on Tea

In Cairo a boy's balcony higher than a man's deathbed.

The boy is sipping tea,

The view is angular like a fracture.

Surrounding the bed, women in wooden chairs.

They signal mourning with a scream.

Family men on the street run up the stairs and drink raven tea.

On the operating table in Solwezi a doctor watches a woman die.

Tea while the anesthetic wears off,

While the blade is waiting, tea.

The doctor says the woman knows god is sleeping

Outside heaven in a tent.

God is a refugee dreaming of tea.

Once upon a time an ocean married a sea to carry tea around.

Land was jealous.

So it turned into desert and gave no one wood for ships.

And when ships became steel,

Land turned into ice.

And when everything melted, everything tasted like tea.

Once upon a time there was a tea party in Boston.

Tea, like history, is a non sequitur.

I prefer it black. The Chinese drink it green.

Arda Collins (1974–) *It Is Daylight,* 2008

Born in New York City, Arda Collins studied at the Iowa Writers' Workshop and the University of Denver. She is the recipient of the May Sarton Prize and the American Academy of Arts and Sciences Poetry Prize. Collins currently teaches at Smith College, where she is the Grace Hazard Conkling Writer in Residence.

From Speaking in the Fall

Was that the river?
No, it wasn't the river, oh, it was the sink.

We don't need a known reason, I say,
we can have our own ones;
we don't even have to know what they are;
they're from before all this,
they're from before everything,
from when the universe was a dark and cold place with nothing in it.
I feel that there is no telephone.
I see myself
as a cat who has learned how to imitate talking on the phone
through observation,
has learned how to pick up the receiver with its paw
and turns to look at the viewer
as though in mid-sentence; or maybe as a person
who has never seen a phone, and says blah blah blah
to the dial tone. The silence that once existed
in the dark cold universe: translated, the empty sound
is a place—the inside of the phone. Infinity,
I say, there it is.
This is where we all go to
when we touch each other;
this is what supernatural is.
I feel I can break

away everything. Today dark arrives
at a new hour.
Welcome, hour,
thank you
for transparenting yourself.
I will go quietly
into another room
into quietry
for you;
it'll just be us.

Poem #9

And felt ashamed at this
clarity
though I've made a mess out of it
but knew
listening to the neighbor shovel
heavy ice in the driveway
and the sun was out
that it was a thing to go forward to;
Finally willing to talk to the trees,
maybe for the first time
ever
and like feeling ashamed
at what they would say to me;
confusion at the shrubs now looks good;
all the things that are called
that I don't know how they're called—
I'm brought to the low
approaching world below the upper air
contrite at how it continues
at my back,
while looking through the closet,
moving through the sheltered rooms

in the gentle passing of things I remember,
that I can stand still any moment in here
something will happen;
to think, now far away, about going down the beach road
past the marshes in late afternoon
and the marsh grass touched the edges of my eyeballs;
all the world inside this old afternoon
light won't become
come closer
stay there.

Elegy

She asks me if the great aunt has been around lately.
What do you mean by lately? I say.
I've been doing too much of this recently.
She doesn't say anything.
No, I tell her. No.
I think it's because I've been shirking my duties;
she thinks this.
Maybe she's right, or maybe she's not right at all;
we can't always agree;
I don't think I've seen her,
I say,
because she answered the question. Remember?
After the great aunt died,
I saw her all the time.
She never said anything,
which I assumed was a reflection of my own
failings. I decided she wasn't saying anything
because she was mad, at me,
and also in general. She was a kind and stubborn person when alive.
She had survived a genocide, and spent the back end of her life
in a small room, coming out to eat farina.
I wish this were not what I had to say,

but in spite of how things seem, or what I think
I might know otherwise,
the truth is that I know almost nothing
about any family members, because
I wasn't there for their lives. Stories
are not the same thing. As she got deeper into being dead,
she became—*tan*;
her white hair was longer,
and she didn't wear it up anymore. Based on a loosely conceived pre-colonial
     aesthetic,
I thought the new hairstyle made her look mannish. In life,
I have never seen her tan;
it occurred to me
that she must have
been tan, when the Turks marched her family across the desert;
but that's the only time I would know about. I never once saw her at a beach.
A dead person with a tan is worrisome:
had she
gone to hell?
That's impossible, I thought. *Genocide?*
Farina?
Doesn't she automatically get her ticket punched?
And that's assuming that hell is anywhere.
This is so stupid, I think,
This isn't—
—what?
This isn't what?
After I saw her a number of times,
starting in the predictable moss-covered stone chambers
and ending on an astringent deck of a ship
heading for probably
a Greek island with one olive tree on it,
I felt an urgent question forming.
I didn't know what it was though.
It came to me though: Is it better to be alive or dead?
She said "It's better alive."

Ken Chen (1979–) *Juvenilia,* 2009

Born in San Diego, California, Ken Chen studied at the University of California, Berkeley, and Yale Law School. Chen works as a lawyer in New York City, where he also directs the Asian American Writers' Workshop. In 2011 he founded Culture-Strike, a national organization designed to bring artists into the migrant justice movement.

My Father and My Mother Decide My Future and How Could We Forget Wang Wei?

> *The suitcase open on the bed.*
> *My grandfather is packing up his organs.*
> *When he is done, he takes a taxi to my grandmother's house for*
>   *supper.*
> *Exits the empty car to Taipei alley.*
>
> *Dissolve. Now the Los Altos lot.*

So did you listen to him, my Father says taking his keys out of the ignition. You should become a lawyer but your grandfather says anything is fine. As long as you're the best.

> My Father stays, my Mother stays silent. I sit and suck my thumb.

I saw your painting. It was beautiful, my Mother says to Wang Wei, restrained beside me by backseat-belt and streetlight world—Wang Wei who says:

> In the silent bamboo woods, sitting along
> Playing strings and bellowing long.

But America is allergic to bamboo, my Father says to Wang Wei. They love skill sets, cash and the first person singular,
the language of C++ not our English. Steps out,
shuts the door, puts gas pump by Acura trunk. My father's son
does not understand, forgets the Chinese

he never remembered. But my mother holds words in her mouth:
The Peking opera soundtrack of my childhood.
You sound like it. I'd listen to it on the radio. You know, when I had to
sweep the floor. And then Wang Wei:

> Nobody knows but the deep grove
> and the luminous moon that glows in response.

California moon not glow—or as the translation might say, irradiates
    instead
like beige screen before my Mother, now at HP after Taipei and
    degree in Home Ec
and divorce. My Mother like the moon which rents light from its past,
my Mother who says, looking at the dashboard, You should listen to
your father. I don't know. Here he comes.
    My Father unlocks the door and says, Dropped the keys in the
toilet. But that's what life is like. You're young, my Father says,
I'm not sure to me or Wang Wei, You don't understand
the world, the world which loves those who
enter it and then Wang Wei:

> Red hearts in the southern country
> Spring comes with stems enlarging.
> I didn't know you two were still together.

We're not, my Father says. He is unsentimental and gestures
at the wish that furnishes the mind of his son.
    Your son? asks Wang Wei. He has seen me and become real, as
though a ghost could die into a man. Not the monk you quite expect,
Wang Wei wears a cowboy's deadened face and stares
at you not unlike an establishing
shot. He says, Who are you?
    Like the scene in the movie, where the actors
find the camera and say Stop
looking at me, they quit the car and stand. And I say:

> Wish you'd gather some, caught me
> More of this thing that is longing.

And Wang Wei asks Who are you?
And my Father says Decide.

He is only waiting to die, my father tells my mother who tells me

> March into Grand Hotel while red fire flays it
> Pall-bearing waiters lay him on circular table
> He dead then why his lips still suck Marlboro Lights?

At Taipei Station, I Saw This City Undress!

> Yes, he is dead and what can we do
> I met a man infected by English and he said please let me practice
>   on you

My grandfather shuffles into the black alleyways
like a specter whose scene in the Act has ended
My eyes follow him as he steps on the floor tiles, black and chipped teeth
My grandfather says, *Come back in two years when I am eighty because I*
    will die then

Graffiti outside a fourth-floor University window. *Who kill my soul?*

> They have some problems stripping the veins from his chest but slowly
> he manages to crawl into
> a glass jar that we slide into a birch box
> His picture on the front
> The hallway is walled with birch boxes

Living room lit by dimming cigarette:
Can I get you anything from California?
No.
He says in Chinese—This is only what will happen to everyone

Adjust your eyes to the unlit room.

Yes, No, Yes, the Future, Gone, Happy, Yes, No, Yes, Cut, You

The first sentence of this poem is not about you.
    In this respect, it is unlike the last sentence and my heart.
Is the heart a thing that can be about something?
    We were about
    to break up and after that, we broke up.
Did it have to end in this—I mean, was there anything
else I could have done?
    See fifth-to-last sentence.
When dinner wilts into memory,
when the frost florescent bars in parking lots
spangle out like bones blooming from a tree,
when I busy myself out towards sleep, wheel around,
adorned-in by alone from every direction,
when the moon outdopples the ambulance siren and the evening
pollutes itself with reference, suffused by our lost
elbow-clasping smoky-tender moist and utmost shirtless plucked-up naked
    nights—
when I miss you, does that make the first sentence false?
    Because I think about you more now that
    my life no longer mentions you.
If statement is when
antecedent and consequent clap their hands: having thought
for a while, having understood
what we have built behind us, let me ask
what is the wilderness
charring the scene before me?
    It is called the future, the branches feathery
    and lowing in the wind.
Now call the consequent a painting and why don't I see you in this painting?
    Now that you are no longer here, a scar floats as halo
    above my scalp and when you come back, I grow jealous
    of your talents.

What are my talents?

    You are so good at being happy, a skill I too
    practice (or try to practice) and despise.

Well, don't worry—I've been to the future and seen that scar
evaporate into a crown. Will you call me in September?

    The conversation was boring—fat pauses like
    lakes and I didn't know what to say.

Did I want to hang up?

    No, never. I must have loved you.

Are questions like relationships?

    Questions have answers, unless they are questions nine or two.

What are questions for?

    One can use a question mark for many things. For example: as a
    sickle for cutting people's hearts off.

How can you cut someone off with a question?

    You know, like when I said, "Yeah, but we're still in love with
    each other, right?" and you told me the answer.

Katherine Larson (1977–) *Radial Symmetry,* 2010

Katherine Larson grew up in Arizona. She earned a degree in ecology and evolutionary biology at the University of Arizona and a degree in creative writing from the University of Virginia. The recipient of the Kate Tufts Discovery Prize, a Ruth Lilly Fellowship, and the Union League Civic and Arts Foundation Poetry Prize, Larson has worked as a molecular biologist and field ecologist.

Statuary

The late cranes throwing
their necks to the wind stay
somewhere between
the place that rain begins
and the place that it ends
they seem to exist just there
above the horizon at least
I only see them that way
tossed up
against the gray October
light not heavy enough
for feet to be useful or
useless enough to make
gravity untie its string. I'm sick
of this stubbornness
but the earthworms
seem to think it all right
they move forward
and let the world pass
through them they eat
and eat at it, content to connect
everything through
the individual links

of their purple bodies to stay
one place would be death.
But somewhere between
the crane and the worm
between the days I pass through
and the days that pass
through me
is the mind. And memory
which outruns the body and
grief which arrests it.

Risk

In the dream, I am given a monkey heart
and told to be careful how I love
because of the resulting infection.
Suddenly a hard-boiled egg with no yolk,
I pitch down a great hill in a holy city,
past the flaming beakers of ethanol,
the lapis bowls in which Science
would peel me apart. And when I skid
into a fleshy patch of grass,
I unroll into a grub. A grub with the mind
of a girl, a girl with the lips of an insect.
A voice says, *Metamorphosis*
will make you ugly. I answer:
Radiance will change its name.
In the heat I squirm and shrug
out of my summer suit and breathless
split into a cotton dress. It is almost
evening. There are fireflies.
On the lawn of my childhood house,
an operating table, doctors,
a patient under a sheet. I walk up.

Under the webbing of IVs,
a surgeon hands me a silver comb
and I start brushing the patient's hair
like I did my mother's when I was a girl.
The nurse lifts the sheet.
It isn't my mother. It's the monkey.
I bend my ear to its dying lips
and it says: *You haven't much time—*
risk it all.

Metamorphosis

> It is astounding how little the ordinary person notices butterflies.
> —Nabokov

We dredge the stream with soup strainers
and separate dragonfly and damselfly nymphs—
their eyes like inky bulbs, jaws snapping
at the light as if the world was full of
tiny traps, each hairpin mechanism
tripped for transformation. Such a ricochet
of appetites insisting *life, life, life* against
the watery dark, the tuberous reeds. Tell me—
how do they survive passage? I rinse our cutlery
in the stream. Heat so heavy it hurts the skin.
The drone of wild bees. We swim through cities
buried in seawater, we watch the gods decay.
We dredge the gods of other civilizations.
The sun, for example. Before the deity became a
star. *Jasper scarabs excavated from the hearts of*
kings. Daylight's blue-green water pooling at the
foot of falls. Sandstones where the canyon spills
its verdant greens in vines. Each lunar
resurrection, each helix churning in the cells

of a sturgeon destined for spawning—
Not equilibrium, but buoyancy. A hallway
with a thousand human brains carved out of crystal.
Quiet prisms until the sunlight hits.

Eduardo C. Corral (1970–) *Slow Lightning,* 2011

Eduardo Corral was born in Casa Grande, Arizona, and studied at Arizona State University and the Iowa Writers' Workshop. The first Latinx poet to win the Yale Series of Younger Poets, Corral was a founding fellow of the CantoMundo Writers Conference, an organization that supports Latinx poets via an annual poetry workshop and conference. Corral's awards include a Whiting Award, a National Endowment for the Arts fellowship, and the Hodder Fellowship from Princeton. He teaches at North Carolina State University in Raleigh.

Acquired Immune Deficiency Syndrome

I approach a harp
    abandoned
in a harvested field.
    A deer leaps
out of the brush
    and follows me

in the rain, a scarlet
    snake wound
in its dark antlers.
    My fingers
curled around a shard
    of glass—

it's like holding the hand
    of a child.
I'll cut the harp strings
    for my mandolin,
use the frame as a window
    in a chapel
yet to be built. I'll scrape

off its blue
lacquer, melt the flakes
down with
a candle and ladle
and paint
the inner curve
of my soup bowl.

The deer passes me.
I lower my head,
stick out my tongue
to taste
the honey smeared
on its hind leg.

In the field's center
I crouch near
a boulder engraved
with a number
and stare at a gazelle's
blue ghost,
the rain falling through it.

Caballero

Only symmetry harbors loss.
—Lorna Dee Cervantes

Throatlatch.
Crupper. Martingale. Terret. My breath
tightens around him,
like a harness. Once a year
he eats a spoonful of dirt
from his father's grave.

In his sleep
he mutters lines

                    from his favorite flick,
          Capulina

Contra Los Vampiros.
Summers he hunts underground water with a
          dowsing rod made
                    from the sun-bleached spine
of a wolf. When a word stalls
          on his tongue he utters,
                              Sufferin succotash.
                    Stout. Apache-
                              dark. Curious
                    and quick.

          He builds up the bridge
of his nose with clay. Mornings he sings: Dices
          que me quieres pero
                    mi tienes trabajando. He spits
     into a tin cup each time
          lightning strikes. In the small
                              of his back I bury
                    my hands. Once,
                              lost in the desert,
                    he ate beak-

          punctured pitayas;
pissed on his fingers to keep them warm. Weekly
          he plays poker with other
                    mojados. The winning hands
     teach him more English. Sawmill.
          Three Kings. Presto.

                              He pronounces
                    my name beautifully.
                              His thumb: flecha
               de sal,

          gancho de menta.

In Nogales he bought a whisky-colored mutt.
He named it Nalgas.
He slipped a canary into
his father's coffin: its pecking,
its hunger, smoothing
the creases
of the face.
With an old sock
and black coffee

he polishes his boots.
Rosa salvaje. Corazón salvaje. The inner-
most part of a castle
is the keep. Andale, pues.
When I ride him at night I call out
the name of his first horse.

Monologue of a Vulture's Shadow

I long to return to my master
who knew neither fear nor patience.
My master who years ago spiraled
above a woman
trudging through the desert.
She raised her face & cursed us:
Black Torches of Plague, Turd Blossoms.
She lashed out with her hands,
pinned me to her shoulders.
I went slack.
I called for my master.
I fell across her shoulders like a black shawl.
Now I'm kept on the shelf of an armoire:
perfumed,
my edges embroidered with red thread.
She anchors me to her dress with a cameo of a bird
clutching prey

as if to remind me of when my master flew close to the desert floor
        & I darkened the arroyos

                & the jade geometry of fallen saguaros.

How could I forget?

          Sometimes my master soared so high

              I ceased to blacken the earth.

What became of me in those moments?

          But the scent of decay always lured my master

              earthward.

As my master ate, I ate.

Will Schutt (1981–) *Westerly,* 2012

Will Schutt was born in New York City and graduated from Oberlin College and Hollins University. His honors include a fellowship from the Stadler Center for Poetry and the Amy Lowell Traveling Poetry Fellowship. He has also received a fellowship from the National Endowment for the Arts for his translations from the Italian of Edoardo Sanguineti. His translation *My Life, I Lapped It Up: Selected Poems of Edoardo Sanguineti* was published in 2018. Schutt lives in Baltimore, Maryland.

Fragment from a Coptic Tunic

They draped it over the dead.
        That's how it survived
(frayed, mealy, spotted)
              as a language 10% of the population
speaks inside a temple
             survives on the outskirts of a slum.
Spanish, Hindu, Arabic,
             Greek, each museumgoer's headset
murmurs in the room.
            Last week, twenty-six
Christians were shot in Cairo.
           Neighbors marched the corpses
through the streets, their shirts
             pursed in the heat or parted
by a strange wind. I wonder
             what the salvo of utter faith feels like
compared with the slightly dull
             sensation I get, skimming half
the story ("shock—surprise—
             anger"), squaring the paper
("interim—uprising—alongside—
             against") and planting it in my pocket
like a curved blade in a sheath.

Westerly

Even up close it's hard to tell
whether the white and blue
church tower is defunct or half-finished
or, like every third house
block after prim block, let for summer.
Only an odd patch of moss
flecks the siding, and thin ginger-colored
stains make a noncommittal
braid, like wicker or wings at rest.
From our third-floor window
long scarves of water push
right up against the houses.
They seem to clip the gutter spouts.
If one were Elizabeth Bishop
one might hear it turn into a tidy music.
Tidy and resolved, the way
history says, "Look West, Future-looker,"
and kids worry a blue vein
of hope in their spiral notebooks.
At night after each boat has pulled in
behind the artificial bulwark
moonlight saddles a galvanized tub
of orange marigold and sedum,
and green and burgundy rosettes
creep upward like weird insect antennae
trucking the earth off to Westerly,
Rhode Island, where nirvana is a long time
coming, or untidy, unresolved,
the way stupid hope won't shut up.

After A Silvia

Mirava il ciel sereno,
Le vie dorate e gli orti,
e quinci il mar da lungi, e quindi il monte.
— Giacomo Leopardi

Remember? You used to thumb
through the pages of *Seventeen*
eyeing each snapshot of other
girls on the slopes of girlhood.
The song you sang at school
drifted through the quiet rooms
and out the street. Vague, whatever-will-be,
May took up the air. I dropped
my books. I shoved my papers in a drawer—
half my life sewn shut inside
my father's house—and cupped my ear
to catch the sound of your voice
as you hauled your heavy workload home.
I'd look out at the clear sky,
the bright streets, people's yards,
all the way down to the sea
and all the way up the hillside.
No words really fit what I felt.
The hopeful pitch of then.
To think of that time tightens my chest
and grief ploughs through me.
Shock and blowback, tricks and masks—
why is it nothing keeps its word?
What's with all the lights burning in the distance?
Before winter starved the grass
or some compliment was paid
your modest, nothing-special looks,
some narrow sickness buried you.

Whatever boyhood I had
fate hijacked too. Old friend, is this that
world we stayed awake all night for?
Truth dropped in. Far off,
your cool hand points the way.

Eryn Green (1984–) *Eruv,* 2013

Eryn Green grew up in Park City, Utah, and studied at the University of Utah and the University of Denver. He teaches at the University of Nevada, Las Vegas, and is completing his second book of poems.

The Disaster Takes Care of Everything

There is somewhere
the perfect you in a room
with no boundaries and full
of light—the torch
of chin, hips, thighs, throat
light—my hands
start shaking
smell like flowers
hours after the disaster
all resonant harmonics—traffic
padding down the shoreline tanks
on the beach still in my body
far from any collection of falling
for example airplanes or my—
                    I kept quiet mostly
except when I didn't, shuffled
the self around, measured faults in the ark
looked for correspondence
          what it means

carrying carry

          tender mercy, looking

down at you through

          the trees again

again saying *don't devolve*

into a lesser you

don't be base—

Entropical (the Bulk)

Out-stubborned
emotional sea-urchin
in the shallows (stabbed me) in the shallows of the heart—
I'm the only one without a camera
which makes for difficulties, and the sun
you can't even look at it
even as it sets. I no longer have the right
to ask you who
does that look like? Do
these messages get through?
I know. I wanted to
tell you, right now
my dad is dancing funny
in front of everybody
by the iceplants
just so perfect so
I go out to the water
at the wrong time
don't talk for hours
think through it—only one answer
break up, diffuse
carelessly unto
this wave that floats
the bulk, the wastage
left with

I, this hole in my chest, left
with weekends
emotional

fur traps, no good
            reasons
a test, the affections
a thin freezing
twig of a man, someone saying almost
comically handsome, good
so long as I keep moving, so long
as my feet don't hit the ground
                    oat grass

        globe flower

                    bamboo world

        balsa wood

If I miss you like crazy still
not going to let it beat me. There
is someone calling my name
from the back of a restaurant
like woken from a spell, I should be
clear this is a love poem

Found Well

Not forgotten, just not there
white flowers
in a column, sea shaped air
receding every morning
I stare, saying I am sure
something will happen

I want to be in love and all
the birds keep laughing
opening, opening
Levi I think the heart doesn't skip
but leaps, sends off between

limbs its dream and fingers
crossed helplessly

And what do I want? Music
moved beyond me—cradle
and smell of a new home
from the one I've known
a brand new nursery
I've never seen
sawgrass, meant more
than I do right now
when I'm not looking
and my beer foams over
as I call your name. I gently blow
over the corona. All the white
laughter happens. All flowers

Ansel Elkins (1982–) *Blue Yodel,* 2014

Born and raised in Anniston, Alabama, Ansel Elkins graduated from Sarah Lawrence College and the University of North Carolina, Greensboro, where she currently teaches. Elkins's honors include fellowships from the National Endowment for the Arts, the North Carolina Arts Council, and the American Antiquarian Society.

The Girl with Antlers

I tore myself out of my own mother's womb.
There was no other way to arrive in this world.
A terrified midwife named me Monster
and left me in the pine woods with only the moon.
My mother's blood dripped from my treed head.

In a dream my mother came to me and said
if I was to survive
I must find joy within my own wild self.

When I awoke I was alone in solitude's blue woods.
• • •
A woman found me and took me to her mountain home
high at the end of an abandoned logging road.
We spent long winter evenings by the fire;
I sat at the hearth as she read aloud myths of the Greeks
while the woodstove roared behind me.
She sometimes paused to watch the wall of shadows
cast by my antlers. The shadows danced
across the entire room like an oak's wind-shaken branches.
• • •
The woman was worried when I would not wear dresses.
I walked naked through the woods.
She hung the wash from my head
on hot summer days when I sat in the sun to read.

The woman grew worried when I would not shed
my crown with the seasons as the whitetails did.
"But I am not a whitetail," I said.

. . .

When I became a woman
in the summer of my fifteenth year,
I found myself
suddenly changed in the mirror.
My many-pronged crown had grown
into a wildness all its own;
highly stylized, the bright
anarchic antlers were majestic to my eye.

The woman saw me and smiled. "What you are I cannot say,
but nature has created you.
You are fearfully and wonderfully made."

When night came it brought a full moon.
I walked through the woods to the lake
and knelt in the cool grass on its bank.
I saw my reflection on the water,
I touched my face.
You are fearfully and wonderfully made.

Reverse: A Lynching

Return the tree, the moon, the naked man
Hanging from the indifferent branch
Return blood to his brain, breath to his heart
Reunite the neck with the bridge of his body
Untie the knot, undo the noose
Return the kicking feet to ground
Unwhisper the word *jesus*
Rejoin his penis with his loins
Resheathe the knife
Regird the calfskin belt through trouser loops

Refasten the brass buckle
Untangle the spitting men from the mob
Unsay the word *nigger*
Release the firer's finger from its trigger
Return the revolver to its quiet holster
Return the man to his home
Unwidow his wife
Unbreak the window
Unkiss the crucifix of her necklace
Unsay *Hide the children in the back*, his last words
Repeal the wild bell of his heart
Reseat his family at the table over supper
Relace their fingers in prayer, unbless the bread
Rescind the savagery of men
Return them from animal to human, reborn in the long run
Backward to the purring pickup
Reignite the Ford's engine, its burning headlights
Retreat down the dirt road, tires speeding
Backward into rising dust
Backward past cornfields, past the night-floating moths
Rescind the whiskey from the guts
Unswallowed, unswigged, the tongue unstung
Rehouse the flask in the field coat's interior pocket
Unbare the teeth, unwhet the appetite
Return the howl to its wolf
Return the shovel to the barn, the rope to the horse's stable
Resurrect the dark from its heart housed in terror

Reenter the night through its door of mercy

Sailmaker's Palm

My black-haired bride was made of sails.
She was a ship; her wedding sails were white.
I made her dress with yards of canvas.

Winding stitch after stitch, I sewed all night.

I was a child to the wind.
I listened to it like a father.
I put an inwardly spiraled shell to my ear
to hear what the sea had to say.

A web spun between weeds. Like a memory
I keep forgetting
of being kissed for the first time at the sea;—
her wind-whipped red hair, her bathing suit of cobalt blue.

What is memory but wind
blowing through you?

My bride was a full-rigged ship
being launched to sea. On her maiden voyage
she was thrown into the wild green Atlantic.

At the hour of my death
carry me to the graveyard by boat
as on Bequia, island of the cloud,
where the dead were ferried by oarsmen
who rowed *de dead stroke:*—
they took one stroke through water,
            then feathered the oars,
took the next stroke through the air,
            then feathered the oars.
The oarsmen of the island
transported both body and spirit
into the afterlife.

I saw my wife sailing beneath the light
of a full moon. Her bright sails illumined,
she rides across a ghostly topography.

The shipwright ran a ragged hand down the entire length
of the vessel's hull from stern to stem.
He looked up at the wooden figurehead—

bare breasted, her hair all around her.
Her wild blank eyes unpainted.

When a sailor dies at sea
the ship's sailmaker sews the dead man into a canvas shroud.
Stitch by stitch, the sailmaker closes him tightly round
with twine; he works his way from foot to head.
And the last stitch
he sews through the dead man's nose.

Death, Captain,
is not what I feared it would be.
I was blown through death.
Death blew through me.
I was sewn into the wind itself
as a singing voice blown out to sea.

Noah Warren (1989–) *The Destroyer in the Glass,* 2015

Born in Nova Scotia, Canada, Noah Warren studied at Yale University. A former
Wallace Stegner Fellow in Poetry at Stanford University, he is now in a doctoral
program in English at the University of California, Berkeley, and is completing a
second book of poems, Ark.

Like the Pelican

The shape of the pelican
swings back and forth
across the mouth
of the Cove of Now and Then.

So winter blooms, hot, stark—
three black notes,
you, me, this, float
together from the ark

revolving: wary we touch
fingertips and as our tongues
meet strung nerves thrum and the sea's lungs
boom our chord—a clutch

of heart in teeth—now hollower notes—
listen—
        shark rots on sand,
a breeze drains the land,
and two stars wink out

in rhythm—break open to theme and so prove eternity
is choice and death, choice—
love, its voice—
spread your gaze through my gaze, all pity

for the dying union, drown: this dark water
swallows planets,
dissolves the granite
cape, the reefs of bone—dark water

trickle through my cells, my eyes, persist in me
like the pelican
that I may learn
to see and not to see

Thou in Time

With the mower passing over
the lawn this August morning

shirtless, lightheaded

it is such easy going, you just
push it along and the fresh swathe
follows after, good machine,

and what Mother called the smell of *order*
wafts up from the headless
plants

         around you, around you—

and who has no excuse like you, none?
You cry quietly, birdsong
occurring here and there, as you observe
the sun sinking
into the torn trunks

of trees . . . numbed on the porch
beneath the yellow porch light, you let
mosquitoes settle on your forearms, chest, and throat
and drink deep
motionless, by the hundred

then you rub yourself, and cherry juice—

Please take pity,
speak to me,
come inside.

Look—
I am drinking the rose, now
I drink the thorns.

Empathy

I was the tree all afternoon,
drawing my life from the air.

Thrushes' grace made me haunt of music.
Light streamed into me and was woven

into a gold-green tapestry
that I unmade, made, and laid

to abandon on the golden grass.
When the sun dragged the last light

back into himself, I sighed,
but did not lower my worshipful arms.
• • •
Tonight I see you are the sky,
pierced by a million diamond nails,

your children, that may be dead.
Into nothingness, into me

the light escapes its birth—
but you are torn

and vast, all hide.
The zone of deepest black,

the most riddled, is your heart:
it stretches to your very edge

which now glows wan,
now crumbles away to bluish ash.

. . .

Morning

I study to live my death well.
Through the chilly forest,

my mind ravens on ahead
of my life

like a silent, monstrous bulldozer
chased by a chariot with bells.

Airea D. Matthews (1972–) *Simulacra,* 2016

Airea Matthews grew up in New Jersey and studied at the University of Pennsylvania and the University of Michigan. She has received the Rona Jaffe Writer's Foundation Award and a Kresge Literary Arts Award, among other honors. Matthews teaches at Bryn Mawr College, where she directs the creative writing program.

The Mine Owner's Wife

The bone china had been laid out. The napkins, threadbare, antiqued, yellowing. One gold-rimmed plate with butter in the trench. The wife asked, "How was your day?" His coal-mine mouthshaft widened, to make an utterance, managed only soot and one canary. Canary's wings, blackened and broken, tangled in the web above their heads, suspended in the chandelier's pendalogue. A spider eyed dinner, sharpened its knifeclaw. The mine owner dragged his fork's sharpened tine against his lip, rent his tongue. He bled all over the napkin, made pink the butter dish. His wife handed him her crystal goblet. He wrung his tongue over her glass, spilled garnet into her bowl. Filled his flute. They toasted.

And, this, every single night.

If My Late Grandmother Were Gertrude Stein

I. *Southern Migration*

Leech. Broke speech. Leaf ain't pruning pot. Lay. Lye. Lie. Hair straight off. Arrowed branch and horse joint. Elbow ash. Row fish. Row dog. Slow-milk pig. Blue-water sister. Hogs like willow. Weep crow. Weep cow. Sow bug. Soul narrow. Inchway. Inches away. Over the bridge. Back that way. Fur. Fir needles in coal. Black hole. Black out. Black feet. Blame. Long way still.   Not there.   There. Here.   Same.

II. Feed the Saw

Old Crow. Liquor. Drink. Drunk. Girdle. Grits. Grit. Tea. Grit tea. Tea git. Get shaved. Shook. Shucked. Shit. Flour. Flower. Lard and swallow. Hardedge chew. Chipped tooth bite. Tool chip. Bite. Bloat. Bloat. Bloat. Blight seat. Blight sit tea. Be light city. Down town dim. Slight dark. Old Arc. New Arc. New Ark. New work. Newark. Lark-fed. Corned bread. Bedfeather back. Sunday-shack church fat. Greased-gloved. Dust-rubbed. Cheap-heeled shoe. Window seat. Mirror eye. Window. I. Window. Window. When though. When though. Wind blow. November. December. No cinder. No slumber. No summer. Branch. Branched. Blanched. Fried. Freed.   Fly.   Want. What.   Want. What. Graves want.

III. Miscegenation

Good. Smooth. Curly haired baby. Baby rock-a-bye. My baby. Mama rock-a-bye that baby. Wrestle the earth, baby. No dirt. No. Dirt-shine. Shine. Shine-neck. Porcelain. Tin. Tarnish. Powder milk. Pout her. Milk. Powder-silk inheritance. Front the washtub. Top the bed. Bin. Leaky numbers run in. Run in. Run on. Red fevers hold your palm. Sweat it out. Hot. Hot. Heat the rest. Pretty melt that wax. Wide flower. Ellis-Island daddy. O, Daddy's bar. Banned. Mongrel hum. Come. Come now. Little bones bend. Old crack. Creak. Crank. Crick. Curly Q. Fuck. Them. Then   fuck them. You hear me. Walk through good-haired baby. Half   of you.   Belong.

IV. Gertrude Stein

Who. Bills mount. Picasso. Who. Matisse. Who. Mortgage. No currency canvass. Pay brushes. Stroke. Stroke. Bridge. Brittle. Blend. 10 miles daybreak. 10 miles they break. We broke. No brick. Widgets in the envelope. No railroad green. Agriculture. Pea snap. Earth under nails. Spine and stilt woman. Roach-kill heel woman. Roaches in the crawl. Woman, creep. Keep 5th grade. Every where. Wear every where. We're every. Where. Any. How. We sacrifice and hammer. They sacrifice the hammer. Never. Ax and hatchet make callous. Hard hand. Prison-pen privilege. Prison. Privilege pinned. Bar-thorn pinned. Pine cross. Crown.

Weight. Weight. Wait. Iron is harder. Chicken fat can is full of spark.
Spark kill. Ore. Sparkle. Or. Spark cull. Spark. Cull. Hoe. Heave-ho.
Heave-holy. Heavy. Heavy. Heavy lights genius. That is that Gertrude.
Who.

Sexton Texts Tituba from a Bird Conservatory

　—*for Margaret Walker and Molly Means*

FRI., JULY 2, 7:07 PM
"Eat, the stones a poor man breaks,"

FRI., JULY 2, 7:18 PM
Still stale as they were
when Memaw died.
Half-mad on working-class
hunger; plumpness thinned
to a chip of lamb's bone,
legs decayed, necrotic.

FRI., JULY 2, 7:26 PM
Running is a game
for the young. Women
of a certain age, root.

FRI., JULY 2, 9:09 PM
Some rot gashing cane
with dull machetes. Sinking in
clay around 10-foot stalks when
all the while they could have been
coal-eyed peacocks, lean deep-water
ghosts, spunforce bladefeathers,
fear itself.

FRI., JULY 2, 9:11 PM
Can you believe I still carry
the knife my husband gave me?
I gut, hollow and scrape
soft spoil from cavities, but
what's dead is pretty well empty.

FRI., JULY 2, 9:21 PM
Good on you. Makes for easy work.
My people are steel-clad nomads
at the full-metal brink. None
know what's in the chamber,
staring down our barrels.

FRI., JULY 2, 9:32 PM
There's 2 ways to terrify men:
tell them what's coming,
don't tell them what's next . . .

FRI., JULY 2, 9:55 PM
(2/2) deathbed—herons,
black merlins, white-necked
ravens, mute cygnus, Impundulu—

FRI., JULY 2, 9:54 PM
(1/2) Pales lower as light approaches.
Memaw felt all kinds of birds
hovering near her

FRI., JULY 2, 10:07 PM
What did Impundulu want?

FRI., JULY 2, 10:10 PM
Wondered myself. She named
ancestors and gods I'd never
met—
limbs of Osiris in Brooks Brothers,
Isis in Fredrick's of Hollywood,
Jesus in torn polyester.

FRI., JULY 2, 10:12 PM
Ah, the birds wanted them then.

No. She said: *They waitin'...*
for you.
Then she died,
eyes wide,
fixed on me.

FRI., JULY 2, 10:28 PM
Dinn, dinn, dinn—
Dying's last words
mean nothing. What wants you
dead would have your head.

FRI., JULY 2, 10:29 PM
LOL! But I'm not dead, huh?

FRI., JULY 2, 11:21 PM
I'm not dead, right?

SAT., JULY 3, 3:00 AM
Anne? I'm not, right?

Duy Doan (1982–) *We Play a Game,* 2017

Duy Doan was born in Dallas, Texas. After graduating from the University of Texas at Austin he received his MFA in poetry from Boston University, where he worked with, and for a time directed, the Favorite Poem Project. He has been a fellow at Kundiman, an annual conference and retreat for Asian American writers.

Arrangements

hail changes the shape of a city.
the sun, shy above the

sound of shattering.
no beast was ever as wild

as the dimpling of a pond
cooled by hailstones.

out of various glass bottles,
one rhythm approaches

monotony, when it is hardest
to trace what is random.

the illusion of synchronicity:
the gazelle the cheetah.

Lake Hoàn Kiếm

The wind plays with the moon; the moon with the wind.
The moon sets. Who can the wind play with?
—Vietnamese folk song

Meet me on the unlit stretch of lake least fooled
by autumn. Under the youngest willow.

Its thin branches hang over me, its leaves
veil my face from the milk flower playing
matchmaker.

You say you love her sweet scent.
Even the plum blossom isn't so lavish.

One day I will take a wife myself.
If I reach forward, I can touch the water
past the edge of the moon.

I wait for you beyond the temple lights
at the center of the lake, my ankles deep
in a pillar of moon on the water.

Come whisper our secrets to the lake,
make it shiver in unison with the willow.
Shall we become now
worthy of the Lạc-Hồng race?

The Roundworm Travels Up from the Foot

(Having to have a body)
Survival instincts: I turn myself into a smaller target. Thriving instincts: I put
myself into situations where my pupils dilate.

(Boxing)
To make yourself into a smaller target. You're a beautiful silhouette, reveal-
ing only one shoulder at a time, constantly rotating clockwise behind
the heel of your pivot foot.
Avoid the left hook, the left shot to the body, the straight right. Keep your
rhythm.

(Dancing)
In the dark, with the music, there's no need to be a silhouette; your shoul-
ders can be square to others. One goal: to be a string undulating
between two fixed points.

Move sharply and quickly if you're not feeling graceful tonight; slowly if
    you're feeling confident and have nothing to hide or if your pupils are
    especially alive.

(*Mermaid birth*)
The amniotic sac is intact and someone has to puncture it. Then
baby's song: so brave and so beautiful. His rotator cuff, the examining table,
    unused forceps and ventouse.

Silver nitrate
eye drops: then Judy Garland is in color.

(*The roundworm travels up from the foot only to be swallowed again*)
I ran first thing in the morning, sub-24 minute 3-miles. I'm the fastest.
    Today is a big day in a big way. Hot shower, a half-mile walk to the T.
It has been at least 12 hours since I consumed salt. I am cold, fresh water. I
    am the whale
bursting out of the Arctic.

(*Boxing*)
You're beautiful as a silhouette, in and out in and out. Masterful. You made
    weight again;
hydrate back to 134. Don't let your shoulders be square to anyone. Don't be
    the midpoint of the base of an isosceles.

(*Dancing*)
I ran first thing in the morning, sub-24 3-miles. I'm the fastest. Hot
    shower, a half-mile walk to the T.
It has been at least 12 hours since I had salt. On the train, the guy
    sitting across from me has
what must be vomit on his shoes, not caked on but still glistening. Like me,
    he is purged.
He is cold, fresh water.

(*Buckeyes*)
We piled them up
for ammunition. We lay down with them
among the bruised leaves so that we could
rise, shining.

(The roundworm travels up from the foot again)
Shower, Clobetasol foam, Dove Men-Care Post-Shave Balm,
Tretinoin cream, Joico Matte Clay or Molding Clay or Water Resistant Styling
    Glue. An apple.

(Boxing)
Brody fails to make weight

(Dancing)
I'll move
slowly tonight. Madonna, Laurent
Korcia, Iron and Wine.

(Buckeyes)
We piled them up
for ammunition. We lay down with them
so that we could
rise, shining.

(Dancing)
Ecstasy turns us into moths.

I'm an embryo in the mother's womb.
I sleep hidden in you.
Don't give birth to me yet.

(Dilated pupils)
Hyperbole and the coquette.

(Mermaid birth)
The amniotic sac is intact and someone has to puncture it. Then mother's
    wooing: so overwhelming, so alluring. New Order, Erasure, Lorde,
    glitter, eyeliner. Judy Garland is in color.

Yanyi (1991–) *The Year of Blue Water,* 2018

Yanyi was born in China, graduated from Columbia University, and is now a student in New York University's MFA program in creative writing. His honors include a Margins fellowship from the Asian American Writers' Workshop and an Emerging Poets fellowship from Poets House.

Dream Diary

You're awake, then you are standing.
Then the last thing that you dreamed will unfold
its field of memory. What you touch will come
to life: a whole room sprung in the backwards words
of people untalking to you. Walking reverse with such
confidence until you reach another room. There stands
this person who is also a talisman. In the dream,
it doesn't matter when they loved you. In the dream,
when you talk, the butterflies are orange and then blue,
and together you lead the rabble to the square where
you touch this person and then leave them. And on cue
a flock of pigeons will soon want nothing but to return
to you. And on cue the cedars become green and then
stone, this person unmaking love from you and placing
the pieces elsewhere, again, on earth. Until before that.
Until the somewhere else before you agreed to move.
Then you are language, too. Backwards words unstuck to
the dream as the dream began to happen. And the ghosts
inside the many rooms rustle nude inside the blue water.
And the ghosts inside the many rooms illuminate
the many walls.

Form gives space for something to exist. You have to dig in yourself to find what you'll put in it. Places you don't know appear. Poems are a way to ask for what exists, to invite what wants to be visible.

The male dancers are paired with other male dancers. They dance in a way that echoes sameness. Yet that is not what I feel with women, or what draws me to women. When I was a woman, I didn't feel the same as them, or they to me. Our sameness was only a cover. This is the great secret of lesbianism if there is a secret that even I did not know. We do not want the same things. There is no other woman. There is only woman to woman to woman.

The Yale Series of Younger Poets

Judges

Charlton M. Lewis, 1919–1923
Frederick E. Pierce, 1923
Edward Bliss Reed, 1923–1924
William Alexander Percy, 1925–1932
Stephen Vincent Benét, 1933–1942
Archibald MacLeish, 1942–1945
W. H. Auden, 1946–1958
Dudley Fitts, 1959–1968
Stanley Kunitz, 1969–1976
Richard Hugo, 1977–1982
James Merrill, 1983–1989
James Dickey, 1990–1996
W. S. Merwin, 1997–2003
Louise Glück, 2003–2010
Carl Phillips, 2011–

Winners

Howard Buck *The Tempering* (1918)
John Chipman Farrar *Forgotten Shrines* (1918)
David Osborne Hamilton *Four Gardens* (1919)
Alfred Raymond Bellinger *Spires and Poplars* (1919)
Thomas Caldecot Chubb *The White God, and Other Poems* (1919)
Darl MacLeod Boyle *Where Lilith Dances* (1919)
Theodore H. Banks, Jr. *Wild Geese* (1920)
Viola C. White *Horizons* (1920)
Hervey Allen *Wampum and Old Gold* (1920)
Oscar Williams *Golden Darkness* (1920)
Harold Vinal *White April* (1921)
Medora C. Addison *Dreams and a Sword* (1921)

Bernard Raymund *Hidden Waters* (1921)

Paul Tanaquil *Attitudes* (1921)

Dean B. Lyman, Jr. *The Last Lutanist* (1922)

Amos Niven Wilder *Battle-Retrospect* (1922)

Marion M. Boyd *Silver Wands* (1922)

Beatrice E. Harmon *Mosaics* (1922)

Elizabeth Jessup Blake *Up and Down* (1923)

Dorothy E. Reid *Coach into Pumpkin* (1924)

Eleanor Slater *Quest* (1925)

Thomas Hornsby Ferril *High Passage* (1925)

Lindley Williams Hubbell *Dark Pavilion* (1926)

Mildred Bowers *Twist o' Smoke* (1927)

Ted Olson *A Stranger and Afraid* (1927)

Francis Claiborne Mason *The Unchanging Mask* (1927)

Frances M. Frost *Hemlock Wall* (1928)

Henri Faust *Half-light and Overtones* (1928)

Louise Owen *Virtuosa* (1929)

Dorothy Belle Flanagan *Dark Certainty* (1930)

Paul Engle *Worn Earth* (1931)

Shirley Barker *The Dark Hills Under* (1932)

James Agee *Permit Me Voyage* (1933)

Muriel Rukeyser *Theory of Flight* (1934)

Edward Weismiller *The Deer Come Down* (1935)

Margaret Haley *The Gardener Mind* (1936)

Joy Davidman *Letter to a Comrade* (1937)

Reuel Denney *The Connecticut River and Other Poems* (1938)

Norman Rosten *Return Again, Traveler* (1939)

Jeremy Ingalls *The Metaphysical Sword* (1940)

Margaret Walker *For My People* (1941)

William Meredith *Love Letter from an Impossible Land* (1943)

Charles E. Butler *Cut Is the Branch* (1944)

Eve Merriam *Family Circle* (1945)

Joan Murray *Poems* (1946)

Robert Horan *A Beginning* (1947)

Rosalie Moore *The Grasshopper's Man and Other Poems* (1948)

Adrienne Rich *A Change of World* (1950)

W. S. Merwin *A Mask for Janus* (1951)

Edgar Bogardus *Various Jangling Keys* (1952)

Daniel Hoffman *An Armada of Thirty Whales* (1953)
John Ashbery *Some Trees* (1955)
James Wright *The Green Wall* (1956)
John Hollander *A Crackling of Thorns* (1957)
William Dickey *Of the Festivity* (1958)
George Starbuck *Bone Thoughts* (1959)
Alan Dugan *Poems* (1960)
Jack Gilbert *Views of Jeopardy* (1961)
Sandra Hochman *Manhattan Pastures* (1962)
Peter Davison *The Breaking of the Day* (1963)
Jean Valentine *Dream Barker* (1964)
James Tate *The Lost Pilot* (1966)
Helen Chasin *Coming Close* (1967)
Judith Johnson Sherwin *Uranium Poems* (1968)
Hugh Seidman *Collecting Evidence* (1969)
Peter Klappert *Lugging Vegetables to Nantucket* (1970)
Michael Casey *Obscenities* (1971)
Robert Hass *Field Guide* (1972)
Michael Ryan *Threats Instead of Trees* (1973)
Maura Stanton *Snow on Snow* (1974)
Carolyn Forché *Gathering the Tribes* (1975)
Olga Broumas *Beginning with O* (1976)
Bin Ramke *The Difference Between Night and Day* (1977)
Leslie Ullman *Natural Histories* (1978)
William Virgil Davis *One Way to Reconstruct the Scene* (1979)
John Bensko *Green Soldiers* (1980)
David Wojahn *Icehouse Lights* (1981)
Cathy Song *Picture Bride* (1982)
Richard Kenney *The Evolution of the Flightless Bird* (1983)
Pamela Alexander *Navigable Waterways* (1984)
George Bradley *Terms to Be Met* (1985)
Julie Agoos *Above the Land* (1986)
Brigit Pegeen Kelly *To the Place of Trumpets* (1987)
Thomas Bolt *Out of the Woods* (1988)
Daniel Hall *Hermit with Landscape* (1989)
Christiane Jacox Kyle *Bears Dancing in the Northern Air* (1990)
Nicholas Samaras *Hands of the Saddlemaker* (1991)
Jody Gladding *Stone Crop* (1992)

Valerie Wohlfeld *Thinking the World Visible* (1993)
T. Crunk *Living in the Resurrection* (1994)
Ellen Hinsey *Cities of Memory* (1995)
Talvikki Ansel *My Shining Archipelago* (1996)
Craig Arnold *Shells* (1998)
Davis McCombs *Ultima Thule* (1999)
Maurice Manning *Lawrence Booth's Book of Visions* (2000)
Sean Singer *Discography* (2001)
Loren Goodman *Famous Americans* (2002)
Peter Streckfus *Cuckoo* (2003)
Richard Siken *Crush* (2004)
Jay Hopler *Green Squall* (2005)
Jessica Fisher *Frail-Craft* (2006)
Fady Joudah *The Earth in the Attic* (2007)
Arda Collins *It Is Daylight* (2008)
Ken Chen *Juvenilia* (2009)
Katherine Larson *Radial Symmetry* (2010)
Eduardo C. Corral *Slow Lightning* (2011)
Will Schutt *Westerly* (2012)
Eryn Green *Eruv* (2013)
Ansel Elkins *Blue Yodel* (2014)
Noah Warren *The Destroyer in the Glass* (2015)
Airea D. Matthews *Simulacra* (2016)
Duy Doan *We Play a Game* (2017)
Yanyi *The Year of Blue Water* (2018)

Credits

"Battle-Retrospect," "Unsung," and "Romanesque" from Amos Niven Wilder, *Battle-Retrospect*, Yale University Press, 1923.

"Blackberry Winter," "Gold of Beeches," and "Blue Cups" from Marion M. Boyd, *Silver Wands*, Yale University Press, 1923.

"The Woman to the Man," "October," and "Rondeau" from Beatrice E. Harmon, *Mosaics*, Yale University Press, 1923.

"Ode to Loneliness," "Bedouin Lullaby," and "Memories" from Elizabeth Jessup Blake, *Up and Down*, Yale University Press, 1924.

"Volumes," "Study in Clouds," and "Sonnet" from Dorothy E. Reid, *Coach into Pumpkin*, Yale University Press, 1925.

"Balm," "Because Your Heart Was Shy," and "Disillusionment" from Eleanor Slater, *Quest*, Yale University Press, 1926.

"Mountain Rivers," "The Empire Sofa," and "Missing Men" from Thomas Hornsby Ferril, *High Passage*, Yale University Press, 1926.

"Forgive Me," "I Remember a Hill," and "The Sealed Mouth to the Baffled Heart" from Lindley Williams Hubbell, *Dark Pavilion*, Yale University Press, 1927.

"I Have Sat by Many Fires," Punctuation," and "We must not even think of faces known" from Mildred Bowers, *Twist o' Smoke*, Yale University Press, 1928.

"Two Unlamented," "Nocturne in Sepia," and "Stay-at-Home Sonnets" from Ted Olson, *A Stranger and Afraid*, Yale University Press, 1928.

"Prophecy at Love's End," "Crossing," and "Song of the Image Makers" from Francis Claiborne Mason, *The Unchanging Mask*, Yale University Press, 1928.

"Lullaby," "Deserted Orchard," and "Hands" from Frances M. Frost, *Hemlock Wall*, Yale University Press, 1929.

"As Autumn Fields," "The Valley of the Muted Songbirds," and "The Amethyst Gardens" from Henri Faust, *Half-Light and Overtones*, Yale University Press, 1929.

"Two Cinquains," "Farm by the Sea," and "Loveliest of Trees" from Louise Owen, *Virtuosa*, Yale University Press, 1930.

"Document," "Capriccio," and "She Who Lies Motionless with an Arrow in Her Heart" from Dorothy Belle Flanagan, *Dark Certainty*, 1931.

"Road Gang," "The Torn Leaf," and "One Slim Feather" from Paul Engle, *Worn Earth*, Yale University Press, 1932. Courtesy of Hualing Engle.

"Portrait," "A Plea Unheard," and "Sonnet XX" from Shirley Barker, *The Dark Hills Under*, Yale University Press, 1933.

"Sonnet IV," "Sonnet XXII," and "Permit Me Voyage" from *Permit Me Voyage* by James Agee, copyright © 1968 by the James Agee Trust; used by permission of the Wylie Agency LLC.

"Sailing to Europe," "Near a Cemetery Pond," and "In Memory of Robert Menner" from Edgar Bogardus, *Various Jangling Keys*, Yale University Press, 1953.

"Off Chichicastenengo," "Auricle's Oracle," and "An Age of Fable" from Daniel Hoffman, *An Armada of Thirty Whales*, Yale University Press, 1954.

"A Boy," "Errors," and "Answering a Question in the Mountains" from John Ashbery, *Some Trees*, copyright © 1955; used by permission of Georges Borchardt, Inc.

"Father," "Eleutheria," and "Autumnal" from James Wright, *The Green Wall*, Yale University Press, 1957.

"Carmen Ancillae," "A Word Remembered," and "Jefferson Valley" from John Hollander, *A Crackling of Thorns*, Yale University Press, 1958. Courtesy of Natalie Charkow.

"Part Song, with Concert of Recorders," "*Les très riches heures*," and "A Vision, Caged" from William Dickey, *Of the Festivity*, Yale University Press, 1959.

"Technologies," "A Tapestry for Bayeux," and "Cora Punctuated with Strawberries" from George Starbuck, *Bone Thoughts*, Yale University Press, 1960. Courtesy of Kathryn Starbuck.

Alan Dugan, "This Morning Here," "The Mirror Perilous," and "How We Heard the Name" from *Poems Seven: New and Complete Poetry*, copyright © 1961, 2001 by Alan Dugan; reprinted with the permission of the Permissions Company, Inc., on behalf of Seven Stories Press, www.sevenstories.com.

"Perspective He Would Mutter Going to Bed," "The Abnormal Is Not Courage," and "It Is Clear Why the Angels Come No More" from Jack Gilbert, *Views of Jeopardy*, Yale University Press, 1962. Courtesy of Linda Gregg.

"Inferno," "Hansoms," and "Divers" from Sandra Hochman, *Manhattan Pastures*, Yale University Press, 1963. Courtesy of Sandra Hochman.

"Fogged In," "Summer School," and "The Suicide" from Peter Davison, *The Breaking of the Day*, Yale University Press, 1964. Courtesy of Edward Angus Davison.

"Asleep over Lines from Willa Cather," "Sasha and the Poet," and "Sex" from Jean Valentine, *Dream Barker*, Yale University Press, 1965. © Jean Valentine.

"The Face of the Waters," by James Tate, first appeared in *Kayak* and subsequently in Yale Series of Younger Poets Volume 62, reprinted by permission of Estate of James Tate; "The Lost Pilot," by James Tate, first appeared in *Atlantic Monthly* and subsequently in Yale Series of Younger Poets Volume 62, reprinted by permission of Estate of James Tate; "Grace," by James Tate, first appeared in 1967 in Yale Series of Younger Poets Volume 62, reprinted by permission of Estate of James Tate.

"Among the Supermarket," "Joy Sonnet in a Random Universe," and "Encounters And" from Helen Chasin, *Coming Close*, Yale University Press, 1968. Estate of Helen Chasin.

"Happy Jack's Rock," "Watersong," and "Buzzards' Bay" from Judith E. Johnson (formerly Judith Johnson Sherwin), *Uranium Poems*, Yale University Press, copyright © 1969 by Judith Johnson Sherwin (later Judith E. Johnson).

"Fragmenta," "Poem," and "Pattern" from *Collecting Evidence* (1970) by Hugh Seidman, copyright © 1970 by Hugh Seidman; reprinted by permission of the author.

"Poem for L. C.," "No Turtles," and "Photographs of Ogunquit" from Peter Klappert, *Lugging Vegetables to Nantucket*, Yale University Press, 1971. Courtesy of Peter Klappert.

"Maps," "At Stinson Beach," and "Two Views of Buson" from Robert Hass, *Field Guide*, Yale University Press, 1973.

Original versions of "The Beginning of Sympathy," "Talking About Things," and "The Blind Swimmer" as they appeared in *Threats Instead of Trees* are reprinted by permission of the author; revised versions of "The Beginning of Sympathy" and "The Blind Swimmer" were subsequently published in Michael Ryan, *New and Selected Poems*, Houghton Mifflin, 2004.

"Dreaming of Shells," "A Few Picnics in Illinois," and "Going Back" from Maura Stanton, *Snow on Snow*, Yale University Press, 1975; reprinted by permission of the author.

"From Memory," "Las Truchas," and "Year at Mudstraw" from Carolyn Forché, *Gathering the Tribes*, Yale University Press, 1976.

"Leda and Her Swan," "Triple Muse," and "Snow White" from Olga Broumas, *Beginning with O*, Yale University Press, 1977. Courtesy of Olga Broumas.

"The Channel Swimmer," "Martyrdom: A Love Poem," and "The Green Horse" from Bin Ramke, *The Difference Between Night and Day*, Yale University Press, 1978. Courtesy of Bin Ramke.

"Nostalgia," "His Early and Late Paintings," and "Memo" from Leslie Ullman, *Natural Histories*, Yale University Press, 1979. Courtesy of Leslie Ullman.

"Winter Light," "One Way to Reconstruct the Scene," and "In the Pit" from William Virgil Davis, *One Way to Reconstruct the Scene*, Yale University Press, 1980; reprinted by permission of William Virgil Davis.

"The Midnight Sun," "Rejects from the Greenhouse," and "The Fox" from John Bensko, *Green Soldiers*, Yale University Press, 1981. Courtesy of John Bensko.

"Distance," "Cold Glow: Icehouses," and "Another Coast" from David Wojahn, *Icehouse Lights*, Yale University Press, 1982. Courtesy of David Wojahn.

"Flemish Beauty," "Conversation with the Sun Bittern," and "From Stone" from Talvikki Ansel, *My Shining Archipelago*, Yale University Press, 1997. Courtesy of Talvikki Ansel.

"Hermit Crab," "Great Dark Man," and "Shore" from Craig Arnold, *Shells*, Yale University Press, 1999. Courtesy of Rebecca Lindenberg.

"Cave Wind," "Floyd's Lost Passage," and "The River and Under the River" from Davis McCombs, *Ultima Thule*, Yale University Press, 2000. Courtesy of Davis McCombs.

"A Prayer Against Forgetting Boys," "Pegasus," and "Like a Tree" from Maurice Manning, *Lawrence Booth's Book of Visions*, Yale University Press, 2001. Courtesy of Maurice Manning.

"The Old Record," "False Love," and "The Sweet Obsession Bleeds from Singer" from Sean Singer, *Discography*, Yale University Press, 2002. Courtesy of Sean Singer.

"The Prize," "Interviews," and "Exploded" from Loren Goodman, *Famous Americans*, Yale University Press, 2003. Courtesy of Loren Goodman.

"Memories Are Nothing, Today Is Important," "After Words," and "Pilgrim's Progress" from Peter Streckfus, *Cuckoo*, Yale University Press, 2004. Courtesy of Peter Streckfus.

"Dirty Valentine," "Wishbone," and "Road Music" from Richard Siken, *Crush*, Yale University Press, 2005. Courtesy of Richard Siken.

"Nothing to Do Now but Sit and Wait," "And the Sunflower Weeps for the Sun, Its Flower," and "Aubade" from Jay Hopler, *Green Squall*, Yale University Press, 2006. Courtesy of Jay Hopler.

"Nonsight," "Tide," and "The Hunger for Form" from Jessica Fisher, *Frail-Craft*, Yale University Press, 2007. Courtesy of Jessica Fisher.

"Proposal," "Morning Ritual," and "Additional Notes on Tea" from Fady Joudah, *The Earth in the Attic*, Yale University Press, 2008. Courtesy of Fady Joudah.

"From Speaking in the Fall," "Poem #9," and "Elegy" from Arda Collins, *It Is Daylight*, Yale University Press, 2009. Courtesy of Arda Collins.

"My Father and My Mother Decide My Future and How Could We Forget Wang Wei?" "At Taipei Station I Saw This City Undress!" and "Yes, No, Yes, the Future, Gone, Happy, Yes, No, Yes, Cut, You" from Ken Chen, *Juvenilia*, Yale University Press, 2010. Courtesy of Ken Chen.

"Statuary," "Risk," and "Metamorphosis" from Katherine Larson, *Radial Symmetry*, Yale University Press, 2011. Courtesy of Katherine Larson.

"Acquired Immune Deficiency Syndrome," "Caballero," and "Monologue of a Vulture's Shadow" from Eduardo C. Corral, *Slow Lightning*, Yale University Press, 2012. Courtesy of Eduardo C. Corral.

"Fragment from a Coptic Tunic," "Westerly," and "After *A Silvia*" from Will Schutt, *Westerly*, Yale University Press, 2013. Courtesy of Will Schutt.

"The Disaster Takes Care of Everything," "Entropical (the Bulk)," and "Found Well" from Eryn Green, *Eruv*, Yale University Press, 2014.

"The Girl with Antlers," "Reverse: A Lynching," and "Sailmaker's Palm" from Ansel Elkins, *Blue Yodel*, Yale University Press, 2015.

"Like the Pelican," "Thou in Time," and "Empathy" from Noah Warren, *The Destroyer in the Glass*, Yale University Press, 2016.

"The Mine Owner's Wife," "If My Late Grandmother Were Gertrude Stein," and "Sexton Texts Tituba from a Bird Conservatory" from Airea D. Matthews, *Simulacra*, Yale University Press, 2017.

"Arrangements," "Lake Hoàn Kiếm," and "The Roundworm Travels Up from the Foot" from Duy Doan, *We Play a Game*, Yale University Press, 2018.

"Dream Diary," "Form gives space," and "The male dancers" from Yanyi, *The Year of Blue Water*, Yale University Press, 2019.